CULTURE OF WEALTH
1st Edition
By Advocate Leon Perez

'Imagination is more important than knowledge'
'The important thing is not to stop questioning. Curiosity has its own reason for existing'

Albert Einstein

Professor Einstein, who was a proud ethnic-Jew and is still to this day considered to be the greatest scientific mind in history, has stated that imagination is the greatest tool available to humans.

    Based on this premise I have decided to engage with, and attempt to solve, the following question --- a question that has lingered at the back of my mind for decades:

    What has made one of the Western world's smallest and most persecuted minority --- ethnic-Jews --- produce some of the smartest, wealthiest, and most influential people on the planet; including Prof. Einstein himself?

    I believe, with the use of Prof. Einstein's views on human imagination and questioning, it may be possible to answer this question.

    I also believe that an answer to this question may guide all people in finding ways for the creation of wealth in their lifetime --- whether that wealth be financial, or intellectual.

INTRODUCTION

In order to answer the question posed above, an abundance of imagination is required --- imagination, coupled with prior knowledge of true historical facts.

Religion --- which is historically associated with Judaism --- is only able to provide some aspects of the answer to the above question; yet it might also be a hindrance to the question as generally, religious people in modern society --- and within Judaism --- are some of the least economically empowered populations in the Western world. The smartest, wealthiest, and richest ethnic-Jews this book describes are, generally, ultra-secular Jews --- some who even shun their Jewish origin (for various reasons). This contrast between religion and material wealth makes discovering the answers to the main question of this book more of a challenge, and far more interesting.

Today's facts about ethnic-Jews in the modern Western world

There is little doubt that people who originate from ethnic-Judaism are the richest ethnic group in the United States of America. Since the U.S. is still considered to be the richest country in the world, when comparing Jews' overall size to the total world population, they may even be considered as the richest ethnic group on the planet.[1]

In today's upper echelons of American society, being an ethnic-Jew is not necessarily a disadvantage anymore.

President Trump's son-in-law, as well as his closest confidant, Mr. Jared Kushner is an ethnic-Jew; while Ivanka, President Trump's daughter who is married to Mr. Kushner, has converted to Judaism. Former president Clinton's daughter, Chelsea, also married an ethnic-Jew[2] ;as have many other individuals who are part of the most successful people in American society. A large percentage of all successful American ethnic-Jews are married to non-Jews[3], and appear to value their nationality more than their ethnicity. However, subconsciously, most will hold Jewish values with regards to: life; their family life; the manner in which they raise and educate their children, as well as their general way of conduct --- whether that conduct be within a business setting, or their private life.

About eight percent of members in America's congress and senate are also of ethnic-Jewish origin --- especially those that hold positions within the Democratic Party.[4] Many others bear typical surnames that indicate to some Jewish ancestry. The intellectual driving force for the American Federal Reserve Bank has also been Jewish.[5] Many of the current members of the Federal Reserve Bank --- and many of America's financial institution leaders --- are of ethnic-Jewish origin. The new Secretary of Treasury, Mr. Steven Mnuchin, is also of Jewish origin.

---

[1] "World's 165 Jewish billionaires worth combined $812 billion | The ...." https://www.timesofisrael.com/worlds-jewish-billionaires-worth-combined-812-billion/. Accessed 26 Jan. 2018.

[2] "Marc Mezvinsky - Wikipedia." https://en.wikipedia.org/wiki/Marc_Mezvinsky. Accessed 26 Jan. 2018.

[3] "The Vanishing American Jew." http://www.nytimes.com/books/first/d/dershowitz-jew.html. Accessed 19 Feb. 2019.

[4] "How Many Jews Are in Congress? | ReformJudaism.org." 4 May. 2017, https://reformjudaism.org/blog/2017/05/04/how-many-jews-are-congress. Accessed 26 Jan. 2018.

[5] "The Jewish Story Behind the U.S. Federal Reserve Bank – The Forward." 29 Nov. 2015, https://forward.com/culture/325447/the-man-behind-the-fed/. Accessed 26 Jan. 2018.

Although in America being ethnically-Jewish is no longer to anyone's detriment, the same cannot be said about continental Europe and many other parts of the world; as well as some areas within rural and urban America --- especially where a large population of immigrants, that belong to the Islamic faith, are growing increasingly in numbers. A fair amount of said Islamic immigrants being fixed on subconscious: religious; ethnic; and racial induced hate, toward ethnic-Jews.[6]

In Europe, old traditional European anti-Semitic theories have been compounded by new populism conspiracy theories that promote: anti-Semitic; anti-American; and anti-Israel beliefs. Some of said beliefs are imported from various Islamic countries within the Middle-East and North-Africa; even as far as Pakistan and Malaysia --- countries where no Jews are even present, and Israelis are barred entry.

Although to a much lesser degree of extremism, this new type of anti-Semitism is also prevalent in the large Black and Hispanic underprivileged population of America, as said groups are well aware of ethnic-Jews' economic and intellectual domination within the United States. This results in their view of ethnic Jews as simply being a different class of rich white-supremacists.[7]

American anti-Semitism is nevertheless limited, to a large extent, by the media and the Democratic Party's institutions (who are predominantly led by intellectual and secular ethnic-Jews). This is in conjunction with many non-Jewish/assimilated intellectual and secular Americans who share the same values. Said individuals have become very similar to, and assimilated with, secular American ethnic Jews --- a product of the 'cultural melting-pots' of New York and California.

From the purest genetic theories, to the darkest conspiracy theories; the internet is rife with anti-Semitic populist theories as to the reasons behind some ethnic-Jews' economic and intellectual success --- quite a few of these suspicions being anti-Semitic in nature.[8] There has never been any real or proper research conducted to determine the causes for the phenomenon that is ethnic-Jewish intellectual and business prowess.

A mystery of nearly two-and-a-half millennia that has never been properly researched has grown over the years into multiple monstrous anti-Semitic conspiracy theories adopted by many uninformed people around the world.

Surely many modern secular people would like to receive some natural, non-religious explanation to this phenomenon? Many others (especially Jewish people) avoid this question, as it harbours racist connotations and has the potential to further provoke anti-Semitic feelings.

In recent years, some South Koreans --- who are known for their own pursuit of knowledge and innovation, and are generally unprejudiced toward Judaism --- have been attempting to unlock this Jewish mystery. Their logic simply being that if the essence of what makes some Jews so smart can be distilled and ingrained into the current young Korean generation, the generations that follow will become smarter. This would advance the Korean people further

---

[6] "Rising from the Muck: The New Anti-Semitism in Europe: Amazon.co ...." https://www.amazon.co.uk/Rising-Muck-New-Anti-Semitism-Europe/dp/1566635713. Accessed 26 Jan. 2018.

[7] ""Entrenched anti-Semitic views" very rare among whites and Asian ...." 19 Feb. 2014, https://www.washingtonpost.com/news/volokh-conspiracy/wp/2014/02/19/entrenched-anti-semitic-views-very-rare-among-whites-and-asian-americans-common-among-blacks-and-latinos/. Accessed 26 Jan. 2018.

[8] "Conspiracy Theories and the Jews | My Jewish Learning." https://www.myjewishlearning.com/article/conspiracy-theories-the-jews/. Accessed 26 Jan. 2018.

as a leading economic powerhouse in the world. In South Korea, the Jewish Talmud has been identified as a key component of Jewish wisdom; and has been adopted as study material.[9]

Chinese people have also shown marked interest, as they have realised that many well-established merchants around the world --- with whom they trade --- are of ethnic Jewish origin. Many recent innovations that are of interest to them are being produced by companies in silicon valley --- an area teaming with individuals of ethnic-Jewish origin. The small state of Israel, which harbours some incredibly intelligent IT specialists, also produces many innovations that are of interest to the Chinese. The Chinese also notice that America's large corporations with whom they deal --- as well as with whom they engage in fierce global financial battles --- are also heavily manned by secular American ethnic-Jews. One of China's most famous business and financial leader's, Mr. Li Ka-Shing, has opened a branch of the Israeli Technion institute in China. Mr. Ka-Shing, who invests in Israel, believes that there is something in Israeli culture of education and innovation which can benefit China's young generation in their pursuit of Hi-Tech startups in the computing and Cyber fields.[10]

A contentious subject

Many of my friends, Jews and non-Jews alike, had warned me about writing this book with such a contentious topic. Fears and concerns about: anti-Semitic feelings; racial issues; and the animosity of religious people toward me and Jewish people in general, were raised time and again. The potential harm by fanatical Jews and Muslims, who are extremely passionate and uncompromising in their views about the source and history of their religion, was especially worrying.

I was warned by other people about the potential anti-Semitic hatred that this book would exacerbate --- endangering Jewish people around the world. My full answer to those concerns can be found in Chapter 14, which almost completely explains anti-Semitism.

My summarised answer is . . . in a world where everyone, to a varying degree, has hidden: racist; ethnically discriminatory; and anti-Semitic tendencies, most people are hypocrites by nature, and no one can really claim to be on higher grounds (morally) --- despite their intense self-convictions and propagandistic efforts in the media. Anti-Semitism, like racism and any other prejudice, is a natural fact of life.

My book cannot inflame the already elevated levels of anti-Semitism within certain populations --- my hope is that it will actually promote understanding and tolerance in the medium-to-long run of contemporary human history.

In my life, I have noticed that racism has no boundaries. Living for many years in South Africa, I have noticed that today's native South Africans --- who have suffered from racism in the past --- exhibit racism toward other sub-Saharan Africans; rebranding this racism as xenophobia. In addition, their discriminatory policies toward: White; Colored; and Indian

---

[9] "How the Talmud Became a Best-Seller in South Korea | The New Yorker." 23 Jun. 2015, https://www.newyorker.com/books/page-turner/how-the-talmud-became-a-best-seller-in-south-korea. Accessed 26 Jan. 2018.

[10] "Tycoon Li Ka-shing Looks to Israel - China Real Time Report - WSJ." 30 Mar. 2015, https://blogs.wsj.com/chinarealtime/2015/03/30/tycoon-li-ka-shing-looks-to-israel-for-innovation/. Accessed 26 Jan. 2018.

minorities,[11] as well as other Africans within their various tribal makeup,[12] is living proof that the ethnic group which possess the power in a society reveals its hidden racism --- without any shame. Once Hitler had assumed a position of power, a similar process had occurred in Nazi-Germany; at which point it had reached the extreme genocide of Jews and other minority groups.

This violence, induced by racial hate, is also true when various 'left-wingers' and 'politically correct' elites who hold on to power for too long begin demonising others as racists and fascists; in order to continue clinging onto said power. The exact same is done by hard-core conservatives when the political tables turn. In weak democracies, this eventually leads to bloodshed.

Therefore, when people exhibit feelings of anti-Semitism, it is a resounding expression of their own racist tendencies; combined with their hidden feelings of inadequacy, jealousy, or fear. Unfortunately, anti-Semitism --- like racism --- has been a natural fact of life throughout human history; and will continue to be so for the rest of the foreseeable future. It is an instinct that every individual must fight, internally, to quell within themselves --- this is not an easy task.

When a racially prejudiced thought occurs, it should always be understood and considered that all people on this earth are competitive creatures that seek to survive in different, and at times strange, culturally induced ways. Some will resort to extreme conduct such as terrorism, or extreme religious agendas; while others are seasoned manipulators of political and economic situations. Through their competitive actions, all humans are racists (to some degree). Some groups are inherently anti-Semitic; and some will even act upon all of the above unwanted human behaviours. Human behaviour is diverse and complicated.

Given the diversity of human behaviour, I do not believe that my book will make or break anti-Semitism or racism. It may, however, provide intellectual people with a greater understanding about Judaism and ethnic Jews; and hopefully, over the years, this understanding will filter down to the layman. My new, secular approach, in the researching and writing of this book may even eventually help decrease anti-Semitism and racism in the future.

My conviction to find objective truths is stronger than any of the fears and concerns raised by others (even though there is definitely a risk that this book might anger a variety of populations).

Over the long course of history, great men --- in far more hostile environments --- had neither compromised nor adjusted their views to suit public opinion and gain the approval of society. I will therefore humbly set aside any excuses or anxieties for not writing about, or engaging with, this contentious topic.

Moreover, I feel that my personal passion and interest in: history; archaeology; religion; science; and business --- as well as my lifelong curiosity about civilization and the processes of life --- cannot be fulfilled if I do not express my beliefs with absolute authenticity, and honesty. At this stage of my life, writing truthfully seems as though it is the right thing for me to do.

---

[11] "All South Africans Must Be Steadfast In Their Condemnation Of Racism." 4 Oct. 2017, http://www.huffingtonpost.co.za/mbulelo-nguta/all-south-africans-must-be-steadfast-in-their-condemnation-of-racism_a_23228490/. Accessed 26 Jan. 2018.

[12] "Some South Africans still think along racial, tribal lines - academic ...." 23 Jun. 2016, https://www.news24.com/SouthAfrica/News/some-south-africans-still-think-along-racial-tribal-lines-academic-20160623. Accessed 26 Jan. 2018.

Not many people are privileged enough in their lifetime to be in a position where they have the necessary time and resources available to them, to write a book. I should therefore be grateful for such an opportunity; even though writing is more difficult a task than I had originally anticipated --- mentally, and to my surprise, even physically. Back and neck health problems are probably common to writers. After my humble experience, I have now found new respect for writers.

At times, while discussing my will to write this book, I had felt that some people --- whom I knew --- harboured feelings of jealousy and fear; probably because they themselves would have liked to engage in such a project, but could not (and perhaps, out of jealousy, would not have enjoyed witnessing someone else achieve writing a book and potentially succeeding).

Above all, I felt that after many years of enjoying reading; it was time to write, and hopefully disseminate some constructive ideas.

I have also attempted to change --- what I consider to be --- the 'boring and unimaginative' way in which history is written; as well as the way in which it is taught to young people around the world.

Further than all of the above --- and on a lighter note --- at the mature age of 55 years old, I have begun to realise that life is quickly passing by; and if I want to express my beliefs and showcase my ideas, I should hurry up a bit... it is really now or never.

Personal interest

Growing up in Israel as a completely secular person --- and being exposed to the various forms of: Judaism; Judaic history; and Jewish people --- the sole source of Judaism being the complete irrationality of religious writings had always simultaneously intrigued and bothered me. Being a secular person, the question as to what the real source of Judaism was, had occupied my mind for many years.

As I became increasingly economically active, the question as to what the reason was for the disproportional intellectual and economic success some Jewish people in the Diaspora exhibit, intrigued me even more.

My additional personal questions were: firstly; why is there anti-Semitism and so much hate for Jews within the European continent? ; and secondly, how had Jews survived historically inhumane and heinous persecutions --- for over two millennia --- in Christian Europe and the Islamic Arab world? Had it been faith that kept them alive (as religious people claim it to be)? Or perhaps it had been a matter of purely simple fate (due to their widespread geographical distribution in many countries)?

I could not accept or come to terms with the belief that religion, which is largely illogical and full of superstition, is the sole secret to this amazing survival story. It is reasonable to believe that there must have been other more: natural; basic; and secular explanations, underlying or complementing the religious explanation.

My most personal economically based question was: how had it been possible for quite a few Jewish individuals living in the Diaspora --- who are only fairly educated and knowledgeable --- to achieve such amazing economic success? Although I have achieved substantial economic advancements, in my lifetime; it is nowhere close to the achievements of these economic giants. This had been contradictory to my opinion that my academic education and general knowledge, which seemed to be far superior to theirs, should have given me an edge.

Answering this last question may help many hard-working people, around the world, who are confused as to why after so much effort they can never achieve such high economic status

understand that: Jewish history; culture; and way of life, may help individuals and their children further their intellectual and economic success in the future. I believe that such an understanding may also help in the battle against anti-Semitism around the world.

Defining the questions and goals of this book

Throughout European Christian history during the Middle Ages, Jews had been associated with their Bible; and were subject to obsessive: jealousy; hate; and contempt --- as well as the stereotype of possessing and using dark mythical powers. There is no nation in history that had provoked the perverse imagination of the old European Western civilization, quite like the Judaic nation.

Given that recent modern history has witnessed the outstanding economic and intellectual success of ethnic Jews in America --- as well as in other newly developed countries such as Australia and Canada --- there are many questions regarding the nature of the Judaic nation that remain open and are limited to speculation: Why are Jews at the forefront of business, commerce, and finance? Why do they excel in science and technology? What is the secret to their creativity and entrepreneurial spirit?

The answer to these questions may explain what had enabled ethnic Jews to survive for two millennia in the face of horrific persecutions and murder; as well as their expulsion from European countries such as Spain and Portugal, and their expulsion from the Arab world in 1948. It may also explain how the small Jewish State of Israel continues to survive and prosper, whilst being surrounded by numerous large and hating neighboring Arab countries who yearn for its destruction --- including many Arab-Palestinians in Gaza and the West Bank, as well as some Arabs who reside within Israel and hold Israeli citizenship.

A major question that has lingered in the minds of all too many people around the world for many years is: 'What is the secret to Jews' economic riches?' The clues for the answer to all these questions are --- in my opinion --- embedded in a historical evolutionary process. Said historical dimension to the Jewish survival story will become apparent to the reader as they progress through this book.

It should be understood that from the days of the Greek Empire, to our contemporary modern American dominated world; Jews have been the subject of much: controversy; jealousy; and hate, from their surrounding environment. The reasons for this will also become apparent later on in this book.

Historically, for over nearly 2000 years within the Christian world, most views about Jews had been associated with their religion and its conflict with Christianity. This is because the Biblical Old Testament proclaims Jews to be 'the chosen people of God'; while the New Testament portrays the Jewish people as a 'cursed nation' that lost this title due to its betrayal of Jesus Christ. This religious conflict is still ongoing in the minds of many devout Christians, mainly in the economically underdeveloped nations of catholic South America, as well as other poor Christian countries around the world.[13] This religious conflict is futile in the eyes of the modern secular intelligent population of the world --- but it is definitely of some subconscious interest to them.

In recent European history, a pseudo-racial dimension was added to the historical religious conflict between Christians and Jews --- this being the result of mass secularization in Europe,

---

[13] "Anti-Semitism Stirs in Latin America - The New York Times." 15 Aug. 2014, https://www.nytimes.com/2014/08/16/opinion/enrique-krauze-anti-semitism-stirs-in-latin-america.html. Accessed 27 Jan. 2018.

and a burst of Jewish dominance in business and intellectual fields; coupled with the rise of Darwin's evolution theory, and the subsequent development of 'white-versus-negro' racial theories in America, as well as White-Aryan-race theories in Europe's Germany.[14]

The venomous cocktail of religion and racial prejudice, together with the ruthless subversion of the intellectual elite under the Nazi's in Germany, had resulted in the most horrific mass murder of European Jews by Germany's Nazi regime --- murder that had been exacerbated by their anti-Semitic accomplices throughout Europe. This atrocity was committed under the disguised settings of World War II.

The near extermination of the European-Jewish population, as well as other helpless ethnic groups such as the Gypsies, had cast a huge 'dark cloud' over the nature of world humanity and its process of civilization; creating an enormous cultural shock within the more enlightened members of civilization.

Once the atrocities of Hitler's Nazi regime had been revealed, the disconcertion instilled in the emerging powers of the United States and its allies had created a major trend of emerging: anti-Racist; anti-Colonial; and freedom movements --- changing the fortunes of minorities in the modern world. This change of fortunes had led to the unprecedented freedom of ethnic-Jews in the United States of America, as well as other countries such as Canada and Australia --- freedom that had enabled them to actualize their amazing intellectual and economic potential.

The main purpose of this book is to explain the phenomenon that is ethnic-Jews' economic and intellectual success in the modern world; including many other historical questions about the source of Judaism and, Judaism's influences on world history and civilization.

My main claim is that: religious debate, as well as a persistent view of ancient Jewish history through Biblical stories, has obscured much historical and archaeological facts that can be used to explain the Jews, and Judaism, in a clearer and more logical manner. Unfortunately, for over two millennia, both Christians and Jews have fallen into the trap of being intellectually blinded by the debate surrounding the conflict that has been generated by religion.

Another claim of mine is that there is a complete misconception that Judaism is a pure racial class on its own regard. Judaism cannot be so, as it is more of a culture and way of life; and is not solely based on the colour of one's skin and genetic makeup. This claim is only valid when it is acknowledged that racism, like anti-Semitism, is a natural fact of life that exists in all societies --- including all modern countries and ethnic groups. When it comes to Judaism, ethnic culture is more of an issue than racism. For thousands of years, Jewish genes have been scattered amongst every European population that Jews have been a part of --- mainly: Spain; Portugal; France; Germany, and Austria.

For the purpose of this book, my definition of an ethnic-Jew is: someone who has experienced Jewish culture or Jewish behavioural influences within their household; and has at least one parent of Jewish origin.

This definition may seem arbitrary to some people; however, It does carry a reasonable assumption that a person whose parent has raised them in a Jewish home would have adopted some Jewish values and behavioural patterns from said parent. However, if a person 9does not make an effort to instill his/her children with some Jewish identity, then the children can hardly be defined as ethnic-Jews anymore. The question 'Who is a Jew?', is a very complicated one; and does not have a definite answer or conclusion.

---

[14] "Whitman, J.Q.: Hitler's American Model: The United States and the ...."
https://press.princeton.edu/titles/10925.html. Accessed 27 Jan. 2018.

For example: Mark Zuckerberg, who is known to have been raised in a Jewish home, may pass down some of his Jewish values to his children; making them, by my definition, ethnic Jews --- even if his wife, Priscilla Chan, raises their children with some Chinese values. All of this being done within American cultural settings. But, if their children were to marry a person with a different culture to Judaism, and completely disregard Judaism as an integral aspect of their lives (by severing any ties and affinities connecting them to Judaism); then the grandchildren of Mark Zuckerberg can no longer be considered as ethnically Jewish. They will simply be Americans --- holding general American values. There are millions of Americans who bear Jewish names and one of their parents, or grandparents, had been Jewish.

Another hypothetical example of the complexities of the question 'who is a Jew?', is when a child's parents have --- later on in the child's life --- renounced their Judaism. The child may still be considered ethnically Jewish, even if they do not feel like they are, due to the fact that their parents have still exposed them to the Jewish way of life. However, If the child does not raise their offspring in the Jewish culture and Jewish way of life; said offspring can no longer be defined as ethnic Jews, since every trace of cultural identity would have largely been removed.

I do however acknowledge that each case is different, and should therefore be judged on its own merit. I apologize, in advance, to anyone who I mention in this book as an ethnic-Jew even though they may strongly believe that this is not the case. Unfortunately I cannot completely avoid generalizations in this book. This topic is not an exact science, and so there will inevitably be mistakes on my behalf.

A brief about the book

At the beginning of my journey in understanding Judaism and ethnic-Jews, I first describe the current state of affairs of American culture and the way in which it is heavily influenced by American ethnic-Jews. This is followed by a brief description of the world-wide process of Jewish life over the last two-and-a-half centuries; demonstrating the dominance of ideas generated by the Jewish mind, and how humanity --- in modern times --- has been influenced to a great extent by said ideas.

Another assumption of mine is that Judaism has also been greatly shaped by its historic anathema --- namely anti-Semitism. How, and when, this shaping took place is also to be investigated and determined.

The main questions that I would like to answer in this book are: What makes ethnic-Jews so successful in business and intellect? ; and, had the Jewish religious faith been the cause of Jews' survival for over two millennia in a severely hostile environment (as claimed by many religious individuals), or had it been the result of other factors which can be described as 'circumstantial'?

Another major question is: does Judaic culture --- and the ideas and innovations of ethnic-Jews' --- dominate our modern Western world? My claim is that the above questions can be answered by revealing the pillars of Jewish culture, which had been developed over millennia, alongside historical facts about ethnic-Jewish personalities that have changed and moulded world-thought.

In order to prove my assumptions, I shall painstakingly guide the reader through historical and archeological lenses in order to help them discover Judaism. Some questions that will be answered are: 'What is Jewish culture, and can it be quantified?' ; 'Does it lead to intellectualism?' ; and, 'Does it lead to the creation of wealth'?

In this research and discovery process, the Bible will be used sparingly --- especially when there is alternative and credible historical and/or archaeological documentation. This follows the approach adopted by Dr. Sigmund Freud --- another ethnic-Jew who is considered to be the father of psychoanalysis. It is evident that in Dr. Freud's approach to writing his book, 'Moses and Monotheism', the Bible had limited historical value; as it is difficult to distinguish between fact and fiction.[15] In subsequent chapters, it will become apparent that this statement remains true with regard to all religious writings --- such as the Christian New Testament, and the Islamic Quran and Hadith.

This approach is also heavily influenced by the philosophy of Baruch Spinoza --- yet another ethnic-Jew, who is considered by world philosophers as the 'prince of philosophy' and perhaps the first champion of secularism in world history.[16]

The Bible, and other religious scriptures, will still be used --- but only when applicable as corroborative material to historical and archeological facts. The research approach used in this book will be: archaeology as a starting point, followed by historical evidence. At times, Biblical stories or Talmudic writings will be used to demonstrate Jewish philosophical thinking, Jewish values, and Jewish culture.

By acquiring legal knowledge and skills (including an admission as an Advocate in the high court) i have realized that i can use special analytical and investigative tools that resemble legal analysis methods, as I have found those to be most valuable (provided that the user possesses substantial knowledge of the surrounding historical circumstantial evidence).

Archaeologists and historians are generally not conversed with such effective legal tools, and so I hope this to be a pioneering and original approach --- laying the foundation for a different style of writing and teaching history in the future.

For many years, archeology and history have been twisted to meet religious scriptures . . . this is not a correct approach (in my humble opinion). This new approach of mine in researching history will also reveal creative, original, and surprising discoveries of the other Abrahamic monotheistic religions of Christianity and Islam. This will hopefully open the door to a new train-of-thought regarding research on all the subjects raised in this book.

This book also has the potential to serve many people around the world who lack the historic knowledge about Judaism and its contribution to humanity; as well as its amazing journey of nearly 2500 years. This book may also prove to be a more concise way of learning history through secular lenses, as it sifts through massive heaps of religious bias and unrealistic mythical stories. The understanding of Judaism and Jews through this book may hopefully subdue anti-Semitism (by way of information and education).

This book is also directed at Far-Eastern cultures that, due to geographical distance, have hardly ever engaged with Jews and Judaism in the past; although they are undoubtedly influenced by them today (in business). These cultures had also been heavily influenced by Marxist/communist ideas and policies (until recent); Ideas that had been generated by Karl Marx --- also an ethnic-Jew who had been converted out of Judaism at childhood, but held a strict secular view of the world.[17]

Since anti-Semitism had never been a part of Far-Eastern cultures, these cultures have recently realised and recognised that some Jewish populations in the West are highly

---

[15] "Moses and Monotheism: Amazon.co.uk: Sigmund Freud ...." https://www.amazon.co.uk/Moses-Monotheism-Sigmund-Freud/dp/0394700147. Accessed 27 Jan. 2018.

[16] "Baruch Spinoza (Stanford Encyclopedia of Philosophy)." 29 Jun. 2001, https://plato.stanford.edu/entries/spinoza/. Accessed 27 Jan. 2018.

[17] "Religion and Secularism - In Defence of Marxism." 27 Apr. 2011, https://www.marxist.com/religion-and-secularism.htm. Accessed 27 Jan. 2018.

intelligent and successful; and that there is perhaps something worthwhile to learn from their culture.

The Far-Eastern countries would like to unlock the 'Jewish secrets of the mind' for the betterment of their own people. This book may help many South Koreans and Chinese people who believe that the Jewish Talmud holds the secrets; and have, in recent years, begun learning and teaching the Jewish Talmud in private settings and some schools.[18]

This book may be distasteful to hard-core religious populations of all denominations; as it is based on real facts, and strives for logical explanations. It also debunks myths and legends which are dear to some religious populations --- be them Christians, Muslims, or Jews.

To hard-core anti-Semites, this book might add fuel to their fire. My message, however, is that although anti-Semitism will forever be a natural fact of life --- and may have been an Integral part of Judaic evolution over history --- evilness should be internally combatted; and never hinder the search for truth or the improvement of the individual's, and the world's, train-of-thought. Perhaps once a person understands their reasons for hate, they may be able to improve themself; and ease their own suffering from this mental condition.

Finally, this book will attempt to address Jews', and assimilated Jews', confusion and misunderstanding about themselves. With a multitude of religious and secular divisions --- as well as a global spread of ethnic-Jews --- many Jews are confused about their own: culture; heritage; purpose; and future. This confusion has contributed to: tension between secular and religious Jews; hate of other Jews; self-hate, and identity and existential crises within individuals. I believe that this combination of identity and existential crises, together with self-hate, might be in conflict with a person's inner persona; and therefore damaging over their lifetime. Hopefully, this book will help said suffering individuals resolve such matters.

I also hope that the knowledge acquired from this book will act as a mirror placed in front of many ethnic-Jews --- exposing and explaining both Judaism's strengths, and it's weaknesses. Hopefully, ethnic-Jews will in turn better themselves further by correcting their unwanted behaviours; and further promoting humanity and the ideals of civilization --- to everyone's benefit.

Once more, I would like to stress that I am a secular individual with ethnic Jewish origins. My quest is to interpret the history of the Hebrews/Israelites/Jews through: historical; archaeological; and general scientific evidence --- coupled with an analytical process similar to legal critical analysis.

I would also like to believe that this book will help people understand the: myths; legends; and misconception of Jews, through the ages and up to current days. Additionally, it will explain why some Jews are the wealthiest of all populations --- both intellectually, and materially.

My vast and varied education in: science; engineering; business; and law --- together with a fair amount of knowledge in: English; Hebrew; Greek; and Arabic --- has enabled me to arrive at some unique and original understandings of historical and philosophical events. This, according to my belief, may turn out to be a breakthrough; which may eventually lead to new and proper academic research.

Barring known facts, quoted texts, or acknowledged authors; I hereby declare that many of the ideas expressed in this book are my own original ideas. There is a wide gap of knowledge regarding ancient history; so some of my views will be speculative, and may not necessarily

---

[18] "How the Talmud Became a Best-Seller in South Korea | The New Yorker." 23 Jun. 2015, https://www.newyorker.com/books/page-turner/how-the-talmud-became-a-best-seller-in-south-korea. Accessed 27 Jan. 2018.

be true. Nevertheless, I have made substantial efforts to ensure that my ideas are factually based; and, are of high logicality and plausibility.

This book is not purely of academic research and work; therefore, referencing is eased, and facts easily searched on the internet are not referenced --- only: books; articles; and websites, that are easily accessible on the internet and seem to be of high credibility, are referenced.

This book is dedicated to all people who have searched for truth and wisdom; and those who had fought for justice in the world. The list is long . . . but since the book is mainly concerned with Judaic history and its influence on the world, it can be vividly represented by some brilliant Jewish minds. Specifically: Maimonides (Rabbi Moshe Ben Maimon); Baruch Spinoza; Karl Marx; Sigmund Freud, and Albert Einstein --- minds who have wised up, and changed, humanity forever.

I hope that this book will expand the knowledge of many of the world's people who are not Jewish, but instead products of their own powerful and rich cultures.

The title of this book

Creating a title for this book had been an onerous task, as the book deals with many facets of life and encompasses many areas of interests. At first I thought 'The ultimate survivor', would be a suitable title (since this book describes the amazing 'ultimate survival' story of a specific ethnic nation).

One other title that had come to mind was, 'Faith or Fate' --- since it would have been interesting to analyse if the Jewish people's survival had been due to faith in God, or if it had simply been due to a coincidental chain of events (such as the Babylonian exile, or the Jewish-Phoenician blood connection and their seafaring --- which had probably been instrumental in spreading Judaism into Southern-Europe and North-Africa).

Another title I had entertained was, 'The smartest and richest (wealthiest) of them all', but then I had felt that such a title would be pretentious and arrogant; since there are many smart, rich, and wealthy nations on this earth besides the Jewish nation. It had also occurred to me that wealth may encompass material richness, but I would think that true wealth goes beyond purely material possessions.

As I had continued to write this book, I realized that the main activity of Jews over the millennia has been the creation of wealth --- whether that wealth had been in the form of intellectual wisdom, or, material possessions. Jews have relentlessly worked toward creating wealth, as it has guaranteed their survival; but, further than that --- they seem to have developed sublime imaginative powers (which are evident in the works produced by personalities such as: Albert Einstein; Sigmund Freud; and Karl Marx).

This imaginative power is also evident in today's: Silicon Valley; Hollywood; media; sporting organisations, and --- above all --- in financial institutions and world exchanges (such as Wall Street). This heightened imagination seems to be pivotal in modern, finance-based, world economies.

My deep thoughts about the relentless nature of Jewish people, and their historical process of progression towards intellectual wealth, had eventually determined the title of my book. Said relentless physical wealth generation by ethnic-Jews has also proven to be a double-edged sword for them; as, over the centuries, extreme jealousy towards Jews --- and primal feelings of greed and covet --- have manifested within all human populations. These despicable feelings are a substantial part of the anti-Semitic phenomenon akin to, and comparable with, racism. Less of a physical classification, and more of a mental or cultural type of racism; whereby the masses hate a: small; intelligent; and wealthy, elite group.

What eventually intrigued me the most had been the fact that many religious Jews, that can be considered poor by Western standards, do not consider themselves poor and do not exhibit the neglect and deterioration of other poor populations around the world. They never fall to drugs or crime, and their neighborhoods are relatively clean and orderly. Many of them even seem to feel rich within their daily study of scriptures; as well as rich within their way of life amongst their community and family spheres. Therefore, their social culture may be defined as a 'CULTURE OF WEALTH'.

I hope that this introduction has intrigued my readers, and that they will enjoy reading this ambitious book. I would appreciate the readers' feedback on my email: 77lifebooks@gmail.com

I also promise my readers a fascinating second book, that has spawned from the research and understanding I have accumulated during the process of writing this current book. My second book will attempt to unveil the underlying forces that shape life in general, and humanity in particular.

Warm regards and blessings to all my readers and supporters,

Leon Perez

Acknowledgement

I first dedicate this book to my sons. My first written intellectual effort for your benefit. I have written this book so that you will not be as clueless as I was at your age regarding life, and you will feel proud of the many admirable aspects of Judaism. It is also my hope that you will never be complacent, as there are intense life challenges ahead. As per the old Jewish saying . . . 'Know where you come from, and where you are heading to'.

This book is also dedicated to my parents. My late father who had instigated my interest in: archeology; history; philosophy, and life processes. He had possessed an enormous intellectual capacity that was never fulfilled properly. My mother, who has a huge heart, endless patience, and an unlimited internal Judaic optimism.

This book is also dedicated, by default, to all ethnically-Jewish people around the world --- whether they be secular, religious, or agnostic. This book is a tribute to all their contributions, from over more than two millennia, to humanity; as well as their spiritual and survival triumph over the multitude of mental and physical obstacles . . . an understatement regarding the horrors experienced by holocaust survivors.

It is also dedicated to all enlightened and knowledgeable people around the world. All of whom are 'Judaic in spirit' --- the ones who are capable of understanding the book's contents in the face of the ignorance of anti-Semitism and racism . . . people who understand the strengths and weaknesses of humans and social systems in general; be those systems religious, social, or financial.

I also wish to thank all the: people; family; friends, and acquaintances who knowingly --- or otherwise unknowingly --- drove my passion to write on this subject. Whether that drive had been positive, or negative.

My sincere apologies to the many ethnic-Jewish personalities whose contributions to the world --- or to the Jewish nation --- have not been acknowledged in this book. To accomplish this, I would have been required to write an Encyclopedia of thousands of pages. Perhaps, someday, one of my powerful readers can take on such a challenge.

Lastly, I would like to thank all my non-Jewish readers who originate from other powerful human cultures of history. I hope that this book will enlighten your understanding about Jews and Judaism, as well as their influence on civilization.

Whether it be your historical connection, or modern day affiliation with ethnic-Jews --- your help is needed in the battle to combat anti-Semitism, and its disguised forms of: racism; anti-Zionism ; 'anti-Israelism', and all the other 'anti's'.

Modern day anti-Semitism is well hidden beneath slogans of 'a just cause' --- but, it is always championed by the: least tolerant; most hypocritical; and therefore mentally limited, individuals on this planet. At times, disguised and self-entitled 'university graduates' are the leaders of this new type of anti-Semitism. These people are mostly personalities with underlying cultural affiliations and hidden agendas of jealousy, hate, and destruction.

About the Author and his motives for writing this book

I was born on the 8th of March 1963, in the Israeli Negev (desert) town of Be'er Sheva. My father's family had been comprised of a mixture between Sephardic-Greek, and Ashkenazi Eastern-European individuals of Jewish origin. My mother's family had been Sephardic Jews from Morocco. My mother had fled from Morocco to Israel at the age of 15. Her departure had been due to old-age Islamic hostilities towards Jews, as well as the new hope for Jews in their newly established state of Israel. Muslim hostilities had heightened after the establishment of the state of Israel in the year 1948; and about 1 000 000 'Arab' Jews had fled Arab countries to find refuge in Israel and other Western countries.

Unlike: European-Jews; holocaust survivors; and Arab-Palestinian refugees, the stories of around 850 000 'Arab' Jewish refugees fleeing to Israel from the surrounding --- Islamic dominated --- countries of: Egypt; Iraq; Syria; Lebanon; and Iran, are yet to be properly documented or recognized internationally.

For the majority of my childhood, I had grown up in the Israeli town of Be'er Sheva. There, during my tertiary education, I had acquired my first degrees of Chemical engineering and Life sciences. Later on, I found myself looking for job opportunities abroad (due to a massive influx of Russian Jews to Israel, which had made it difficult to find stable employment). I had landed in South-Africa in April 1990, two months after the release of Nelson Mandela from prison which was effectively the start of the political transition from the white-minority-ruled Apartheid government, into the African-majority-ruled African National Congress. During this period, I had managed to further my education by studying at the University of the Witwatersrand in Johannesburg; acquiring a Masters degree in Business Administration. I had also worked as a project manager, and had made my own business (few years later) in the engineering field --- designing and providing machinery and services to the mining, water treatment, and food industries. In addition, I had ventured into other marketing and promotional businesses; as well as various property investments.

In recent years, I have furthered my education to an even greater extent by acquiring an LLB degree at the University of the Witwatersrand. As of February 2017, I have been admitted as an Advocate of the South African high court.

My freshly acquired legal skills had instigated some subconscious passion of mine to write. As a secular person, I had decided to write this book about questions that had bothered me for many years.

These questions being: 'Who are the Jews, really?' ; 'Why has there been so much historical animosity towards Jews in Europe?', and 'What exactly is it that makes some Jewish people exceptional in intellectual activities and business ventures?'

For many years (since the beginning of childhood), I have been very interested in history, archeology, and general knowledge. Since I have not seen any proper secular historical writings use legal tools such as legal critical analysis, legal reasoning, and management of evidence; I have decided to engage in the activity of writing about Jewish historical matters from a secular perspective --- using logical tools which are similar to the above legal concepts and thus sifting through much religious bias in the process.

I am exceptionally fluent and literate in Hebrew. I am sufficiently fluent and literate in English and Greek. I can understand --- and communicate on a basic level in --- Arabic, French, and Afrikaans; as well as some superficial levels of Russian and Spanish.

Growing up, my main hobbies had been basketball and chess. I occasionally play and practice chess --- and at times win local tournaments. Over the years, I have been engaged in the martial arts of: Taekwondo; Judo; Wrestling, and Brazilian Jiu Jitsu. I have been married and divorced twice in my life, and have three boys whom I can only be proud of.

My lifelong passion has always been history (which I believe is taught in a dogmatic fashion with a lack of logical order --- creating confusion, illogicality, and many unanswered questions).

Many questions regarding historical processes remain unanswered. When history is combined with religious writings, a massive confusion occurs between fact and fiction. Any logical person nowadays would have a deep feeling that myths and twists of history are rife --- rendering everything as nonsensical.

At the time of their writing, these twists were originally meant to serve the purpose of theological historians and rulers. These rulers had commissioned said writings for their own: political; military; and social subjugation, agendas. Unfortunately, many modern scholars continue to articulate these historical twists instead of properly questioning them.

I am filled with hope that I will manage to break this trend; and in the process, catalyse debate and discussion --- resulting in creative analysis that will portray history, and historical processes, in a logical manner.

I thank all my readers, and hope that you will greatly enjoy this book. I also hope that you will forgive me for all English language mishaps. If you do enjoy this book, look out for my next book (which will hopefully change people's outlook on humanity and life processes altogether).

Note to my readers: When I had decided to finalize this book; being a novice writer, I had suddenly realized that I was faced with the daunting tasks of editing and creating a cover. Since I think in Hebrew, but write in English; the editing needed had been substantial. Quotes for the editing were expensive, and would have required much of my time. My intense engagement would have resulted in many more months of delay.

Since my principal motives for writing this book --- and the second book coming --- are not purely financial; I had decided to self-publish an eBook, with the help of my youngest son, Yaron Peretz, as an editor and Cover Creator. Therefore, I ask your patience and understanding if you stumble across some editing issues. I truly believe that: the layout of this book; it's novel ideas; and my imaginative process which arrives at some interesting conclusions, will more than compensate for some minor grammar, spelling, or style issues. Perhaps in the near future, a paperback second edition of the book will be published. I again thank my readers --- whoever you are and wherever you live in the world. Thank you very much!

Table Of Contents

Chapter 1	20
How America had been advanced, shaped, and moulded by ethnic-Jews	20 20
The arrival of ethnic-Jews to America	21
Ethnic-Jews' intellectual and economic status in America	21
Historical evidence of the intellectual and business excellence of Ethnic-Jews	26
How can this ethnic-Jewish phenomenon be explained?	28
Chapter 2	30
The origins of Judeans and the Jewish Faith	30
Busting the religious myths: facts, fiction, and clues as to the origins of Judaism	30
Western civilization's great debt to the Jewish people	32
The Canaanites and Judeans, and their legacy	33
The Phoenicians, Israelites and Judeans --- Blood Brothers	36
What can be gleaned from the origins of Judaism	41
Chapter 3	43
Judeans under the Babylonian and Persian Empires.	43
Shaping Judaism as a monotheistic religion.	43
The Myths and Marvel of the Torah within a historical context	50
The Non-religious importance of Jewish Monotheism	55
Chapter 4	57
Under the Greek and Roman Empires.	57
Jews under the Greek and Roman Empires	57
Concluding Remarks	64
Chapter 5	66
From Torah studies to Talmudic studies, and beyond.	66
Building a nation on spiritual pursuits	66
The importance of Jewish deeds	67
Jewish education and its impact on the individual and community	70
The substantive content of Jewish education	72
The Torah as a basic guide to life	73
The influence of Jewish education on our modern world	76
Conclusion and modern day implications of education	78
Chapter 6	81
The Rise of Christianity and Islam, and their impact on Judaism	81

Christianity and Judaism	82
Islam and Judaism	88
Judaism's survival of Islam	111
Judaism accredited	112
Chapter 7	**114**
Between the Muslim and Christian worlds.	114
The Spanish golden era of Judaism	114
The Jewish Kingdom of Khazaria	119
Chapter 8	**121**
In Christian Europe of the Middle-Ages	121
The establishment of Jews in inner continental Europe	121
The community life of Jews in Christian-Europe	123
The Christian crusades and their impact on European-Jews	126
Chapter 9	**130**
The community way of life, and Jewish character building.	130
The Jewish home	130
The synagogue	131
The community as the center of life	132
The Jewish entrepreneurial spirit	133
The storyteller	133
Steadfast, debative and argumentative Nation	134
A brainy nation in the European Middle-Ages	135
What I have learnt from my personal encounter with Jewish characters in the diaspora	136
My own encounter with entrepreneurial Jews in the diaspora	137
My encounters with professional scientific Jews	138
Conclusion	138
Chapter 10	**140**
The age of enlightenment, and the emancipation of Jews	140
Thinking that changed the world	143
Chapter 11	**145**
Within the legal profession --- fighting for human rights	145
The legal profession	145
Fighting for human rights	146
The abolition of slavery	148
Equality for women	149

Chapter 12 153
   From Russia to the promised land of America and the troubled state of Israel 153
      The Zionist movement and the birth of Israel 155
      On the way to America 156
      The way forward 166
Chapter 13 167
   The Inherent conflict between religions, and the new-world religions 167
      The deep-rooted conflict of religions 168
      Turning capitalism into one of America's religions 170
      The religion of financial speculation 173
Chapter 14 177
   Anti-Semitism forever 177
      The holocaust as the pinnacle of anti-Semitism 180
      The arrogant anti-Semite 181
      The new age anti-Semitism 182
Chapter 15 187
   Concluding Remarks 187
      Genetic variation 188
      Cultural variation, and cultural warfare 188
      Competitive traits 189
      Innovation 189
      Tenacity 190
      Business Advancement, Teamwork, and Networking 190
      Lessons for the individual citizen of the world 192
      The Great genetic debate 192
      My next book 193

Chapter 1

How America had been advanced, shaped, and moulded by ethnic-Jews

Summary: This chapter will demonstrate the intellectual and business ability of Jewish people, by stating facts about the recent historical success stories of ethnic-Jews in America and Europe (before the rise of the Nazis in Germany).

More than a 120 years ago, Christian American writer and adventurer Mark Twain (Samuel Langhorne Clemens) had lived in Austria for a few years; witnessing the country's illogical anti-Semitic atrocities committed against its Jewish population. Twain --- who is considered by William Faulkner (an American Nobel prize winner for literature) as the 'father of American literature' --- had observed the Jewish phenomenon in his following excerpt:[19]

'If the statistics are right, the Jews constitute but one percent of the human race. It suggests a nebulous dim puff of star-dust lost in the blaze of the Milky Way. Properly the Jew ought hardly to be heard of; but he is heard of, has always been heard of. He is as prominent on the planet as any other people, and his commercial importance is extravagantly out of proportion to the smallness of his bulk. His contributions to the world's list of great names in literature, science, art, music, finance, medicine, and abstruse learning are also way out of proportion to the weakness of his numbers.

He has made a marvellous fight in this world, in all the ages; and has done it with his hands tied behind him. He could be vain of himself, and be excused for it. The Egyptian, the Babylonian, and the Persian rose, filled the planet with sound and splendor, then faded to dream-stuff and passed away; the Greek and the Roman followed, and made a vast noise, and they are gone; other peoples have sprung up and held their torch high for a time, but it burned out, and they sit in twilight now, or have vanished.

The Jew saw them all, beat them all, and is now what he always was, exhibiting no decadence, no infirmities of age, no weakening of his parts, no slowing of his energies, no dulling of his alert and aggressive mind. All things are mortal but the Jew; all other forces pass, but he remains. What is the secret of his immortality?'

--- Mark Twain ('concerning The Jews,' Harper's Magazine, 1898).

Twain's other observations in his open letter --- regarding the general behaviour of Jews within their European societies at the time --- is of importance when considering Jewish culture. Said observations will, at times, be referred to in the subsequent chapters of this book.[20]

The U.S. is still, to this day, considered to contain the largest ethnic-Jewish population in the entire world --- our journey of exploring the Jewish story will begin there.

---

[19] https://legacy.fordham.edu/Halsall/mod/1898twain-jews.asp (accessed 09/04/2016)

[20] Mark Twain is famous for his literary work on the adventures of 'Tom Sawyer' and 'Huckleberry Finn' as well as his recorded travel adventures around the world which were reported to Americans in the 19th century. Twain is also known for publishing his close friend and former American president Ulysses S.Grant memoirs. His observation of the Jews as an American Christian outsider in his open letter as well as his travel adventure in Palestine in 1865 are of value to the goals of this book.

The arrival of ethnic-Jews to America

America's first immigration of the Jewish population had been Sephardic (of Spanish origin) in nature. Arriving mainly from: the Ottoman Empire's Turkey; the Balkans; Portugal; and the Netherlands, these were mainly Jews whose ancestors had left Spain in the year 1492 (due to religious persecution by the Catholic church).[21]

Some prominent figures have arisen from this community over the years, such as: one of Georgia's first governors, David Emanuel[22]; the first Jewish American senator, David Yulee[23] from Florida; and Judah P. Benjamin of Louisiana[24] (President Jefferson's secretary of war and attorney general, who had also become the second Jewish American senator).[25]

Although highly successful in their new homes in the Southern states of America; it is considered that due to the very small size of the Jewish community, its influence on America's history had been very modest. Over the years, many of them had mingled with the local American population; forming new types of Christian communities.

The second wave of Jews had arrived from Germany, and German territories such as Prussia. These Jews, who had been predominantly Ashkenazi, were estimated to have been around 250 000 --- many of whom had been educated, and were trying to escape German anti-Semitic laws and pogroms during the 19th century.

The third wave of Jewish immigration was considerably large by any scale at the time. During the early part of the 20th century, it is estimated that around 2 000 000 Jews had found their way to America --- mainly from Eastern-Europe . These highly oppressed and poor Ashkenazi Jews filled the area of New York; creating a major hub for religious studies and business. Thereafter, they had spread all over America --- mainly to the metros of California, Los Angeles, and San Francisco.

The last two waves of immigration (especially the latter) are considered to be the catalysts of the profound Jewish influence on America's creativity and 'meteoric' intellectual --- as well as economic --- development over the past 140 years. An assessment of the current intellectual and economic status of ethnic-Jews in America can prove the claim that said ethnic-Jews are of the highest status in America.

Ethnic-Jews' intellectual and economic status in America

It is a fact that in America today; ethnic-Jews, or partly-ethnic Jews, occupy prominent positions in all walks of life. These positions being in: politics; finance; hi-tech and media corporations; entertainment companies; sports commissions; the wholesale and retail

---

[21] "Jewish Immigration to America: Three Waves | My Jewish Learning." https://www.myjewishlearning.com/article/jewish-immigration-to-america-three-waves/. Accessed 28 Jan. 2018.
[22] "David Emanuel - National Governors Association." https://www.nga.org/cms/home/governors/past-governors-bios/page_georgia/col2-content/main-content-list/title_emanuel_david.default.html. Accessed 28 Jan. 2018.
[23] "YULEE, David Levy - Biographical Information." http://bioguide.congress.gov/scripts/biodisplay.pl?index=Y000061. Accessed 28 Jan. 2018.
[24] "BENJAMIN, Judah Philip - Biographical Information." http://bioguide.congress.gov/scripts/biodisplay.pl?index=b000365. Accessed 28 Jan. 2018.
[25] "Judah Phillip Benjamin | Civil War Trust." https://www.civilwar.org/learn/biographies/judah-phillip-benjamin. Accessed 28 Jan. 2018.

industry; academic institutions, and largely all esteemed professionals --- namely doctors, lawyers, and accountants.

Anti-Semitic sources will quickly point out that although only comprising a mere 2% of the U.S. population, ethnic-Jews --- and/or partially-ethnic Jews --- control 25% of the economy; and around 22% of all academic posts. 14% of all American doctors are Jewish. However, their high numbers have been shrinking in recent years due to a massive influx of doctors from the far east into the US. An estimated 25% of the total amount of lawyers in America are Jewish; while Jewish accountants are estimated to encompass 25% of their respective profession.[26] Jewish wealth within the U.S.A. --- and around the world --- is mind-boggling.[27]

There are slightly over 110 American ethnic-Jews (over 203 of half or three-quarters-Jewish ancestry worldwide which represent around 25% of Nobel laureates worldwide) who have been awarded the Nobel prize for their achievements --- mainly in the fields of: medicine; physiology; chemistry; physics, and economics. Some of their discoveries have advanced and changed humanity's ability to deal with disease in the most profound way; and have advanced technology beyond belief.[28] Most discoveries are complicated to describe to the layman --- a simple one being that of Selman Waksman[29] and his discovery of streptomycin (the first antibiotic to be found effective against Tuberculosis).

Although they had not received a Nobel prize for their inventions, Jonas Salk[30] and Albert Sabin[31] had alleviated the world from the dreaded polio disease by developing vaccines. Polio had been monstrous disease that had crippled hundreds of millions of human beings from all over the world. Salk and Sabin were both American ethnic-Jews.

Ethnic, or partly-ethnic, American Jews have been overwhelmingly instrumental in the Hi-tech industries of America. Individuals such as: Larry Ellison[32], the founder of Oracle; Paul Allen, the co-founder of Microsoft [33]; Sergey Brin[34] and Larry Page[35], the co-founders of Google; Steve Wozniak[36] the co-founder of Apple; Irwin Jacobs[37] of Qualcomm; the legendary CEO of Intel, Andrew Grove[38], Andrew Rubin[39] who is considered the "father of the Android

---

[26] "Jewish Dominance Of America - Facts Are Facts - Rense." http://www.rense.com/general59/sdom.htm. Accessed 28 Jan. 2018.
[27] "Jewish Wealth by the Numbers - Taki's Magazine." 1 May. 2013, http://takimag.com/article/jewish_wealth_by_the_numbers_steve_sailer/print. Accessed 28 Jan. 2018.
[28] "Jewish Nobel Prize Winners - Jinfo.org." http://www.jinfo.org/Nobel_Prizes.html. Accessed 28 Jan. 2018.
[29] "Selman A. Waksman - Biographical." https://www.nobelprize.org/nobel_prizes/medicine/laureates/1952/waksman-bio.html. Accessed 28 Jan. 2018.
[30] "About Jonas Salk - Salk Institute for Biological Studies." https://www.salk.edu/about/history-of-salk/jonas-salk/. Accessed 28 Jan. 2018.
[31] "The Legacy of Albert B. Sabin | Sabin." http://www.sabin.org/legacy-albert-b-sabin. Accessed 28 Jan. 2018.
[32] "Larry Ellison - Forbes." https://www.forbes.com/profile/larry-ellison/. Accessed 28 Jan. 2018.
[33] "Paul Allen - Wikipedia." https://en.wikipedia.org/wiki/Paul_Allen. Accessed 28 Jan. 2018.
[34] "Sergey Brin - Inventor, Computer Programmer, Engineer - Biography ...." 2 Nov. 2016, https://www.biography.com/people/sergey-brin-12103333. Accessed 28 Jan. 2018.
[35] "Larry Page - Wikipedia." https://en.wikipedia.org/wiki/Larry_Page. Accessed 28 Jan. 2018.
[36] "Steve Wozniak - Wikipedia." https://en.wikipedia.org/wiki/Steve_Wozniak. Accessed 28 Jan. 2018.
[37] "Irwin M. Jacobs - Wikipedia." https://en.wikipedia.org/wiki/Irwin_M._Jacobs. Accessed 28 Jan. 2018.
[38] "Andrew Grove - Wikipedia." https://en.wikipedia.org/wiki/Andrew_Grove. Accessed 28 Jan. 2018.
[39] "Andy Rubin - Wikipedia." https://en.wikipedia.org/wiki/Andy_Rubin. Accessed 2 Mar. 2019.

system"[40], and the latest and most famous ethnic-Jew in recent years . . . Mark Zuckerberg[41] of Facebook. These individuals have moulded and shaped America's Hi-tech industries. At every significant field in said industry, one will find an ethnic (or partly-ethnic) Jew. At times, one needs to dig further; as many individuals still hide their ethnic-Jewish origins due to the historic complications of being identified as a Jew. Some like Larry Page try to erase any trace of their Jewish origins completely.

The reader can easily search the following individuals in various American industries in order to discover their Jewish origins. We will begin with the entertainment industry:

Hollywood had literally been founded by Jews. The 'Golden Age' of Hollywood is marked by individuals such as: Marcus Loew and Louis Mayer (founders of Metro-Goldwyn-Mayer Studios); Adolph Zukor (founder of Paramount pictures); Albert, Sam, Harry and Jack Warner (founders of Warner Brothers Studios); Joseph Schenk (co-founder of Fox movies); and Harry Cohn (founder of Columbia pictures). The industry had almost been completely founded and dominated by Jewish entrepreneurs. Many producers, directors, and actors have also been Jewish in origin. We are all very familiar with famous directors such as Steven Spielberg and Woody Allen. Much is also known about Jewish actors such Seth Rogen, Adam Sandler, and Mila Kunis who declare their Jewish origins --- but little is known about actors such as Jack Black and Scarlett Johansson who are discreet about their Jewish origins. In addition to these personalities, very little is known about --- or remembered of --- iconic American actors such as: Harrison Ford; Mel Brooks; Tony Curtis (Bernard Schwartz); Kirk Douglas (Issur Danielovitch); Lauren Bacall (Betty Joan Perske); and Paul Newman (who stated that he considers himself as a Jew without religion, and that being Jewish is 'more of a challenge' for him). The full list is overwhelming in its length and depth. This points to the heavy influence of Jewish culture (and Jewish values) on American culture.

The influence of American Jews on mass media is also apparent: Warner communications had been founded by Steven Jay Ross (Rechnitz); Viacom had been co-founded by Sumner Murray Redstone (Rothstein), who is also Chairman Emeritus of CBS; the current president and CEO of CBS is Leslie Moonves (an individual of Jewish heritage); NBC is owned by Comcast, which was founded by Ralph Joel Roberts and Julian A. Brodsky (both of which are of Jewish heritage). These four companies represent 66.6% of 'The Big Six', which includes News Corporation and Disney. The latter two also include smaller companies that had been purchased from former Jewish owners, and were merged --- they are still influenced by executives, managers, and owners of ethnic (and/or partially-ethnic) Jewish origin. Disney is of particularly special interest, since it had been founded by Walt Disney --- an accused anti-Semite who would turn in his grave if he knew the multitude of ethnic-Jews managing his founded firm. Said ethnic-Jews include current Chairman and CEO Robert Allen Iger, and his predecessor Michael Eisner; as well as the current president of Marvel Studios --- Kevin Feige. Other specialised media such as Bloomberg T.V. (created by Michael Bloomberg) also reveals Jewish dominance in the communication of financial news.

Searching up the creators of popular American comic-book heroes will also leave the readers astounded. Superman had been created by Jerry Siegel and Joe Shuster; while Spider-Man by Stan Lee (Stanley Martin Lieber), who had been the president and chairman of Marvel Studios --- a company that owns other popular American cartoon heroes such as:

---

[40] "How Android was created - Business Insider." https://www.businessinsider.com/how-android-was-created-2015-3. Accessed 2 Mar. 2019.
[41] "Mark Zuckerberg - Wikipedia." https://en.wikipedia.org/wiki/Mark_Zuckerberg. Accessed 28 Jan. 2018.

The Hulk; Iron-Man; Thor; The Fantastic Four, and Daredevil (among others). Batman was created by Bob Kane (Kahn) and Bill Finger. All of the above mentioned had been Jewish, and had possessed incredible creative power.

American literature is laden with ethnic-Jewish writers. From the classics of Franz Kafka and Arthur Miller, to Isaac Asimov in the science fiction field and many other well-known American authors.[42]

This creative power is overwhelming and dominating in all aspects of the American entertainment industry. From sports shows to comic shows; host shows, reality T.V. shows, and political T.V. programs. It is overwhelming how many: writers; producers; directors, and presenters are of Jewish origins. Many will hide or deny their Jewish origins; many will change their names for a stage name that is more palatable and sounds 'American', and many will not even be aware that they themselves have Jewish links within their family.

In comedy and stand up comedy shows, most readers will be familiar with: Jerry Seinfeld; Mel Brooks; Louis Szekely; Roseanne Barr; Woody Allen; Billy Crystal; Jon Stewart; Chelsea Handler; Adam Sandler, and Larry David. There are many more well-known individuals within the industry, including famous historical icon Walter Matthau.

Both David Benioff and D.B. Weiss --- co-writers, co-creators, and co-showrunners for the T.V. series currently taking the world by storm, 'Game Of Thrones' --- are two other ethnic-Jews leading the entertainment industry.

Ethnic-Jewish talk show host celebrities such as: Jerry Springer; Joan Rivers; Larry King, and Barbara Walters are also well known in the US, and around the world --- including CNN news anchor Wolf Blitzer.

Many popular reality shows had also been created by people of Jewish origin. The most recent programs being 'The X-Factor' and 'America's Got Talent', which were created by Simon Cowell and Brian Friedman. Cowell's paternal ancestors are of Jewish origin, while Friedman is an ethnic-Jewish American.

In American sports, the situation of Jewish ownership and dominance is somewhat mixed. It may come as a relief to the reader to find that only an estimated 50% of the NFL owners are of ethnic-Jewish heritage. Leading the list is Paul Allen --- the late owner of the Seattle Seahawks, who was previously mentioned as the co-founder of Microsoft; followed by Stephen Ross, who purchased the Miami Dolphins in 2008. Proceeding them are Malcolm Glazer, owner of the Tampa bay buccaneers, and Joan Tisch --- owner of the New York Giants. The NBA is almost entirely owned, and managed, by Jewish Businessmen --- the current Commissioner of the NBA being Adam Silver, also an ethnic-Jew. To mention a few, Paul Allen and Steve Ballmer --- who were prominent in Microsoft --- own the Portland Trail Blazers, as well as the Los Angeles Clippers. The current Golden State Warriors are owned by Joe Lacob --- another ethnic-Jew, who is also a venture capitalist.

Ethnic-Jews are also involved with, and take the lead in, all major wholesale and retail business in America. As the list is too long, I will only mention the Lauder family (who own Estee Lauder cosmetics). Ron Lauder is also the current President of the World Jewish Congress.

The 'Diamond On The Crown' of America's business is the world financial system. In 1987, Alan Greenspan --- titled 'The Honourable Alan Greenspan' --- had been appointed by President Ronald Reagan as Chairman of the Federal Reserve Bank of America. Greenspan went on to be trusted by four consecutive Presidents, and had been the most influential

---

[42] "Best Jewish Authors | List of the Greatest Jewish Writers - Ranker." https://www.ranker.com/list/best-jewish-authors/ranker-books. Accessed 28 Jan. 2018.

Chairman of the Federal Reserve Bank of America (in modern times). Greenspan had been replaced by Ben Bernanke, who was then replaced by Janet Yellen --- all of whom are ethnic-Jews. This trend reveals the continual Jewish leadership of the Federal Reserve Bank of America for the past 30 years.

The Federal Reserve Bank had been founded on American legislation initiated and guided by Paul Moritz Warburg[43] --- a German-Jewish banker who had immigrated to the United States, and had been appalled by the unsophisticated American financial system at the time. This was when financial panics were frequent and interest rates were erratic; sometimes soaring to 100% annually.

Then come most of the financial powerhouses which include: Goldman Sachs, run by Lloyd Blankfein; Blackrock, founded by Larry Fink; Pacific Investment, co-founded by Bill Gross; Icahn enterprises, founded by Carl Icahn; and a long and wide list of other companies. Even the legendary investor, Mr. Warren Buffett of Berkshire Hathaway, credits a big portion of his financial success to his former employer and mentor Professor Benjamin Graham (Grossbaum)[44] --- who is considered to be the 'father of value investing'. Mr. Buffett had been quoted saying that besides for his biological father, Professor Graham had the greatest influence on him for the duration of his entire life. Buffet even named his son 'Howard Graham' in Professor Graham's honour.

What is apparent from all of the above is that a process has taken place, whereby America has been becoming more Judaic in the sense of business and intellect; while Jews have become more American in unique settings of secular freedom and liberalism. As the process continues, the entire Western World is becoming more Judaic in its outlook. This is evident, as what we: see; hear; laugh about; cry about; or are surprised about, has hidden influences from ethnic-Jews.

Much of recent technology such as: Google; Facebook; Apple; and Microsoft, had been made, or influenced, by ethnic Jews. The content on the internet and media is highly influenced by Jewish writers, producers, and showmen/women. Substantial amounts of medicine we use today had been made by Jewish scientists and doctors; and our views about space and the universe are shaped by Jewish physicists like Albert Einstein and Niels Bohr (also of Jewish origin).

Once we realize that the situation of ethnic-Jewish influence placed in front of us is real and a fact of the modern world; it is natural to ask: 'How did this happen?' ; 'When did this process start?' ; 'Why aren't we influenced by much larger ethnic groups that arrived at, or were brought to, America earlier?' ; and 'Why are we not influenced as much by the British, Germans, Irish, French, Italians, Greeks or Africans?'

Can the hidden secrets for the intellectual and business excellence of this minor ethnic group be revealed, distilled, and used to everyone's advantage?

---

[43] "Paul M. Warburg | Federal Reserve History."
https://www.federalreservehistory.org/people/paul_m_warburg. Accessed 28 Jan. 2018.
[44] "10 Little Known Benjamin Graham Quotes and Facts - Wall Street ...." 9 Apr. 2013,
http://blog.wallstreetsurvivor.com/2013/04/09/investor-profile-benjamin-graham/. Accessed 28 Jan. 2018.

Historical evidence of the intellectual and business excellence of Ethnic-Jews

The overwhelming excellence of Jews in: Science; technology; finance; and the various other professions in American society, is not unprecedented. Nearly a century earlier in Germany, Jews had reached the top of German society --- that is until their demise caused by the racist and indoctrinated Nazi regime. The prolific English historian Sir Arthur Bryant[45] described the situation in 1924 Reichstag governed Germany. Although comprising close to only 1% of the German population, Jews had been the business superstars of Germany; controlling 57% of the metal trade, 22% of the grain trade, and 39% of all textile manufacturers. More than 50% of members of the Berlin Chamber of Commerce were Jewish, as well as an astounding 85% of the Stock Exchange brokers. 23 of the official 29 theatres had Jewish Directorship. Authorship was under the complete dominance of Jews.[46] Jakob Wassermann[47], in his book 'My life as a German Jew', recalls that theatres in Berlin were closed on the Sabbath as the majority of the management and workers had been Jewish. Nahum Goldmann[48] also describes how Jewish economic dominance in Germany had been absolute; highlighting the fact that Jewish business had even made substantial inroads into the large shipping business that had been totally dominated by non-Jews.[49] It is documented that the largest German electrical concern AEG[50], and its subsidiary Telefunken, had been founded by Emil Moritz Rathenau[51] --- an ethnic-Jew who is credited for the electrification of Germany. His Son, Walther Rathenau[52], had been Weimar Germany's Foreign minister. Rathenau was later assassinated by an extreme right-wing nationalist terrorist group. Until the year 1938, approximately 33% of all German Nobel Prize winners had been Jewish; some of whom had been forbidden by Hitler to receive the prize.[53] The most famous scientist is Albert Einstein[54], who had received his Nobel prize in 1921 for his most outstanding contributions to mankind in the field of physics.

---

[45] "Sir Arthur Bryant | British historian | Britannica.com." https://www.britannica.com/biography/Arthur-Bryant. Accessed 28 Jan. 2018.
[46] "Jewish Dominance Of America - Facts Are Facts - Rense." http://www.rense.com/general59/sdom.htm. Accessed 28 Jan. 2018.
[47] "My Life As German And Jew : Jacob Wassermann : Free Download ...." https://archive.org/details/mylifeasgermanan027953mbp. Accessed 28 Jan. 2018.
[48] "Nahum Goldmann | Israeli Zionist leader | Britannica.com." https://www.britannica.com/biography/Nahum-Goldmann. Accessed 28 Jan. 2018.
[49] "The Autobiography of Nahum Goldmann: Sixty Years of ... - Amazon.com." https://www.amazon.com/Autobiography-Nahum-Goldmann-Sixty-Jewish/dp/0030813379. Accessed 28 Jan. 2018.
[50] "Welcome to AEG." http://www.aeg.com/. Accessed 28 Jan. 2018.
[51] "The Life of Emil Rathenau | German 2798- Emil Rathenau - Osu." 14 May. 2015, https://u.osu.edu/berlin2798ranthenau/2015/05/14/personal-life-and-schooling/. Accessed 28 Jan. 2018.
[52] "The Assassination of Walther Rathenau | History Today." http://www.historytoday.com/nigel-jones/assassination-walther-rathenau. Accessed 28 Jan. 2018.
[53] "Nobel Prize Facts." https://www.nobelprize.org/nobel_prizes/facts/. Accessed 28 Jan. 2018.
[54] "Albert Einstein - Biographical." https://www.nobelprize.org/nobel_prizes/physics/laureates/1921/einstein-bio.html. Accessed 28 Jan. 2018.

This unprecedented success of German-Jews had been the result of nearly 90 years of emancipation and relative peaceful existence --- this being after subjection to horrendous atrocities from their Christian-German neighbours for nearly a thousand (1000) years.

It is well known that the emancipation of European-Jews had begun with Napoleon in the early part of the 18th Century.

By analysing Napoleon's response to the question as to why he had emancipated the Jews (a question asked by his physician Dr. Barry O'Meara who had interviewed him in exile) we can learn that apart from all the prejudice associated with Jews, they had been perceived by Napoleon as wealth generators.

'I should have drawn great wealth to France as the Jews are very numerous, and would have flocked to a country where they enjoyed such superior privities. Moreover, I wanted to establish an universal liberty of conscience.'[55]

Following the emancipation of Jews in Europe, it is documented that they had risen to prominence in many European countries --- until their demise by the Nazis. This will be expanded upon in chapter 10.

Some four hundred years earlier, Jews had been expelled from Spain by the then new Christian conquerors of the Iberian Peninsula. Before said expulsion, Jews had been prominent in business for hundreds of years during the Islamic rule of the Iberian Peninsula. A more extensive account of the Jewish-Spanish era is written in Chapter 8.

The most recent evidence regarding the brilliance of the Jewish mind is the recent technological successes within the state of Israel. Today, Israel is globally renowned for its innovations in Informational Technology. Sophisticated electronic innovations such as 'Mobileye Autonomous Driving Systems'[56], had recently been bought by Intel for $15 billion. Others innovations include: 'Waze GPS navigator'[57], which had been bought by Google for nearly $1 billion; and 'Orbotech'[58], which had been purchased by KLA-Tencor for $3.4 billion, as well as many other Israeli companies and innovations which are usually bought for hundreds of millions of dollars by American technological giants such as: Apple; Microsoft; Facebook, and Google.

Based on these facts, it can be reasonably assumed that Jewish-American domination, in terms of intellect and business, is a result of hidden traits within the Jewish culture --- traits that have been built over many years. One of the goals of this book is to identify said traits (as well as other contributing factors to the success of Jews' that have remained hidden within the Jewish culture).

The discourse around whether or not Jewish prowess is genetically inherited may not be that important after all, as it can be reasonably assumed that the survival of beneficial genes is an expression of an environmental pressure to survive (which is linked to the culture of a community). Further discussion regarding genetics will take place in subsequent chapters.

---

[55] "Napoleon And The Jews - Aish.com." 11 Aug. 2007, http://www.aish.com/jl/h/h/48945221.html. Accessed 28 Jan. 2018.

[56] "Why Intel is buying car-vision company Mobileye for $15.3B ...." 13 Mar. 2017, https://www.computerworld.com/article/3180164/car-tech/why-intel-is-buying-car-vision-company-mobileye-for-153b.html. Accessed 28 Jan. 2018.

[57] "Waze - Wikipedia." https://en.wikipedia.org/wiki/Waze. Accessed 28 Jan. 2018.

[58] "Orbotech." https://www.orbotech.com/. Accessed 21 Mar. 2018.

How can this ethnic-Jewish phenomenon be explained?

Nowadays it is a researched fact that American Ashkenazi-Jews, as an ethnic group in America, possess the highest IQ on the planet --- with an average of 112-115 points.[59] This score is 12-15 points higher than the mean, which is an IQ of 100. The gap widens even further at the narrow end of the IQ scale.

While the general population muster 4 people with an IQ of over 140 per 1000 individuals, American Ashkenazi-Jews will produce 23 such individuals per 1000 Jewish people . . . that statistic is nearly 6 fold in frequency.[60] This is significant, as it can partly explain the Academic, Professional, and Financial success of ethnic-Jews in North America.

It is obvious that, in many intellectual fields, an individual with an IQ of 140 will perform far better than an individual with an IQ of 100 --- however, this will only be true if both parties exert equal amounts of effort in attempting to achieve a specific task.

What about two individuals with the exact same IQ score of 140? Such individuals, whether they be Jewish or not, should turn out to be equally successful (given that all other parameters are equal). Considering this simple logic, and taking the relatively small quantities of the Jewish population in America (around 2%) versus the general population into account, we still remain in a perplexing situation; as it seems that in most scenarios, the Jewish individual will turn out to be more successful --- despite the fact that the number of Jewish individuals with an IQ score of more than 140 is only one tenth of all Americans who possess the same IQ score or higher. Some simple arithmetic may better explain this point.

If the total population of America is 320 million people, and only 6.4 million of which are considered to be of Jewish origin, then the number of Jewish individuals with an IQ score equal to --- or greater than --- 140 will be 147,200 (nearly 150,000); while the general American population will have 1,280,000 (nearly 1.3 million) such individuals. The result of this calculation being that amongst all Americans who have an IQ equal to, or greater than, 140; 10.3% of such individuals belong to the ethnic-Jewish population. Yet, it is apparent that the dominance of ethnic-Jews in the various fields of business (and other professions) treads into spheres of influence reaching heights of: 20%; 25%; 30%; 40%, and even up to 70% in certain high-end lucrative fields such as the media, business, and finance. This is a huge discrepancy between expectation and reality. It is also important to consider that within the general American population, there are millions of individuals who possess substantial amounts of Jewish genes --- even though they are no longer ethnically-Jewish. Some of said individuals may contribute to the generation of high IQ individuals in America. Since the immigration of just over 2 million Jews to America in 1880, the Jewish population's growth rate has been less than half of the general American population's growth rate --- this indicates to a high rate of ethnic-Jewish assimilation into the general American population.

The simple statistical calculations shown above indicate that IQ alone cannot explain the Jewish phenomenon; and that there may be many other factors at play that determine this current state of ethnic-Jewish dominance. These factors include: favourable environmental conditions; individual motivation and work ethic; group work efficiency, and cultural differences from the general population that influence productive living (such as abstinence from alcohol or drugs). Aside from these characteristics, there are many other hidden factors that are not easily identifiable or quantifiable. What is of certainty is that most of these factors are rooted,

---

[59] "Natural History of Ashkenazi Intelligence - MIT."
http://web.mit.edu/fustflum/documents/papers/AshkenaziIQ.jbiosocsci.pdf. Accessed 28 Jan. 2018.
[60] ibid

in one way or another, in Judaic culture or makeup; as people are usually a reflection of their culture.

My assumption is that even individuals of second or third generations will hold certain characteristics from their predecessors' Jewish culture. These characteristics do, however, eventually dilute and wane; as people often remove themselves from their own heritage, and adopt other cultures and ways of life. Some characteristics of their initial culture then lose priority, while other foreign characteristics of the adopted culture gain favour. Overtime, a new and modified culture develops --- be it for better or for worse is a matter of personal interpretation.

Based on my assumptions, the primary task of my research will be to explore, identify, and quantify characteristics and traits that Judaic culture has installed into individuals over the years. This, I believe, will bring me closer to acquiring some tangible answers as to the reason for the phenomenon of Jewish intellectual and business domination.

In order to achieve this task, it is necessary to gain a substantial understanding of the many historical processes and changes that had been instrumental in the formation of Judaic culture.

Beginning with the origins of Judaism will provide insight into the national and communal interactions within the general environment that had existed at the time. Further exploration of the interactions that had occurred between other nations of antiquity will reveal the influence said nations had on the development of Judaism. These macro processes build character (in terms of nationality), which in turn influences the behaviour of an individual and determines the various aspects of their character. Many of these traits are be passed down to future generations; and, over many years, some national or ethnic characteristics are built.

Throughout our journey of exploration, original and surprising insights about the history of other nations and religions will emerge. These insights may assist in forming a better understanding of the world we live in today --- including the composition of its population, its perils and opportunities, and possible ways to advance and improve the lives of all humanity. Our journey will begin in the 6th century BCE, whereby historical and archaeological documentation is of significance. The origins of the Jewish Bible can also be traced to that time period (as will become apparent).

Chapter 2

The origins of Judeans and the Jewish Faith

Summary: This chapter will attempt to establish the true historical roots of ethnic-Jews. It will demonstrate a huge gap between religious scriptures and historical/archeological facts regarding the origins of ethnic-Jews. Said archeological and historical facts will point to the huge influence that the Persian Empire and their Zoroastrian religion had on the creation of Judaism. The role that Babylonian culture had played in the creation of Judaism will also be made apparent. The chapter will end on the surprising gift that Judaic people had given to the modern world (apart from the Bible's morals), in the hope that modern humanity will begin to understand and appreciate Jewish peoples' contributions to civilization.

Busting the religious myths: facts, fiction, and clues as to the origins of Judaism

The religious Jewish population, as well as all Christian populations, will refer to the Biblical stories of the Torah as the starting point of the Jewish nation --- from the stories of Abraham, Isaac and Jacob; all the way through to the life in, and exodus from, Egypt under the leadership of Moses. This being followed by the conquering of Canaan and the life of the Israelites in their God's promised land; and thereafter, the era of the Kings: Saul; David; Solomon; and their descendants, until the destruction of the first Temple and the Babylonian exile.

For centuries, many historical books written by: Jewish; Christian; and secular authors, had partially been based on the Biblical Torah --- the result being that the Bible had acquired the status of a historical document. One such example is Paul Johnson's famous book 'A History of the Jews'.[61]

The biggest problem with the Torah's stories is that there is no archaeological evidence whatsoever to support them. Beyond the Torah, and the Biblical stories, there is scant archaeological evidence to support the existence of even a few of the Bible's royal personalities. Only King Ahab of Israel, as well as a handful of the Judean kings before the destruction of the first temple, is archaeologically documented --- all other stories of the Bible completely lack archaeological or historical evidence to support them.[62] This lack of evidence makes it difficult to believe the Biblical stories of the Torah, as these stories are not valid grounds on which to unveil the true origins of the Jewish people.

Scrutinizing archaeological and historical evidence prior to the destruction of the first temple, and comparing it to the archaeological and historical evidence at the time of return from the Babylonian exile, may enable us to assess the outline of the origins and formation of Judaism as a monotheistic religion and arrive at a plausible conclusion.

As previously mentioned, the first noteworthy observation is that there is absolutely no evidence of the existence of the Torah before the destruction of the first temple (leading into the Babylonian exile) . . . not even a trace of important documentation such as the Ten Commandments --- the core principles on which the Torah is based. Upon return from the

---

[61] "A History of the Jews: Amazon.co.uk: Paul Johnson: 8601400093931 ...."
https://www.amazon.co.uk/History-Jews-Paul-Johnson/dp/0060915331. Accessed 28 Jan. 2018.
[62] "Is the Bible supported by modern archaeology?."
http://www.sciencemeetsreligion.org/theology/bible-archaeology.php. Accessed 28 Jan. 2018.

Babylonian exile however, the Torah becomes the heart and central focus of the Jews and their existence.

The alphabet used is a crucial clue that indicates to which time period the Torah had been written in. The Torah is written in a script that is almost identical to what is termed by linguistic experts as the 'Imperial Aramaic script'[63]. Aramaic had been the lingua Franca of the Assyrian and Babylonian Empires (also known in history as the Chaldeans). This alphabet had also been adopted at a later stage in history by the Persians . . . after they had conquered the Babylonian Empire.

Imperial Aramaic script is different to the ancient Hebrew and Phoenician alphabet; in the sense that although the Aramaic alphabet had been derived from the Hebrew and Phoenician alphabet, the shape of its letters had been modified to look more square like --- making it visually different from the original ancient Hebrew/Phoenician alphabet.[64]

The fact that the Bible had been written in this type of script and not the ancient Hebrew script is a strong indication that it had been written either during the Babylonian captivity; or, during the Persian rule of the Middle-East thereafter. Therefore, the Bible must have been written by people who wrote and understood the Aramaic alphabet. The audience for this writing had to have been people who were literate in this alphabet. Babylonian-Jews were naturally the most suited candidates to be the audience addressed for the Torah and Biblical stories.

It is impossible for the audience to have been the Judeans prior to the Babylonian exile, as they had used the ancient Hebrew/Phoenician alphabet and would not have recognised even a single character of the Imperial Aramaic writings.

Many historians consider ancient Hebrew to be a sister language to Phoenician. This language had been used by Jews in Judea during the time period prior to the Babylonian exile. It is therefore logical to assume that the Torah, as well as ancillary books of which the Bible is comprised, had been written either during or after the Babylonian exile leading into the period of the Persian Empire's rule of the Middle-East.

If it is conceded that the Torah and other Biblical stories had been written either during or after the Babylonian exile --- then many religious myths can be easily shattered. In all likelihood (to the disapproval of religious people around the world who strongly believe in the Bible) the first myth that can be busted is the myth of prophecy.

At the time during which the Bible was written, most prophetic stories which appear in the Bible (such as the destruction of the Assyrian Empire and its capital city of Nineveh) had already been historical facts that had occured before the Bible was even written. The prophecy of the reconstruction of the second Temple is therefore also proven void, since the Temple had either been in preparations for construction before the Bible was written; or, the process of construction had already begun during the time in which the Bible was written.

These religious prophetic myths can be dubbed, or described by a secular person, as 'Hindsight Pseudo-Prophecy'. This 'Hindsight Pseudo-Prophecy' is only of value to the hard-core religious believer. Modern secular people will not entertain such prophetic beliefs --- especially when presented with the above known historical facts.

Archaeology can further enhance one's understanding of the differences between Judaism prior to the Babylonian exile, and Judaism after the Babylonian exile; thus providing extra tools in helping one understand the source of Judaism and the Jewish people.

---

[63] "ScriptSource - Imperial Aramaic." http://scriptsource.org/scr/Armi. Accessed 28 Jan. 2018.
[64] "Aramaic language and alphabet - Omniglot." https://www.omniglot.com/writing/aramaic.htm. Accessed 28 Jan. 2018.

Archaeological evidence of small personal artifacts from the pre-Babylonian exile era (that had once been in Judea), indicate that it had been common to possess statues of 'Baal' and 'Asherah' (Male and Female Gods) which had been considered the Gods of all nations in Canaan. The Judeans partook in the customs of the Canaanites; their male God was named 'Yahweh', and alongside this God resided a female God named 'Asherah'. Judaism had not originally been a purely monotheistic religion, but rather a dual-theism worship for a God and his Goddess consort. Male and Female Gods. The Bible constant warning against the idol worship of Baal and Asherah corroborate with the archeological findings of a male and female Gods, it just does not name the male God Yahweh but Baal which was the principle male God of the Phoenicians.

Dr. William Dever, a famous archaeologist, has made some YouTube videos on this subject.[65] It has been noticed that during the post-Babylonian exile era, the custom of the possessing statues of the dual Gods had been discontinued. At times, only the statue of the Male God had been found; and in later periods, following the return from Babylonian captivity, statues or images of any God had become scarce.

The return from the Babylonian exile seems to have set the Jewish nation on an entirely new moral and philosophical path --- the path of the Torah. A path which revolves around a faceless God (Yahweh) and his laws given to the children of Israel; laws which are written in the Torah and are mandatory.

In order to understand why this transformation had occurred, it is necessary to scrutinize the Babylonian exile; and the Persian occupation of Babylon. This will be dealt with in the following chapter.

Western civilization's great debt to the Jewish people

The Babylonian and Persian influence on the formation of Judaism should not detract from the intellectual capacity of the Judeans that had existed before the Babylonian exile. King Nebuchadnezzar's decision to transfer the Judeans from Canaan to Babylon had specific reasoning linked to their intellectual capability.[66] The following may shed some light on their historical intellectual capacities.

It is generally taught that the Latin alphabet (the English language being its latest historical form) had been introduced to Europe by the Phoenicians[67] (according to the historical accounts of the Greek Historian, Herodotus).[68]

It is of no difficulty to recognise that the Hebrew letter 'Aleph' became the Greek letter 'Alpha', which in turn became the Latin letter 'A'. The Hebrew letter 'Beit' became the Greek letter 'Beta', and later the Latin letter 'B'. This trend continues with most of the characters of the alphabet. The most terrible aspect about this selective modern European teaching is the fact that the Phoenicians are tacitly or unknowingly credited for the invention of the alphabet used by the modern world --- even though, according to archeological findings, they had

---

[65] https://www.youtube.com/watch?v=_ZADRRdaUG8 (accessed June 2016)
[66] "Who was Nebuchadnezzar? - Got Questions." 10 Feb. 2011, https://www.gotquestions.org/Nebuchadnezzar.html. Accessed 29 Jan. 2018.
[67] "Phoenician alphabet and language - Omniglot." https://www.omniglot.com/writing/phoenician.htm. Accessed 29 Jan. 2018.
[68] "History of the Greek alphabet - Wikipedia." https://en.wikipedia.org/wiki/History_of_the_Greek_alphabet. Accessed 29 Jan. 2018.

probably not invented it. The question is, if the Phoenicians had introduced the Europeans to the Alphabet; who had actually invented the Alphabet?

Today, it is archaeologically documented that the alphabet had probably been invented by Southern Canaanites bordering the Egyptian Pharaonic Kingdom[69] --- but who exactly were those Southern Canaanites?

Again, by sidelining the stories of the Torah and instead turning to archeology, one finds that it is somewhat accepted nowadays by archeologists that the Israelites/Judeans --- among others such as: the Phoenicians; Ammonites; Moabites; and Edomites --- had most probably been the Canaanites the Bible describes.[70] The most Southern Canaanite nations bordering Egypt had been the Israelites and Judeans --- amongst whom the oldest Hebrew/Phoenician inscription was found.[71] Said inscription is believed to pre-date any such inscription in Phoenicia itself.

All these nations are now extinct --- all except the Jews, who claim Judean descendance. Why do they not receive any credit in the modern world's historical education books for the invention of the alphabet? Is it possible that Europeans are reluctant to credit Jews for such an important invention?

The invention of the alphabet is perhaps the most important innovation in the entire history of civilization throughout the Western world.

Over the course of civilization, the alphabet had provided quick and easy recording, storage, and transfer of information between humans. All books, electronic media, and technological advancement are a result of the implementation and application of the alphabet. It is impossible to comprehend how the world would have been without the alphabet --- we are simply accustomed to it and take it for granted. The world owes a huge moral debt to Judaic people (solely based on the strong probability that Judeans had invented the alphabet).

The least that should be done to pay back this debt would be the adjustment of learning material in schools, so as to accurately inform students about the instrumental role Judaic people had played in the formation of the alphabet. That could possibly be one of the best ways to fight anti-Semitism within continental Europe and the Arab world. Why doesn't UNESCO embark on such an education program?

The Canaanites and Judeans, and their legacy

The story of the Judaic people begins in a place known as the fertile crescent[72] in the Middle-East. This area, which stretches from modern day Iraq through: Syria; Eastern-Turkey; Lebanon; Israel; and Egypt, is considered to be the cradle of Western civilization.

The massive Euphrates and Tigris rivers on the one side of the fertile crescent, and the Nile river on the other side, had allowed for an abundance of crops to grow; crops which could sustain large populations.

---

[69] "Proto-Sinaitic / Proto-Canaanite scripts - Omniglot."
https://www.omniglot.com/writing/protosinaitc.htm. Accessed 29 Jan. 2018.
[70] "Ancient DNA reveals fate of the mysterious Canaanites | Science | AAAS." 27 Jul. 2017,
http://www.sciencemag.org/news/2017/07/ancient-dna-reveals-fate-mysterious-canaanites. Accessed 30 Jan. 2018.
[71] "Inscription bearing name from Davidic era found at ancient site | The ...."
https://www.timesofisrael.com/inscription-bearing-name-from-davidic-era-found-at-ancient-site/.
Accessed 29 Jan. 2018.
[72] "Fertile Crescent - Ancient History Encyclopedia." https://www.ancient.eu/Fertile_Crescent/.
Accessed 20 Feb. 2018.

The narrow corridor in the middle is the Biblical Canaan, consisting of parts of: Modern Syria and Lebanon; Israel; Arab-Palestinian territories, and Jordan. It is possible that this area could have only sustained much smaller populations; and, over the course of ancient history, had been subject to invasions from the much larger Egyptian Pharaonic Kingdoms[73] of the South, as well as the Assyrian[74] and Babylonian[75] Empires of the North-West and North-East, respectively.

This power struggle between the Northern Empires and the Pharaonic Kingdom had stretched over thousands of years. This power struggle is archaeologically and historically documented, as well as being corroborated by some Biblical stories.

Aside from the Biblical stories about the multitude of small nations that had occupied Canaan, archaeologically documented nations are: the Judean Kingdom[76] in the South and Central mountain ridge (which nowadays includes Jerusalem); the Philistines,[77] in a narrow coastal strip (today consisting of the Gaza strip and some parts of Southern-Israel); the ancient Kingdom of Israel[78] (just North-West of Judea and Philistine and partly along the coast bordering Phoenicia in the North); The Phoenicians[79] (along the coast of what is today northern modern Israel and Lebanon); the Arameans[80] (to the North-East), and smaller desert-dwellers such as the Nabateans[81], Edomites[82], Moabites[83] and Ammonites[84] (on the Eastern parts bordering the Jordanian desert).

Aside from the Philistines --- who are documented as an invading nation from somewhere in the Mediterranean (Possibly the Island of Crete) --- all the other nations mentioned above are considered Semitic, and had been related by shared languages and the worship of similar Gods.

Since these nations had been subject to overwhelming invasions and constant warfare, their character was naturally shaped by battle. They were, however, constantly active in seeking strategies to aid them in the pursuance of survival. The Judeans' strategy had included fortifications (as well as mountain dwelling in, and around, Jerusalem); while the

---

[73] "The Kingdoms of Pharaohs - A Brief History, Ancient Egypt." https://www.ancientofegypt.com/the-kingdoms-of-pharaohs/. Accessed 20 Feb. 2018.

[74] "Assyrian Empire: The Old Kingdom - History." https://www.historyonthenet.com/assyrian-empire-the-old-kingdom/. Accessed 20 Feb. 2018.

[75] "Babylon - Ancient History Encyclopedia." https://www.ancient.eu/babylon/. Accessed 20 Feb. 2018.

[76] "Kingdom of Judah - New World Encyclopedia." 19 Jun. 2014, http://www.newworldencyclopedia.org/entry/Kingdom_of_Judah. Accessed 20 Feb. 2018.

[77] "Philistine | people | Britannica.com." https://www.britannica.com/topic/Philistine-people. Accessed 29 Jan. 2018.

[78] "Kingdom of Israel - New World Encyclopedia." 5 Aug. 2015, http://www.newworldencyclopedia.org/entry/Kingdom_of_Israel. Accessed 20 Feb. 2018.

[79] "Who Were the Phoenicians? - National Geographic Magazine." http://ngm.nationalgeographic.com/features/world/asia/lebanon/phoenicians-text.html. Accessed 29 Jan. 2018.

[80] "Who were the Arameans? - Got Questions." https://www.gotquestions.org/who-Arameans.html. Accessed 29 Jan. 2018.

[81] "Nabataea: Who were the Nabataeans - Nabataea.net." http://nabataea.net/who.html. Accessed 29 Jan. 2018.

[82] "Who were the Edomites? - Got Questions." 16 Sep. 2012, https://www.gotquestions.org/Edomites.html. Accessed 29 Jan. 2018.

[83] "Who were the Moabites? - Got Questions." 7 Apr. 2011, https://www.gotquestions.org/Moabites.html. Accessed 29 Jan. 2018.

[84] "Who were the Ammonites? - Got Questions." https://www.gotquestions.org/Ammonites.html. Accessed 29 Jan. 2018.

Phoenicians' action had been to expand their frontiers through seafaring and trade into the Mediterranean Basin. The Nabateans had ventured into the desert expanses of what is now modern-day Saudi-Arabia and Jordan, establishing desert trade routes.

According to Biblical stories (which can not be confirmed) the ancient Kingdom of Israel, which had bordered Phoenicia and Judea, was largely allied to Phoenicia. It rivaled Judea to its South, and Aram-Damascus to its North-East. Upon its destruction by the Assyrian Empire's invasion (assessed at around 720-740 BCE), the Kingdom of Israel had ultimately been proven the most vulnerable.[85] Ironically, after King Pekah had paid tribute to the Assyrian King (King Tiglath-Pileser III) in a request for military support against the Arameans and Judeans; the Assyrian King had completely destroyed the Arameans, rendering them an Assyrian province, as well as his tributor --- the Kingdom of Israel.[86]

The archeological fact that Phoenicians are related to Israelites and Judeans is also corroborated in the Hebrew Bible. The relationship between: the Judean King (King Solomon); the Phoenician King (King Hiram); and the building of the first temple, is described in the Bible.[87] According to the Bible, King Hiram had dispatched hundreds of craftsmen and cedar timber from Lebanon to help build the temple in Jerusalem. The joint shipping trade to far places like Tarshish (possibly Corsica Island or Southern-Spain), is also mentioned in the Bible.[88]

For the purposes of this book, what is most important in this Biblical story is the physical connection between Phoenicians and Judeans; as well as the repeated theme of King Solomon's drive to acquire wisdom.[89] The importance of acquiring wisdom is stressed on numerous occasions. King Hiram's appreciation of the wisdom of the Judean King --- as well as the complex and profitable relationship that Phoenicians had shared with the Judeans --- is also emphasized.

This teaches us that the composers of the Torah had realised that learning and the acquisition of wisdom is one of the most paramount tasks for humans in order to survive in this world.

Today we know (as we have known for many thousands of years) that without the search for wisdom, most of mankind would have still been subject to the powers of nature --- namely: natural disasters; disease; hunger, and poverty.

Wisdom (which becomes knowledge) must be preserved and handed down from generation to generation. Through the invention of an easily learnable and applicable alphabet, Judeans --- via their Phoenician brethren --- have contributed immensely to the world. This way of written communication has been the basis upon which civilization has: created; conveyed; preserved, and disseminated a wealth of knowledge over the millennia --- knowledge that had been easy to pass down over generations. (A much harder and cumbersome task for the

---

[85] "When and how was Israel conquered by the Assyrians? - Got Questions." https://www.gotquestions.org/Israel-conquered-by-Assyria.html. Accessed 30 Jan. 2018.
[86] "Arameans - Wikipedia." https://en.wikipedia.org/wiki/Arameans. Accessed 30 Jan. 2018.
[87] "Phoenician Design of King Solomon's Temple - Phoenicia.org." https://phoenicia.org/temple.html. Accessed 30 Jan. 2018.
[88] "Bible Map: Tarshish." http://bibleatlas.org/tarshish.htm. Accessed 30 Jan. 2018.
[89] "1 Kings 3 - Solomon Asks for Wisdom - Solomon made - Bible Gateway." https://www.biblegateway.com/passage/?search=1+Kings+3. Accessed 30 Jan. 2018.

preceding methods of writing being Egyptian hieroglyphics[90] and Assyrian and Babylonian cuneiform writing).[91]

The alphabet is primary evidence of the creation of wealth by Judean people. This innovation itself should prompt all nations of the modern world to revere the Jews for being the most significant contributors to civilization (on a global scale), as well as being a key nation behind modern wealth creation.

The ability to transfer information reliably and efficiently is the most significant human innovation in the history of mankind. It should be credited as a gift to civilization from the Judaic nation. The Hebrew alphabet had later been adopted and modified by: the Arameans; the Assyrians; the Babylonians, and the Persians. It had also been adopted by the Phoenicians (who had disseminated it to Greece and Rome via their seafaring Mediterranean routes). It had been modified to become the Latin alphabet --- the very basis of the English alphabet, which now dominates the world.

The Phoenicians, Israelites and Judeans --- Blood Brothers

As previously mentioned, it is an archeological fact that Phoenicians, Israelites, and Judeans had been connected --- this is even corroborated in the stories of the Bible. The Israelites, Phoenicians, and Judeans had all: spoken the same language; shared the same alphabet; and fought the same Assyrian and Chaldean (Babylonian) enemies of Mesopotamia to the North, and the Pharaonic enemies to the South.

The Pharaonic Kingdom had been the first large enemy to occupy these Canaanite nations. This occupation had lasted from around 1500 BCE to 1150 BCE, and is fairly well-documented with archeological artifacts (including the discovery of the Amarna letters of ancient Egyptian archeology).[92] This Egyptian occupation had stretched as far North as the Euphrates river (bordering the Assyrians and Babylonians).

This Egyptian Pharaonic occupation of Canaan had ended with what is now known in archeology as the late collapse of the Bronze Age.[93] This collapse is not entirely understood, and may have been the result of climate change, drought, or famine. What is clearly evident is that many cities around the Mediterranean and Middle-East had been destroyed and burnt to the ground.

These circumstances, and the chronological proximity of Egyptian occupation --- as well as the collapse of the Bronze Age --- is as close as it gets to the Biblical stories of Jacob and the famine in Canaan; followed by the story of Moses, and the Egyptians' enslavement of the Hebrews. (The latter story ending in the Hebrews' eventual freedom from bondage and exodus out of Egypt). Both being Biblical stories that cannot be confirmed by any means.

It is worthwhile mentioning that during this historical period (at around 1350 BCE) a religious theme close to monotheism had taken place under the Pharaoh 'Akhenaten'[94] and his Queen

---

[90] "Egyptian hieroglyphs - Wikipedia." https://en.wikipedia.org/wiki/Egyptian_hieroglyphs. Accessed 30 Jan. 2018.
[91] "Cuneiform - Ancient History Encyclopedia." https://www.ancient.eu/cuneiform/. Accessed 30 Jan. 2018.
[92] "Amarna Letters - Ancient History Encyclopedia." 6 Nov. 2015, https://www.ancient.eu/Amarna_Letters/. Accessed 30 Jan. 2018.
[93] "What Caused the Mysterious Bronze Age Collapse?." 20 May. 2015, http://etc.ancient.eu/interviews/what-caused-the-bronze-age-collapse/. Accessed 30 Jan. 2018.
[94] "Ancient Egypt Pharaohs: Akhenaten (Amenhotep IV)." http://ancientegyptonline.co.uk/akhenaten.html. Accessed 30 Jan. 2018.

'Nefertiti'. This is also the approximate time period in which archeology pinpoints evidence of the first ancient Hebrew (or Proto-Sinaitic) alphabet in the Sinai region.[95] It may also point to the physical origins of Judeans as desert people who had invaded Canaan either during, or after, the collapse of the Bronze Age --- a possibility that corresponds with Biblical stories and even hints at the idea that Judaic people had first been desert-dwellers before capturing Canaan.

During Akhenaten's 17-year reign, there had been a systematic effort to abolish polytheism in the Pharaonic Kingdom; and replace all Egyptian Gods with a single God --- the God of the Sun, 'Aten'.[96] It is likely that this push for monotheism had an impact on the Judeans and Canaanites under Akhenaten's rule; and may have been a precursor to the Judean and Israeli almighty God, Yahweh, and his female consort.[97] In many instances, Akhenaten and his wife Nefertiti appear together as a divine couple. Nevertheless, as mentioned earlier this dualism of male and female Gods is still far from the Judaic monotheism we know today.

It has been archaeologically established that by the 9th century BCE, the Kingdom of Israel had bordered the Phoenician cities to the North-West; and Judea to the South-East. King Ahab had been the first Israelite King in all of history to be documented. King Ahab had been one of the defeated Kings inscribed on the monolith of the Assyrian King, King Shalmaneser III.[98] The Kurkh Monoliths describe the battle of Qarqar (estimated at 853 BCE). According to archaeologists, the alliance (which possibly also included Phoenicians from Tyre) had been defeated by the Assyrian King.

The Bible corroborates with these archeological records. It describes the relationships that had existed between Israelites and Phoenicians. The marriage between King Ahab to the Phoenician Queen, Queen Jezebel,[99] is the most famous example.

The Bible detests the Queen for her beliefs in the Baal and Asherah (male and female) Gods. These Gods, which had been adopted by King Ahab, are re-introduced into --- and spread within --- Israel. Aside from this Biblical story (which is probably a modification of real historical events in order to suit the drive for monotheism) there is little to suggest that there had been any conflict whatsoever between the Israelis and the Phoenicians. On the contrary, it appears as though these nations had been 'Blood Brothers'; as they had shared a language, literature, and possibly many other aspects of each other's culture. Both nations had also been under threat from the same large enemies.

This close relationship between the Phoenicians/Israelites and Judeans is of the utmost importance in unfolding Jewish history in the upcoming chapters, as these tribes had been closely intertwined through marriage, a shared language, and trade. It is also important to note that the neighbouring Israelites had been in alliance with the Phoenicians in defending their countries against the mighty Assyrian Empire to the North.

---

[95] "Ancient Scripts: Proto-Sinaitic." http://www.ancientscripts.com/protosinaitic.html. Accessed 22 Feb. 2018.
[96] "Pharaoh Akhenaten: A Different View of the Heretic King | Ancient ...." 27 Jan. 2016, http://www.ancient-origins.net/ancient-places-africa/pharaoh-akhenaten-different-view-heretic-king-005249. Accessed 30 Jan. 2018.
[97] "Yahweh | Britannica.com." https://www.britannica.com/topic/Yahweh. Accessed 30 Jan. 2018.
[98] "Biblical Archaeology: Bonus 34 - Kurkh Stelae Monolith Inscription." 28 Dec. 2014, http://biblicalarchaeologygraves.blogspot.com/2014/12/bonus-34-kurkh-stele-monolith.html. Accessed 30 Jan. 2018.
[99] "How Bad Was Jezebel? - Biblical Archaeology Society." 17 Sep. 2017, https://www.biblicalarchaeology.org/daily/people-cultures-in-the-bible/people-in-the-bible/how-bad-was-jezebel/. Accessed 30 Jan. 2018.

Taking into account the fact that their language and culture are almost identical, it is of logical inference that Israelites had lived amongst Phoenicians; and vice-versa. This had been especially true during war times, when populations had fled from the large Assyrian and Babylonian armies.

Nowadays, the connection of Phoenicians to Jews is affirmed through genetic testing.[100] Lebanese individuals, who are descendants of ancient Phoenician populations (mixed with the various nations that had occupied them), bear the closest genetic similarity to Jewish populations. In light of this, it is of interest to investigate the archaeological and historical path of the Phoenicians alongside that of the Israelites and Judeans.

The Phoenicians had lived along the North-Coast shores of the Middle-Eastern Mediterranean sea in city states. From the sea settlement of Dor and the city of Acre, located today in modern Israel (just North of Tel Aviv), through: Tyre; Sidon; and Byblos, which are located along the coast of modern Lebanon.

In addition to rich archeology documenting the Phoenicians existence in those areas for thousands of years, there is historical evidence of the Greek Historian Herodotus visiting the temple of Melqart (King of the earth, 'Melek' being King in Hebrew) in Tyre, at around 450 BCE. By Herodotus' accounts, it is widely accepted amongst Greek historians that the Phoenicians had taught the alphabet to the Greeks; and that the Greeks had borrowed many Gods from the Phoenician pantheon --- simply renaming them with Greek names.[101]

Over the years, the Phoenicians had developed a flourishing sea trade in the Mediterranean with: Egypt; Greece; Rome; Spain, and North-Africa. They had also established settlements on the shores of: Cyprus; Sicily; Malta; Spain, and North-Africa. The famous Greek poet Homer,[102] accounts for Phoenician ships trading in the Mediterranean in the following manner:

'They dominated the Mediterranean Sea and Grew rich trading precious metals, wine, olive oil and timber from the cedars of the Lebanon. They established emporiums and colonies from Cyprus in the East to Italy, North-Africa and Spain in the West.'[103]

Outside their traditional cities on the coasts of Lebanon, their most well-known city was Carthage (modern Tunis)[104]. This prosperous city had clashed with the rising Roman Republic (The first and second Punic wars)[105]. The name of Carthage's famous leader, General Hannibal, is also a testament to its Semitic origins[106] --- 'Graced in the eyes of Baal' ('Han' means 'Grace' in ancient Phoenician and Hebrew, and 'Baal' is the name of the well-known prime Canaanite God --- therefore, 'Hannibal').

---

[100] "Phoenicians Left Deep Genetic Mark, Study Shows - The New York ...." 30 Oct. 2008, http://www.nytimes.com/2008/10/31/science/31genes.html. Accessed 30 Jan. 2018.
[101] "Phoenician Religion -- Pagan." http://arclab.usc.edu/profilecoin/html/religion.html. Accessed 30 Jan. 2018.
[102] "BBC - History - Historic Figures: Homer (circa 750-650 BC)." http://www.bbc.co.uk/history/historic_figures/homer.shtml. Accessed 30 Jan. 2018.
[103] "Who Were the Phoenicians? - National Geographic Magazine." http://ngm.nationalgeographic.com/features/world/asia/lebanon/phoenicians-text.html. Accessed 30 Jan. 2018.
[104] "Carthage - Ancient History Encyclopedia." https://www.ancient.eu/carthage/. Accessed 30 Jan. 2018.
[105] "Punic Wars | Summary, Causes, Battles, & Maps | Britannica.com." https://www.britannica.com/event/Punic-Wars. Accessed 30 Jan. 2018.
[106] "Hannibal - Ancient History - HISTORY.com." http://www.history.com/topics/ancient-history/hannibal. Accessed 30 Jan. 2018.

The Phoenicians had somewhat departed from historical accounts on the shores of Lebanon after their bitter resistance war against the Greek conqueror Alexander the Great over the city of Tyre at around 332 BCE.[107]

Thereafter, they had effectively vanished altogether into their other colonies at around 146 BCE --- Fifty-five years after their legendary Carthaginian general, General Hannibal, had been defeated by the Romans. As mentioned earlier, these wars are known as the Punic wars.

The Romans had effectively taken control over all Phoenician settlements around the Mediterranean sea --- including Spain. So what had happened to the entire Phoenician population?

There is no historical account of exactly what happened to the Phoenician population; however, Jewish populations began to sprout all over former Phoenician colonies in Spain and North-Africa under the Roman Empire's rule at approximately the same time that Phoenicians had vanished . . . Later, historical accounts of substantial Jewish populations in Spain and North-Africa suggests that at least some Phoenicians had turned to Judaism.

A vivid example of this suggestion is Josephus Flavius'[108] (a Jewish/Roman official historian) account of a Jewish settlement in the Egyptian city of Alexandria (which is also recorded to have had a large Phoenician population). Josephus claimed that there had been numerous Jews from the onset of the year 332 BCE, when Alexander the Great had founded the city in his name. Later on, a further 120,000 Jews were brought to the city as captives by the Alexandrian derived Ptolemies who had ruled Egypt after warring in Judea with the Alexandrian derived Seleucids; consequently draining the large Judean population out of Judea and Syria to inflate the population in Alexandria.[109]

It is known from this historical record that Phoenicians --- alongside Jews --- had been of substantial number in Alexandria. The Bible corroborates with the account that there had been populations of Jews in Egypt at the time. Following the assassination of the Babylonian installed Jewish Governor, Gedaliah, in 597 BCE; the Jews had fled from Judea to Egypt in fear of Babylonian retribution.[110]

Simultaneously, as the Phoenicians seem to vanish suddenly from all historical records, there had been a resurgence of Judea in the Middle-East with the uprising of the Maccabees[111] against the Hellenistic Seleucids.[112] The Maccabees had formed an alliance with the rising Roman Republic; acting as a counterbalance to the Alexandrian derived Hellenistic Seleucid Empire, which had been led by Antiochus III. Religious Jewish accounts of the Maccabees as champions of Judaism should be examined with caution, however, as most of the Maccabees (Hasmonean) descendants bore Hellenistic names and appear to have been heavily influenced by the Greek culture.

The alliance between Judea's Hasmonean dynasty and the Roman Republic had faltered when the Roman general Pompey eventually defeated the Alexandrian derived Seleucid

---

[107] "Alexander 2.7 - Livius." 19 Aug. 2017, http://www.livius.org/articles/person/alexander-the-great/alexander-2.7/?. Accessed 30 Jan. 2018.
[108] "Flavius Josephus | Jewish priest, scholar, and historian | Britannica.com." 15 Nov. 2017, https://www.britannica.com/biography/Flavius-Josephus. Accessed 30 Jan. 2018.
[109] "Alexandria - Jewish Virtual Library." http://www.jewishvirtuallibrary.org/alexandria. Accessed 30 Jan. 2018.
[110] "Gedaliah - Jewish History - Chabad.org." http://www.chabad.org/library/article_cdo/aid/4825/jewish/Gedaliah.htm. Accessed 30 Jan. 2018.
[111] "Maccabees | priestly Jewish family | Britannica.com." https://www.britannica.com/topic/Maccabees. Accessed 30 Jan. 2018.
[112] ibid

Empire in Syria.[113] General Pompey had then Intervened in the power struggle between the Hasmonean[114] dynasty brothers Hyrcanuss II[115] and Judah Aristobulus II[116] over Judea; using this struggle as an opportunity to overtake Judea. He had effectively imposed Roman rule in Judea at around 63 BCE; appointing Hyrcanuss II as King. Not too many years later --- after bitter internal struggles within the Hasmonean royal family --- Herod the Great[117] had been crowned as 'King of the Jews' by the Roman Senate.

The importance of all this historic documentation regarding Jews and Phoenicians is that both nations had originated from Canaanite roots. They had shared history en route to other Mediterranean locations as far as Spain; and, at the same time that Phoenicians seemed to have vanished from the records of history, Jews seemed to have settled all over Southern-Europe and North-Africa.

It is plausible, and logical to assume, that within some of these communities a transformation had occurred. This transformation --- tilted as 'The Balance' --- had been from Phoenician dominated polytheistic communities, to Jewish monotheistic communities. Since both had been Semitic nations of antiquity who had shared common roots, they must have had some common ground for such a process to occur.

The spread of Jewish communities all over the Mediterranean, coupled with a strong religious belief system, had substantially decreased the risk of the complete annihilation of Jews (as history later on proves). This spread of Jewish communities all over the Mediterranean gives new meaning to the popular risk management saying, 'don't put all your eggs in one basket'; in this case, it is 'don't put your entire population in the same territory'. This should be a factor to consider when observing over two millennia of historical Jewish survival.

From this point onwards in history, wherever and whenever Jews had been in jeopardy; some were able to escape and settle elsewhere amongst their established brethren communities in neighboring countries and territories. When times were conducive again in the place that had previously been hostile towards Jews, a new Jewish community would be re-established.

This is unlike other small, and even some bigger, nations that had dwelled in one fixed area --- eventually, and inevitably, being completely annihilated. Most Canaanite nations had vanished in this fashion at some point in history. The: Arameans; Edomites; Ammonites; Moabites; Nabateans, and Philistines are among said nations which had ceased to exist.

It can be reasonably argued that the fate of the 'Blood-Brother Nations' (the Phoenicians and Judeans) was to survive under the Jewish religious belief. This had been the result of their unique physical settled position on the shores of the Mediterranean Sea. A position that had expanded their frontiers due to pressure from the larger occupying Middle-Eastern Empires such as the Assyrians, Babylonians, and Persians --- empires that had eventually collapsed in clashes between themselves (in conjunction with the rising Greek and Roman Empires).

---

[113] "Pompey - Ancient History Encyclopedia." 27 Jan. 2013, https://www.ancient.eu/pompey/. Accessed 30 Jan. 2018.
[114] "Hasmonean Dynasty | Judaean dynasty | Britannica.com." https://www.britannica.com/topic/Hasmonean-dynasty. Accessed 30 Jan. 2018.
[115] "John Hyrcanus - Wikipedia." https://en.wikipedia.org/wiki/John_Hyrcanus. Accessed 30 Jan. 2018.
[116] "Aristobulus II - Wikipedia." https://en.wikipedia.org/wiki/Aristobulus_II. Accessed 30 Jan. 2018.
[117] "Herod the Great - Livius." 28 Jun. 2017, http://www.livius.org/articles/person/herod-the-great/. Accessed 30 Jan. 2018.

The skills that had been developed by these communities may also prove to be important contributing factors to this epic Jewish survival story. These skills had been: first, an effective alphabet which had promoted literacy; secondly, advanced technological seafaring skills; thirdly, their acute trading skills, and finally, their uncompromising drive to preserve their ethnic identity via a strong religious Jewish belief system which promotes literacy.

This drive for survival had been fiercely prompted by their formation of a unique religion centered on the premise of being 'the chosen nation of God'[118]. They had fervently believed that so long as they had followed the laws of God (written in the Torah), they would not only survive --- but they would also, eventually, become a 'beacon of light to the Gentiles'.[119] No-one had chosen the Jews . . . the Jews had chosen themselves. They alone had decided to become 'the chosen nation' --- with all the positive and negative historical ramifications that would accompany this title.

A noteworthy observation is that the Jewish nation had been the nation to eventually represent all Semitic nations of antiquity. This time displaying the relentless drive of the Phoenicians --- venturing into unknown territories and, again, upholding features of relentless wealth creation via trade and establishment of new communities all over the Mediterranean Basin.

Jews are still to this day renowned for their trading skills and resultant wealth creation. Nowadays --- unlike in antiquity --- trade wealth can be accurately measured monetarily. This can clearly exhibit ethnic-Jewish domination in business around the world within many countries; many of whom trade with the emerging markets of the far East. However, it is not as easy to measure the hidden wealth of knowledge (with regard to the practices and methods of performing this trade). The hidden knowledge of mental and intellectual wealth creation; passed on to future Jewish generations. This hidden wealth eventually becomes part of the culture within communities.

Verbal and numerical literacy are essential basic skills in the creation of monetary wealth, since documentation and accounting is of the utmost necessity when managing material wealth. Literacy is therefore the foundation of wealth creation, which in turn becomes a tool that forms the basis of the creation of secondary wealth --- material wealth. This literary wealth had been a scarce resource in antiquity (as will be demonstrated in the following chapters).

Judaic people were prized for possessing this foundational wealth --- sometimes at the high cost of their freedom. But mostly, this skill had saved their lives in the very cruel world of antiquity.

In good and peaceful times, it had given them an advantage over surrounding non-Jewish populations who had not been as literate.

What can be gleaned from the origins of Judaism

Based on everything that has been discussed thus far, we can learn that although the Judeans' religion had not been a purely monotheistic religion at first (with its dual male and female Gods); it had been the closest religion to the concept of monotheism among the Semitic people of the region.

---

[118] "9. The People of God in God's Perfect Plan | Bible.org." 17 May. 2004, https://bible.org/seriespage/9-people-god-god-s-perfect-plan. Accessed 30 Jan. 2018.
[119] "Light Unto the Nations - Wikipedia." https://en.wikipedia.org/wiki/Light_Unto_the_Nations. Accessed 30 Jan. 2018.

Judeans and Israelites were of close ethnic similarity to the Phoenicians, as they had spoken the same language, and had shared the same alphabet --- an alphabet which had originated from the southern borders of Judea in the Pharaonic Egyptian Kingdom.

At that time in history, the invention of the alphabet had pushed the boundaries of human thought; as it had suddenly been possible for ideas to be conveyed to --- and stored for --- future generations in a far easier manner than ever before. This had made the: Judean; Israelite; Phoenician, and Aramean nations more intellectually advanced than their huge traditional enemies (namely the Pharaonic Egyptian Kingdom in the South, and the Assyrian/Babylonian Empires in the North).

The latter --- who possessed huge armies and eventually conquered Canaan --- had adopted the aramaic alphabet and language; making it the lingua-franca for the entire Middle-East.[120]

As had been discussed above, the Judean people --- much like their Phoenician brethren --- had been appreciative of wisdom, and constantly developed survival skills in the face of the overwhelming Assyrian/Babylonian threat. These skills had involved seafaring and trading, as well as the establishment of colonies and settlements along the shores of the Mediterranean Sea. Said colonies and settlements had increased their chances of survival in the long course of history.

It is very important to realize and internalize the fact that at first, Judaic people had not been religiously monotheistic in nature. This is partly corroborated by the Bible itself, as it describes many stories about Israelites and Judeans practicing idol worship.

Once it is accepted that Judeans had not been monotheistic in antiquity, questions that immediately spring to mind are: how; where; and when, did Judeans become monotheistic? These questions will be answered during my attempt to discover the real story behind the origins of Judaism; based on historical facts, as well as some degree of corroboration from Biblical accounts regarding: Babylon's conquering of Judea; the subsequent destruction of the Temple in Jerusalem; the exile of the most intelligent Judeans to Babylonia, and the eventual return to Judea (as well as the re-establishment of the Jewish Temple in Jerusalem).

---

[120] "Aramaic language - Wikipedia." https://en.wikipedia.org/wiki/Aramaic_language. Accessed 30 Jan. 2018.

Chapter 3

Judeans under the Babylonian and Persian Empires.

Summary: This chapter will further discuss the development of Judaism as a true monotheistic religion. It will lead to some reasonable assumptions regarding the true origins of the Jewish Bible and its main purpose being the rebuilding of a nation. The Jewish Torah --- which had been purposefully constructed to build the Jewish nation --- will be compared to other human literature at the time. This comparison, and the subsequent influences the Torah had on civilization's mores and legal systems up to modern times, is highlighted. The Torah had been a brilliant literary masterpiece for its time, and another great gift from the Jewish people to civilization.

'By the rivers of Babylon we sat and wept when we remembered Zion…
….If I forget you, Jerusalem, may my right hand forget its skill. …' **Psalm 137 NIV**

Shaping Judaism as a monotheistic religion.

The fact is --- history books barely reveal anything about Judean captivity in Babylon, and the Persian Empire's rule thereafter. It is astonishing that the Babylonians' defeat by the Persians is the only event to be documented during that time --- thereafter, the Babylonians inexplicably vanish from the records of history. The Persians' rule of Babylon for over 200 years (until the rise of Greece under the leadership of Alexander The Great) also lacks sufficient information regarding the development/formation of Judaism. The establishment of the Greek Empire is also poorly explored in history books.

Historical clues that point towards the full truth behind the Persian and Babylonian eras come from the Bible itself, and can be found within the stories of the late prophets (especially within the books of Daniel,[121] and Ezra and Nehemiah).[122] Other strong clues include the few bits of archaeological evidence regarding the Persian Empire, and the Babylonian Empire that had preceded them, in the forms of artifacts such as the cylinders belonging to Cyrus the Great,[123] and Nabonidus (the King of Babylon) respectively.[124]

---

[121] "Daniel 1 - Daniel's Training in Babylon - In the - Bible Gateway."
https://www.biblegateway.com/passage/?search=Daniel+1. Accessed 30 Jan. 2018.
[122] "Ezra-Nehemiah - Bible Hub."
http://biblehub.com/library/mcfadyen/introduction_to_the_old_testament/ezra-nehemiah.htm. Accessed 30 Jan. 2018.
[123] "British Museum - The Cyrus Cylinder."
http://www.britishmuseum.org/research/collection_online/collection_object_details.aspx?objectId=327188&partId=1. Accessed 31 Jan. 2018.
[124] "British Museum - cylinder."
http://www.britishmuseum.org/research/collection_online/collection_object_details.aspx?objectId=327140&partId=1. Accessed 31 Jan. 2018.

Over the course of modern archaeology, enormous efforts had been made in order to reconcile archaeological findings with Biblical documentation. Many of the first archaeologists had some religious bias (in favour of Christianity) towards the correctness of Biblical stories. Their religious faith in the Bible was such that they had been adamant in their belief that proper excavation will reveal the Bible's divinity and correctness.[125] This attitude had contributed to great confusion, with many findings being incorrectly interpreted (only to be revised later) during attempts to link the findings to specific Biblical writings. One such example is 'Solomon's stables' in Megiddo, Israel;[126] assigning the archaeological finding in Megiddo to the Biblical story of King Solomon --- even though there had not been any concrete inscription, or any indication of one, of the name 'Solomon' (or the name of any Judaic King for that matter) in the archaeological finding.

Among the many historians and archaeologists who had rigorously excavated all over Israel (in what turned out to be a futile attempt to discover the Torah and Biblical stories such as the ancient Kingdoms of Israel and Judah, and further back into the exodus from Egypt) not one of them seemed to have addressed the possibility that perhaps the real story behind the origins of Judaism as a monotheistic religion had not begun in Judean and Israeli lands . . . perhaps the real beginning of Judaism, as we know it today, had originated in the land of Mesopotamia/Babylonia.

Not enough attention has been given to this period; a period that --- in all probability --- had actually defined Judaism as we know it today. A period in which the stories of both the Torah, and the Bible, were most probably written. The period of the Babylonian exile and the Persian occupation. The time in which Judaism begins to demonstrate signs of true monotheism.

Since this period in Judaic history is abysmally documented --- both archaeologically and historically --- it is incredibly difficult to even speculate about the chain of events that would have occurred throughout history leading up to the formation of Judaism.

The following hypothetical assumptions and conclusions had been validly arrived at through the use of analytical tools similar to those used in the legal profession in order to draw up a verdict as close to the truth as possible. Critical analysis of Biblical texts (our main source of evidence) and logical reasoning taking the surrounding circumstantial historical evidence into account are key techniques used.

First and foremost, the most compelling circumstantial evidence of Persian influence on Judaism's transformation into monotheism being the Persian rule at the time; as well as the Persian religion and customs that had prevailed (along with small amounts of information about the Babylonians who had preceded the Persians).

Oscillating back and forth throughout the history of that period --- while at the same time observing and always considering the end result of Judaic people becoming monotheistic --- can enable a reasonable deduction as to what had transpired, as well as to why history had unfolded in the way it did.

To commence this process, some initial main assumptions must be made. These assumptions will be as follows:

The first assumption is that although we know and revere the Torah as being of high value and significance with regard to the formation of, and shaping of, Judaism; it does contain a substantial amount of myths that had been constructed from pure imagination. This

---

[125] "Is the Bible a true story? - Archaeology - Haaretz.com." 1 Nov. 2017, https://www.haaretz.com/archaeology/MAGAZINE-is-the-bible-a-true-story-latest-archaeological-finds-yield-surprises-1.5626647. Accessed 31 Jan. 2018.

[126] ibid

assumption will be proven highly probable through the discussion and assessment of some of the Torah's stories.

It should be clear from the onset of our analysis that although the Torah consists of many myths; they are well thought-out myths which had been created to serve as catalysts for long term --- and short term --- nation building, as well as for various political purposes.

The Torah --- a well thought-out and well-constructed document with a fundamental and deep purpose of creating and 'gelling' a nation. It had bestowed a purpose unto the people it was built to serve; whose action it meant to promote --- action that would result in the liberation and independence of the Judaic people existing during that era. The Torah had also enabled certain leaders to encroach their rule upon said Judaic people.

The second assumption is that the Biblical accounts of Ezra and Nehemiah --- regarding the stories of the Judaic peoples' return to Judea under the Persian occupation after the Babylonian exile --- had actually been true historical events. At the time, these events had been documented by the same leaders who had either written the Torah themselves; or brought it with them to Judea from Mesopotamia (Babylonia). This assumption has some solid basis, as the Biblical accounts of the Persian Kings are very close to what is known by archaeological and historical documentation outside the Bible.

In human nature, the need for recognition is a strong motivator --- this can point to what the real interests of the Judaic leaders had been at the time; enabling us to document their admirable roles in the resurrection of a Jewish nation in Judea.

The third and most important assumption is that during this entire period, an underlying historical process --- which can be defined as 'Cultural Warfare' --- had occurred. This cultural warfare, under the circumstantial Persian occupation, had ended in the demise of the old Babylonian culture; which further lead to the rise of Judaism as the prominent force within the Semitic world. This assumption is based on the fact that Judaism had spread and expanded all over the Middle-East during the Persian rule, and had been well entrenched within most of the Persian Empire at the time of the Greek and Roman occupations. Within the same time frame, Babylonian culture had died altogether.

There are many instances throughout history in which the process of Cultural Warfare had occurred between the conquered, and their conquerors. Usually, the conquered populations --- which are physically weak --- fight back mentally and culturally, in an effort to eventually defeat their physically dominating conqueror.

This third assumption is not a 'Black and White Fallacy'. The culture of the conqueror and the culture of the conquered often merge together to form a new culture that may be more resilient in different aspects.

This process had been distinctly visible in many later periods within historical settings such as the Mongolian occupation of China. During this event, the Mongols had eventually assumed Chinese culture. Another example would be the Islamisation of the Mongols who had conquered Iraq; as well as the Islamisation of the Turkic tribes in Asia minor (known today as Turkey).

It is important to recognize Cultural Wars, as they occur constantly; and change a nation's character. Even today we are witnessing Cultural Warfare between: nations; religions; secular movements, and social systems. Western societies and Islam in general --- as well as radical Islam in particular --- are currently engaged in a tacit and open warfare with each other.

This phenomenon of Cultural Warfare is able to explain and reveal many things about Judaism, Christianity and Islam. Very similarly rooted and uncompromising religions that originate from different times, and had ventured on different paths throughout history --- paths that will be explored in later chapters. Let us resume exploring the formation of the Jewish religion as we know it today.

The short and probable story goes as follows:
Under the Persian Empire, Jews had been granted the freedom to return to Judea. Among all exiled communities brought to Babylon by the Babylonian Kings, the Jewish community had undoubtedly been of some significance to the Persians; since once the Persians had conquered the Babylonians, the Persian King had allowed Jews to return to their ancestral land of Judea (which had been under his newly established Empire). The King had also permitted them to rebuild their destroyed Temple in Jerusalem in honor of their God.

Why would the Persian King, King Cyrus the Great[127] be so kind and generous to one specific nation out of his vast empire? This contribution by King Cyrus had been of tremendous importance to Judaism --- he is the only non-Jewish figure in the Bible to be revered as a Messiah.[128]

Setting aside religious Jewish explanations rooted in the books of Ezra and Nehemiah about 'God's will' prompting the Persian King's decision --- there had been real-life practical reasons for this generosity; as well as religious reasons from the Persian perspective.

In those days, religion had been the centerpiece of a nation's existence. Religion was one-and-the-same with real-life practicalities and logic. Back in those times, rulers had listened to --- and took advice from --- clergy (an example would be the supposed 'Dreams From God' experienced by Kings). This has been shown, archaeologically, in the Nabonidus cylinder inscription; and is corroborated by Biblical stories in 'The Book of Daniel'.

What is known about Persian-Jewish relations at the time can shed light upon the formation and expansion of Judaism.

The books of Ezra and Nehemiah, as well as legends such as the scroll of Esther, suggest that there had been many periods in which the relationship between Jews and Persians thrived. From later historical periods, documentation from the Egyptian city of Alexandria imply that the Persian Empire had used army garrisons of Jews to control Egypt, and other parts of the southern Middle-East.[129]

The width and breadth of Judaic expansion during the reign of the Persian Empire, and the Persian rulers' co-operation with --- and protection of --- Jews; indicate that there had been some sort of pact between the two parties. Perhaps a tacit pact to spread monotheism within the Persian-Empire.

It is therefore suggested that from a political and religious perspective, it had made much sense to the new Persian rulers of Babylon to grace Babylonian-Judeans with the opportunity to rebuild their Temple in Jerusalem (with the condition that it be a monotheistic Temple).

As the Persians conquered the cities of Susa and Babylon --- and shortly thereafter declared the city of Susa as their capital --- relationships between the Jewish inhabitants in the city and the Persian elite, had been cemented. Perhaps even as a backlash against the former Babylonian rulers.

It is very likely that after more than three generations in Mesopotamia, said Jewish inhabitants were already heavily influenced by Babylonian culture. However, they had still been distinguishable enough to be treated favourably by the Persian conquerors.

---

[127] "Cyrus the Great | Biography & Facts | Britannica.com." 29 Nov. 2017, https://www.britannica.com/biography/Cyrus-the-Great. Accessed 1 Feb. 2018.
[128] "Isaiah 45 NIRV - "Cyrus is my anointed king. I take - Bible Gateway." https://www.biblegateway.com/passage/?search=Isaiah+45&version=NIRV. Accessed 1 Feb. 2018.
[129] "Ancient Sudan~ Nubia: Investigating the Origin of the Ancient Jewish ...." http://www.ancientsudan.org/articles_jewish_elephantine.html. Accessed 31 Jan. 2018.

The Persians would undoubtedly trust their close neighbours and new internal allies far more than any remote population within their Empire (such as the polytheistic Phoenicians, as well as other polytheistic exiles that had existed within the Babylonian Empire).

The conflicts of Judeans with Samaritans[130] --- whom according to the Bible had also been exiled by the Babylonians and relocated to the land of Israel --- can demonstrate the Persians' favouritism towards Judeans. According to genetic studies, Samaritans are also very similar to Jews. When taking such information into account, the Samaritans exile into the remaining populations of Judeans and Phoenicians in Samaria during the Babylonian era (as claimed in the Bible), might only be partially true.[131] The stories of clashes between Samaritans and returning Judeans from Babylon that came to rebuild the Temple and their resolution demonstrates the favouritism that the Jews had enjoyed under Persian rulers.

The end result being that the Persians' new 'Babylonian/Jewish' allies had been allowed to travel to Judea and rebuild, and cement, the Jewish population in and around Jerusalem and Judea in order to form a stable Judean state allied with the Persian Empire.[132]

What about the religious aspect of allowing Judeans to build a Temple for their God? This is a defining question with regard to Judaism. In answering this question, it would be beneficial to understand the new, Persian-ruled environment in which the Jews had lived under during their time in Mesopotamia. So . . . who had been the dominant God there at the time? Obviously it would have been the Persian God, since as the Persians had ruled.

It is historically and archaeologically documented that the Persian Empire's religion had been the Zoroastrian religion.[133] Examining the foundational beliefs of the Zoroastrian religion and comparing them to Jewish beliefs may therefore be a worthwhile exercise that reveals interesting similarities.

The Zoroastrian religion had consisted of a single God named 'Ahura Mazda'[134] (the nurturing, supporting, or established light) who had created the world . . . not much different to the Jewish belief in a single omnipotent entity. The worship of Ahura Mazda had taken place within constructed Temples in which fire had been employed --- this had also occurred within the Jewish Temple. In the book of Leviticus, one can find the corroborative descriptions regarding burnt offerings. 'The fire must be kept burning on the altar', and 'Every morning the priest is to add firewood and arrange the burnt offering on the fire, and burn the fat of the fellowship offerings on it.'[135]

The term 'Ahura' means enlightened; and, a Hebrew speaker listening carefully will notice the similarity to the Hebrew word for 'light' --- 'Ha-ora' (האור) ('the light' in Hebrew). The word 'Mazda', or 'Masda', also has Aramaic or Hebrew roots; 'Saad' or 'Masad' in Hebrew meaning nurturing, supporting, or established.

The Zoroastrians believed that fire (pronounced 'Asha') had been the purest spiritual form of their God. First, the Hebrew word for fire is 'Eish' --- a pronunciation not very different to

---

[130] "Religion of the Israelite Samaritans : The Root of all Abrahamic ...." https://www.israelite-samaritans.com/religion/. Accessed 31 Jan. 2018.
[131] ibid
[132] "Yehud Medinata - Wikipedia." https://en.wikipedia.org/wiki/Yehud_Medinata. Accessed 31 Jan. 2018.
[133] "BBC - Religion: Zoroastrianism." http://www.bbc.co.uk/religion/religions/zoroastrian/. Accessed 31 Jan. 2018.
[134] "Ahura Mazda - Ancient History Encyclopedia." 13 Mar. 2017, https://www.ancient.eu/Ahura_Mazda/. Accessed 31 Jan. 2018.
[135] "Leviticus 6:12 The fire on the altar must be kept burning; it ... - Bible Hub." http://biblehub.com/leviticus/6-12.htm. Accessed 31 Jan. 2018.

'Asha'. Secondly, fire had always been part of the Jewish religion --- more specifically in the religious act of performing the Mitzvah (Hebrew word for 'deed') of lighting shabbat (Sabbath) candles every friday night. Fire has also been used, in a traditional sense, in the lighting of 'Ner Neshama' (spiritual candles) on many religious Jewish occasions;[136] customs from time immemorial in Judaism. 'Spirit candles?', you may be wondering --- who's spirit? Perhaps it is the spirit of the ancient Persian God whom had shaped Jewish monotheism. At least some religious Jewish interpretation is that the lighting of candles is practiced to remind people of God's presence.[137]

According to Persian belief, the Zoroastrian God (enlightened nurturer) had revealed the truth to humans via his prophet, 'Zoroaster', who had been born into a culture of polytheism; eventually having a revelation that there is only one true God, after which he had proceeded to denounce all other Gods and declare them to be false. A similar story to that of Abraham's, in which he smashes idols.[138] This theme of a specific 'chosen' individual experiencing a profound metaphysical epiphany also appears in different settings in Judaism; particularly within the Biblical story of the burning bush, whereby the truth to the people of Israel is revealed through Moses the prophet.[139] The use of fire in this revelation story is again strikingly similar to the Zoroaster's encounter with the fire that had enlightened him.

Many other motives encapsulated in Zoroastrian religion (such as: heaven and hell; good and evil; and the end of days) are also of significance in Judaism, as well as within the Abrahamic religions that had followed; namely Christianity and Islam. Another important aspect of the Zoroastrian religion is the fact that membership of the religion is acquired by birth, and not by conversion. Judaism holds a very similar standard. The Zoroastrian Persian Empire did not, by any means, coerce others into joining the Zoroastrian religion. It seems as though their religion had been ethnically based in order to exclude others.

Similarity between the images of the Ahura Mazda God (minted on archaeologically discovered coins of the era) and the Jewish God is also striking. The Zoroastrian God is depicted as a King being lifted by the wings of eagles; while the Jewish God just so happens to also be portrayed as a King sitting on a chariot equipped with none other than the wings of eagles.[140] Notice how similar wings are displayed on the well-known logo of the Japanese auto-manufacturer Mazda. It seems as though the Japanese founder of the Mazda car manufacturer, Mr. Matsuda, had utilized some knowledge of history when deciding on what his motor company's name and logo was to be (that is, two wings within a circle).[141]

The wings of eagles seem to be a recurring theme in the portrayal of ancient Gods. Even the statues of Babylonian and Assyrian Gods had sported large eagle wings. The motif of wings also appears as a prominent feature on the Jewish 'Ark of the Covenant' which had, according to tradition, housed the spirit of their God.[142]

---

[136] "The Symbolic Meaning of Candles in Judaism - ThoughtCo." https://www.thoughtco.com/what-do-candles-represent-in-judaism-2076656. Accessed 31 Jan. 2018.
[137] ibid
[138] "Abraham and the Idol Shop - Wikipedia." https://en.wikipedia.org/wiki/Abraham_and_the_Idol_Shop. Accessed 31 Jan. 2018.
[139] "Burning bush - Wikipedia." https://en.wikipedia.org/wiki/Burning_bush. Accessed 31 Jan. 2018.
[140] "Yehud Medinata - Wikipedia." https://en.wikipedia.org/wiki/Yehud_Medinata. Accessed 31 Jan. 2018.
[141] "The Evolution of the Mazda Logo and Brand – Inside Mazda." https://insidemazda.mazdausa.com/the-mazda-way/mazda-spirit/mazda-brand-marks-logotypes-history/. Accessed 31 Jan. 2018.
[142] "Ark of the Covenant | National Geographic." https://www.nationalgeographic.com/archaeology-and-history/archaeology/ark-covenant/. Accessed 31 Jan. 2018.

Based on all that has been analysed so far, as well as the easily identifiable and striking similarities between Judaism and the Persian Zoroastrian religion (coupled with the ample use of Babylonian legends in the Torah which will be demonstrated below); there is reason to suspect, with a high degree of probability, that Judaism --- as we know it today --- had been formed during the Persian Empire's rule of Babylonia.

The people who had formed this religion may have been a mixture of Judaic people, Babylonians, and other exiled semitic nations such as the Phoenicians and Arameans. All these semitic nations had lost their national identity in Mesopotamia under Persian rule. For these semitic nations, Judaism may have become the popular group identity with which to assimilate into (in order to gain favour as monotheists under Persian rule). At the time, polytheistic Phoenicians seem to have been an exception to this hypothesis; as they had been the last group to lose their national identity (despite existing as a shrinking minority within Phoenicia itself).

At some stage, these newly-shaped Semitic individuals had searched for some degree of freedom and self-determination. What could have been more desirable than the opportunity to leave the heavily populated land of Babylon, and settle into the relatively unpopulated land of Judea instead?

This had been the beginning of an exodus story that had changed the course of Jewish history. As we shall discover, it is a remarkable story of the 'quest for freedom'; based on an uncompromising belief in one God, and his covenant with his 'chosen people' --- promising freedom and prosperity. A story that had inspired generations of Jews and non-Jews alike. A story that had followed persecuted populations for generations. A story that had even shaped America --- nearly 2000 years later --- on the 'Mayflower' voyage from England to America, as is evident in the written 'Mayflower compact'. The 'Mayflower' voyage had been a journey in which the first American settlers sought freedom and self-determination away from their motherland in England.

It is important to keep in mind that the return of the Jewish people to Judea (from Babylon) had not completely drained Babylon of its Jewish populace. On the contrary, most of the newly formed Jewish population had been comprised of smaller nations that had assimilated into Judaism after the Persian conquering. Some original Jews had remained in Babylon. This newly formed Babylonian Jewish Population had even begun to grow in numbers; eventually establishing the most respectable Talmudic centers in Mesopotamia.

The Babylonian Talmud briefly discusses the Judaic people who went to build the second Temple in Jerusalem. It undermines them, referring to them as the 'assimilated', 'lower-class' sections of the Judaic nation. This implies that the 'cream-of-the-crop' upper-class Jews had remained in Babylonia. It is a known fact that a very large population of Jews had remained in Babylonia, and had flourished for nearly 1200 years after the resurrection of the second Temple (until the formation of the Umayyad Caliphate and the Abbasid Islamic Caliphate thereafter). A much smaller community of Jews had even prevailed throughout the Mongolian occupation of the Abbasid Islamic Caliphate, as well as throughout the Mongols' subsequent Islamisation and persecutions of Jews and Christians in Iraq.[143]

As has been demonstrated above, the Torah --- which corroborates some of the Persian Empire's historical accounts --- seems to be part history, and part mythology; however, it becomes the center focus of Judaic people. One of the questions that can be raised is: 'How

---

[143] "History Crash Course #43: The Jews of Babylon - Aish.com." 1 Sep. 2001, http://www.aish.com/jl/h/cc/48949881.html. Accessed 31 Jan. 2018.

is the Torah different from other preceding mythologies of antiquity?' 'Had it been novel in any way?' 'Had it enhanced Jewish intellect further than the intellect of other nations at the time?'

The Myths and Marvel of the Torah within a historical context

As we know, Persian Kings had bestowed the honor of restoring Judea and building a Temple for the Jewish God upon Ezra and Nehemiah. Accounts in both the Bible and the Talmud describe the difficulty of their task.

Ezra and Nehemiah found that the remaining Judeans in Judea had been worshipping all types of Canaan Gods, as well as giving special praise to the Phoenician gods of Baal and Asherah. They had mingled with Phoenicians, Arameans, and other related tribes such as Moabites and Edomites. This situation is described in the book of Ezra.

Such circumstances raise the simple question: 'How could such a diverse and differing mix of people be remoulded into a new nation?'

The answer to this question has been demonstrated many times throughout history. Installing a common identity and purpose into large groups of people will inevitably build them as a nation. This can be done through education, as well as the implementation of a legal system that endorses and rewards cohesiveness; while punishing undesirable acts of liberal pluralism.

How does one 'educate' people on becoming a nation? a relatively sound way is by promoting a belief in a shared historical past --- which then leads to the idea of a shared future. This is done by building a past heritage based on: folklore stories; mythologies; legendary heroes, and symbols --- isn't that all the Bible (as well as the Christian New Testament and Islamic Quran that had been created thereafter) is?

The answer in general terms is yes --- the Bible is indeed comprised of various stories, mythologies, and legendary heroes. It is, however, somewhat different to other preceding folklore texts in history in the sense that it contains laws by which the people had been required to live. Strict laws, which had supposedly been God-given.[144] At times, contravention of these laws would trigger the extreme capital punishment.[145]

This had made the Torah a unique invention at the time; as it had incorporated mythologies which had attempted to explain the creation of the world (as well as other philosophies as to the nature of life itself). But above all, the Torah is unique in the sense that it contains laws that act as a guide to life itself: personal; family; communal, and national laws.

It is important to look at the Torah in perspective, and compare it to other known texts of the Middle-East and Mediterranean Basin at the time. The 'Iliad and Odyssey' of the Greeks, for example, had been a brilliant mythological text[146] --- full of heroes and heroic acts. The supernatural Achilles and Patriotic Hector; the villain Agamemnon and Odysseus the Wise. Gods had also been involved, and human nature had been tested to its full extent. A wonderful

---

[144] "The Laws Of The Basic Principles Of The Torah - Jewish Virtual Library."
http://www.jewishvirtuallibrary.org/the-laws-of-the-basic-principles-of-the-torah. Accessed 31 Jan. 2018.
[145] "The Death Penalty in Jewish Tradition | My Jewish Learning."
https://www.myjewishlearning.com/article/the-death-penalty-in-jewish-tradition/. Accessed 31 Jan. 2018.
[146] "The Iliad & The Odyssey: Summary & Characters - Video & Lesson ...."
https://study.com/academy/lesson/the-iliad-the-odyssey-summary-characters.html. Accessed 31 Jan. 2018.

story to read, know, and tell. Nevertheless, it has limited value as to how one should lead one's life.

The same is true for all ancient mythological texts at the time (such as Rome's Romulus and Remus story,[147] as well as the ancient epic Babylonian story of Gilgamesh).[148]

So --- it seems as though the Torah is a unique script (relative to its time in history). However, I have yet to prove my initial assumption that the Torah is a constructed mythological book that was well thought-out. To do that, it is necessary to analyse Biblical texts (to some extent).

In the Bible, 'The Book of Daniel' describes some Jews in Babylonia --- including Daniel himself --- as being exceptionally bright boys who had been mentored by the religious Babylonian clergy to serve the Babylonian King in matters of wisdom. They had excelled beyond expectation, and it is attested that their intellectual ability had been exceptional.[149] All these Jewish boys had equivalent Babylonian names.

Is it possible for these people to have been the scribes of the Torah? According to the story, they had most certainly possessed the necessary skills to complete such a task.

The following analysis of the Torah may provide more clues as to the identity of its scribes, as well as to its chronological formation.

When reading through the Torah, one can only imagine what had happened to the Babylonians who so suddenly vanished from history books (while Judaism seemed to have flourished under the Persian Empire). The Torah's historical accounts had come to an abrupt chronological end at the time of the Persian Empire's rule --- no accounts of, prophecies, or even hints to, the coming Greek and Roman Empires had been present. Can we glean further into history by analysing the stories of the Torah in greater detail?

The Torah begins with 'The Book of Genesis', which is similar in its mythology to the Babylonian story of 'Marduk The God of Light'[150] (in terms of the creation of the world). In Babylonian mythology, the prophesied destruction of cities --- and their subsequent resurrection --- is also similar to Biblical prophecies.[151]

Further striking similarities are the story of Noah's ark compared to the Babylonian epic of Gilgamesh (which also includes the story of the garden of Eden, as well as the story of Cain and Abel). It does not require much imagination to realise that the Biblical stories within 'The Book Of Genesis' had most probably been derived from the Babylonian myths in the Babylonian epic of Gilgamesh.

Many Babylonian words such as 'Shamash' ('Sun in Babylonian) and 'Shemesh' (שמש) ('Sun' in Hebrew) or 'Enlil' (in Babylonian) and 'Elil' (אליל) (in Hebrew) meaning 'a God' are also similar --- this points to some shared distant origins. The Bible confirms this shared origin, as is evident in the story of Abraham and his birth city of Ur (probably 'Uruk', of which the name 'Iraq' is a derivation of). Is it possible that the mixed Babylonian-Jewish populations had formed the 'new Judaism' (as was claimed in the previous section)? Many of said individuals

---

[147] "Romulus and Remus - History Learning Site." https://www.historylearningsite.co.uk/ancient-rome/romulus-and-remus/. Accessed 22 Feb. 2018.

[148] "The Babylonian Epic of Gilgamesh - WisdomWorld.org." http://www.wisdomworld.org/additional/ancientlandmarks/BabylonEpicOfGilgamesh.html. Accessed 31 Jan. 2018.

[149] "Book of Daniel Summary - Shmoop." https://www.shmoop.com/daniel/summary.html. Accessed 31 Jan. 2018.

[150] "Marduk - Ancient History Encyclopedia." 9 Dec. 2016, https://www.ancient.eu/Marduk/. Accessed 31 Jan. 2018.

[151] ibid

had actually been former Babylonians assuming new identities as Jews. After all . . . camouflage is a great survival strategy --- especially when it had been necessary to escape the ruling Persian occupiers persecution.

This suggestion may bother many religious Jews, but the probability of such an occurrence is extremely high; especially when taking the following factors into account:

The first factor is that Judaic people had been raised in, and accustomed to, Babylonian society for nearly four generations before the Persian occupation.

Secondly, the Persian religion had prohibited their own people from mingling with other nations (much like Judaism in later historical periods). This meant that Babylonians had to find some innovative way to survive physically and religiously, as they could not simply assimilate into the Persian religion (the Zoroastrian religion). In those days, everyone had belonged to a faith --- and the new Jewish monotheism could have potentially provided salvation.

Thirdly, out of all exiled Semitic nations in Babylonia; the Jewish belief system in a single God had been the closest to the Persian monotheistic belief system, and would have therefore been the most tolerated and least persecuted Semitic nation by the Persians themselves (and hence the most sought after by the Semitic people at the time).

Based on all these assumptions, it had probably been most convenient for all the exiled Semitic Babylonian tribes (such as the Phoenicians and Arameans) to converge into Judaism --- the only other monotheistic religion besides the ruling monotheistic Persian religion. A religion that would offer them some relief from Persian domination. It had most probably been an attractive refuge to the Babylonians themselves, as they had most-likely attempted to shed their former identity and previous beliefs in a pantheon of fifty (50) gods; eventually falling in line with the new monotheistic trend within the Persian empire.

Judaism had become the Semitic people's religious-ethnic alternative to Persian ethnic monotheism. This had become apparent as Judaism gained momentum within all Semitic people in: Mesopotamia; Syria; Judea; Egypt, and even as far as today's countries of Yemen and Ethiopia (perhaps even as far as Afghanistan to the East) --- all within the Persian Empire's borders at the time.

These genuine ethnic affiliations are substantial, and harbour implications as to the ethnic dynamics of our modern world; helping us understand today's conflicts. Ethnic identities are mostly stronger than religious affiliations. A predominantly ethnically-Semitic Sunni Muslim is far less tolerant towards an ethnically-Iranian (Parsi) Shia Muslim, and vice-versa.

Quite a few Sunni-Muslims will go as far as labeling the Shia, 'Satanic fire worshippers and non-believers' --- hating them even more than Jews who are of a completely different religion. The horror of this is most apparent in the Iraqi and Syrian wars between the Sunni and Shia ethnic Muslim groups, and is expanded upon in chapter 13 of the book which researches the inherent conflict between religions over the course of history.

The important point being made here is that throughout history, ethnicity has been a major influence. When analysing the Persian occupation of Mesopotamia, ethnic influence becomes apparent in the dichotomy between the dominating Zoroastrian monotheistic Parsi religion; and the rise of a new contender in the form of a Semitic monotheistic religion called Judaism.

The potential rivalry between these two religions had never erupted into real conflict, as history had presented new adversaries in the forms of the Greek Empire (followed by the Roman-Empire); disturbing both Persians and Jews in Mesopotamia, Judea, and the Middle-East --- that is, until the formation of Islam (as will be apparent in chapter 6).

In addition to understanding the drive for monotheism, as well as the reasons behind the underlying ethnic conflict at the time, it is possible to discover some clues as to what the strong Babylonian influences on Judaic formation had been.

The use of the Babylonian calendar, and its names for the months of the year, are of extreme significance when assessing the origins of the Jewish calendar and the chronological arrangement of all its festivals.[152]

Without the use of the Babylonian calendar as a template, not one Jewish festival would have been determined. Acknowledging this is extremely important, since religious festivals had played major roles in the development of Judaism. The purpose of these festivals had been to remind people of certain deeds, as well as to re-invigorate people on a yearly basis. Said deeds had been at the heart of the Jewish religion. We can hardly imagine what Judaism --- or any other religion that followed --- would be like without its religious festivals.

Other significant clues as to the extent of the influence of Babylonian culture on Judaism are the Ten Commandments; which resemble the code of conduct of the ancient Mesopotamian King, King Hammurabi,[153] as well as some religious customs such as Shabbat (the day of rest) which had been only partially practiced by the ancient Babylonians (one Shabbat per month, as opposed to four per month in Judaism).

Other minor clues include Jewish names such as 'Mordecai' ('Marduk chai' in Hebrew, meaning the Babylonian God Marduk is 'alive') and 'Esther' (Ishtar, the Babylonian goddess of fertility). Another very important name in the story of the Exodus out of Babylon is 'Zerubbabel' (The Seed of Babylon). These names indicate to Judaism's adoption of Babylonian names just prior to Persian rule. Jews still, to this day, use Babylonian names such as Nimrod, Hanok, and Noah.

Just recently, an archaeological excavation had revealed documentation of a wedding between a Jewish man and a Phoenician woman in Babylonia; confirming that Judaism had been a relatively open religion at the time of its initial formation in Babylon.

The most significant piece of evidence to support my suggestion that Judaism had been created in Babylon is the fact that: from the time of the Persian occupation of Babylonia --- through the Greek, Roman, and Parthian rule of the area --- right up until the Islamic rise in Iraq (Babylonia); a large and well established Jewish population, estimated at 1 million people, had lived in Babylonia/Mesopotamia. At times, this had been the largest Jewish population in the world.[154]

The Babylonian Talmud, which is the most influential book in Judaic thought and the centerpiece of Judaism, is still used by Jews today --- eclipsing the Jerusalem Talmud (which is hardly used nowadays). This reaffirms that the centrality of Judaism had been in Mesopotamia for over more than 1500 years (until the Arab occupation of that area).

Further analysis of the Torah will reveal similarities between the mythological stories in The Book of Genesis; and the mythological stories in The Book of Gilgamesh. Said similarities provide further indication that the Torah had been written in Babylon. In addition to mythology, the Torah serves as a crude philosophical view on world creation through the perceived possible existence of an omnipotent God. However, there is still no write-up in The Book of Genesis describing the realities of life; or any guidance as to how one should live their life in the most optimal way.

---

[152] "Babylonian Calendar and the Bible - Bible Odyssey." http://www.bibleodyssey.org/places/related-articles/babylonian-calendar-and-the-bible.aspx. Accessed 31 Jan. 2018.
[153] "Code of Hammurabi - Ancient History - HISTORY.com." http://www.history.com/topics/ancient-history/hammurabi. Accessed 31 Jan. 2018.
[154] "Historical Jewish population comparisons - Wikipedia." https://en.wikipedia.org/wiki/Historical_Jewish_population_comparisons. Accessed 22 Feb. 2018.

All this changes once The Book of Genesis progresses and begins to tell the stories of the founding fathers of the Hebrew nation --- vindication in the correct path (monotheism), human moral lessons, and laws explaining the desired human conduct begin gathering momentum.

It all begins with the story of Abraham and his revelation regarding the existence of a single, omnipotent God; as well as his covenant with that same God.[155] The first law present in this story is the uncompromising belief in this one-and-only God; another law is that of circumcision, which symbolizes the covenant between man and said God --- a law that physically distinguishes Jews from other populations. Abraham's incentive for abiding by these laws being the reward, promised to him by God, that his offspring would become as many as the sand on the beach or the stars in the sky and will be successful in their endeavours'. Isn't that the ultimate prize of life? producing as many successful descendants as possible. The moral lesson here being that if one respects God, and lives their life according to the laws God has constructed, they will be blessed with the ultimate prize of life --- just like Abraham, the steadfast follower, had been.

The story of the prophet Moses[156] and the exodus from Egypt[157] compound the bulk of the laws in Judaism. Some basic moral laws such as 'do not murder or steal' had already been 'common law' in the Middle-East and, as mentioned earlier, had been documented in the Hammurabi code in 1754 BCE --- nearly 1200 years earlier than the creation of Torah. However, the Torah expands far beyond the Ten Commandments; eventually becoming a marvelous, comprehensive book of law --- a truly great achievement for its time in history. The Torah went on to build and guide an entire nation for thousands of years after its creation. Eventually, it had also become the basis upon which the religions that had divulged from Judaism (namely Christianity and Islam) were founded --- religions that are still prevalent in today's society. The marvel of the Torah had been unprecedented at the time, and will now be further scrutinized so as to unlock answers to its profound influence on Jewish culture.

The question is: 'When exactly had the Torah been written?' --- had it been during Babylonian captivity, or under the Persian occupation? This is difficult to determine, as parts may have been written during both periods. However, considering the Torah's strong monotheistic stance --- which replicates the Zoroastrian religion's stance --- as well as taking the story of Abraham into account; it would be far more logical to assume that the Torah had been written and completed solely during the Persian occupation.

This assumption opens doors to further possibilities that can explain the entire story of the exodus as it is written in the Torah. The exodus --- a major story of deliverance from slavery in Egypt, to freedom in Israel. A story that could easily inspire the diaspora for whom it was written --- the Babylonian-Jewish diaspora. A liberation story without any real trace of archaeological or historical basis. Nevertheless, an inspiring moral story that taps into the deep-rooted human desire for freedom; a desire carried through by ensuing religions (eventually, over generations, evolving into a major modern day legal value and human right --- the right to freedom). A story that had also guided the founding fathers of the U.S.A. while on their voyage on the Mayflower.[158]

---

[155] "Learning from Abraham about the Life of Faith | Bible.org." 1 Jan. 2008, https://bible.org/article/learning-abraham-about-life-faith. Accessed 31 Jan. 2018.
[156] "Moses - Wikipedia." https://en.wikipedia.org/wiki/Moses. Accessed 1 Feb. 2018.
[157] "Exodus: History or Mythic Tale? | My Jewish Learning." https://www.myjewishlearning.com/article/exodus-history-or-mythic-tale/. Accessed 1 Feb. 2018.
[158] "How the exodus story created America :: Michael Freund." 29 Mar. 2013, http://www.michaelfreund.org/13124/exodus-america. Accessed 1 Feb. 2018.

When a nation is under occupation and in need for inspiration; when they are in need for hope of brighter future --- what could be better than a good story that ends in freedom and self-determination? If competent leaders under the Persian Empire's rule needed to write and tell this story to their audience; how would they do it? Would they write that the Persians had been tyrants and enslavers? Surely if they did this, they would be executed by the Persian rulers? Perhaps they would deliberate on how difficult and dangerous a voyage to the holy land would be, thus discouraging their followers? Presumably not.

First they would stress the holiness of this land, and the religious duty to venture there. Then they would describe how it had been done before in ancient times and different lands. What had been pertinent to the land of Mesopotamia and the tyrannical Persian rule, could easily be transversed into the land of Egypt and the Pharaonic rule. This would be done to bestow credibility upon the story as a true historical event --- a model for the action to come.

It must again be stressed that despite the fact that the story of the exodus from Egypt is probably, to a large extent, a pure myth; it is based on the harsh realities of subjugation and slavery that had existed in the world of antiquity. It had inspired humanity's quest for freedom for over many generations, and became the basis upon which various freedom movements had been formed. It had sparked the universal fight for freedom; right up until the days of modern history. The exodus had been expanded upon; describing the wandering of the Hebrews in the desert for 40 years. In this way, it had been able to generate many other laws and concepts that had, in effect, formed the basis of modern-day laws --- family laws, civil laws, and ethical conduct between humans. Some socialist concepts, such as the concepts of charity and social security, are also mentioned as laws within the Torah.

The Torah can be summed up as a story written by wise people who had been ahead of their time in their philosophical outlook. The wisdom and intellectual capacity of the Jewish writers of the Bible had most probably been compounded by the ancient wisdoms of Babylonia and Persia. However, this wisdom could not have appeared without some history of internal capability deeply-rooted within Hebrew culture that had been carried through the generations; capabilities originating from perhaps even as far back as the Canaanites. These capabilities had been that of an innovative nation which had continuously strived to expand their knowledge and cognitive frontiers --- the exact same innovative spirit which had led to the invention of the alphabet.

The Non-religious importance of Jewish Monotheism

Monotheism should be understood by modern secular people as a stepping stone to atheism and agnosticism. Today, since secularism is widespread in the Western world; it is taken for granted that polytheism is a bunch of nonsense (even monotheism is regarded as baloney by the atheists of today's society). But at the time of the Babylonian Empire, whereby people had been raised revering all kinds of Gods and attending various traditional religious ceremonies, it had not been so obvious to them that these Gods were, and are, non-existent; since each of these Gods had been associated with a tangible natural phenomenon. Therefore, the Bible can be considered as the biggest innovation of its time, since it had altered people's psyche from being polytheistic to being monotheistic.

As was discussed above, the writing of the Bible presented an elaborate 'manual' for good-living within a just society. The belief in a single, omnipotent God that had provided this manual was a necessity of the times. The Bible had been further promoted as a gift from God to his 'chosen people'. It had encompassed most of the wisdom and knowledge that had been available to the writers at the time --- the final touch to this wisdom being religious duties that would cement the learning of this manual by the followers of the religion, for generations to come.

As will be apparent in the chapters to come, this manual had not only been instrumental in the lives of the Jewish people, but also --- through its adoption by other cultures, and modification over the centuries and up to modern times --- this manual had changed the course of history in distant lands around the globe. From the establishment of the United States of America, to all over the Americas, Africa, and large parts of Asia.

So what does this period of Jewish history reveal about the Jewish people? Aside from the probability that Ethnic Jews had been involved with, and mingled with, the religious Babylonian elite and were therefore familiar with religious Babylonian traditions and customs; they had also been privy to Babylonian wisdom (which seemed to have been embedded in the well thought-out document of the Torah). The Jewish leaders Ezra and Nehemiah had most probably engaged with the Persian rulers as well, as they had definitely been the Persian religion (the first truly monotheistic religion in the world) --- a precursor to Judaism, and the Abrahamic religions that followed.

The Torah, which had probably been created by Babylonian-Jews during this time, had been a truly unique manuscript for its time in history. It had guided people --- laying out the correct ways of how they should lead their individual and family lives. It had also included important community mores; and had stressed the importance of wisdom, as well as the human need for freedom.

The Torah, and its laws, had initiated the building of a Jewish culture. A culture of: literacy; learning; rule of law, and social mores --- all within a family-oriented lifestyle. In some upcoming chapters, we will begin investigating this new culture and its influences on the individual Jew (as well as on the broader Jewish community).

Chapter 4

Under the Greek and Roman Empires.

Summary: This chapter is mainly a historical background that may eventually explain the background for the decline of Judaism, and the rise of Christianity. The relationship between Jews and the Roman Empire had been recorded by Roman historians; and surprisingly, many people today --- including many Jews --- have barely any knowledge of this time period in history. Analysing Jewish religious zealasy and terrorism during the Roman Empire's rule may contribute to the understanding of modern-day Islamic zealasy and terrorism.

Most of the information regarding this period in history is derived from the writings of the Roman/Jewish historian Josephus Flavius,[159] who had at first been a Jewish rebel leader. He had been captured by the Roman Flavian family in the Jewish-Roman wars. After gaining the favour of General Vespasian he had been brought to Rome, given a new Roman name, and was commissioned to write history books accounting for the events of the Jewish-Roman wars. He also wrote about the history of the Jews prior to Roman occupation (his sources being historic information available at that time).

Jews under the Greek and Roman Empires

The following quote from the Babylonian Talmud puts the Roman Empire's previous need for writers during the Empire's expansion into perspective:

'If all seas were ink, all reeds were pen, all skies parchment, and all men scribes, they would be unable to set down the full scope of the Roman government's concerns'.[160]

As the Roman Empire expanded its borders, it became a massive administrative task to manage this vast Empire. There became a real need for documentation, as well as literate people who had been able to generate and maintain these huge amounts of documentation. Literacy had become a demanded and useful resource for the Romans. Wherever this resource had been found, it was to be taken and used.

Greeks --- and many Jews who had been literate in the Greek language --- became an essential administrative resource for the Roman Empire; whether they came in the form of slaves or free men. Therefore, throughout the Roman Empire, the Jewish people's intellectual capacity had been used extensively by the Romans.

A few hundred years before the Roman occupation --- during the Hellenistic occupation of Mesopotamia and the Middle-East --- Greek became the official language of the new Alexandrian Empire. While Aramaic had still been the mother tongue language of Jews in Judea and Babylon; Jews living in the big cities of Antioch in Syria and Alexandria in Egypt

---

[159] "Josephus - Livius." 5 Jun. 2017, http://www.livius.org/articles/person/josephus/. Accessed 2 Feb. 2018.
[160] "505506 Estimates of the average literacy rate in the Empire range from ...."
https://www.coursehero.com/file/p6p60hk/505506-Estimates-of-the-average-literacy-rate-in-the-Empire-range-from-5-to-30/. Accessed 2 Feb. 2018.

were beginning to lose this original mother tongue language . . . it had gradually changed to the Koine Greek language.

The Bible had been translated into Greek in what was known as the Septuagint translation[161] under the instruction of King Ptolemy II[162] of Egypt. This had been done in order to make the Bible more accessible to the many Greek-speaking Jews in Egypt. Greek had also been taught to growing numbers of Hellenistic-Jews within Judea itself, as Hellenisation was rapidly advancing in Judea and surrounding areas.

A famous literary figure of the time was Philo[163] of Alexandria, who had promoted Greek translations of Jewish life. Philo believed that these translations would be read by non-Jewish Greeks, and would serve as a bridge of understanding between Jews and Non-Jews; ultimately reducing the hostilities of neighbouring Greek citizens towards the Jews in Alexandria.

The Influence of Hellenic culture on Jews in Judea was profound. Many Greek names such as Alexander, Doron, and Helen had been used by Jews. Said names are still common in Jewish communities to this day. There is some evidence to suggest that Greek philosophy had also influenced Rabbinical Judaism; however, this would be to a lesser degree than Hellenic culture.[164] Some academics go so far as to claim that Jewish writings, such as the Kabbalah, had been influenced by Platonic philosophy.[165]

As the Roman Republic rose --- due to successful military campaigns against the Greek Seleucid and Ptolemaic dynasties[166] --- The Greek era was coming to an end, and the worst for Judaism in Judea was on the horizon.

The most influential historical writer about the Roman Empire in Judea was Joseph Ben Matityahu (Josephus Flavius). His extensive writings described Jewish life, and relationships between Jews, the Hellenists, and the Roman Empire.

The historical writings of Joseph Flavius[167] mention that after about 77 years of Hellenisation and prosperity in Judea under the Hasmonean dynasty (also known as the Maccabees) from 140 BCE to 63 BCE; the Roman Republic's General, General Pompey, advanced on the Greek Seleucid Empire that had been weakened by their Parthian enemies surrounding their Eastern borders. During his military campaign, Pompey decided to dominate Judea under direct Roman rule.

Under Roman rule, the Hasmonean descendants had been used as Roman proxies to rule Judea. They had been swapped and changed in the midst of the power struggles and Roman

---

[161] "Septuagint | biblical literature | Britannica.com." https://www.britannica.com/topic/Septuagint. Accessed 2 Feb. 2018.
[162] "Ptolemy II Philadelphus | Macedonian king of Egypt | Britannica.com." https://www.britannica.com/biography/Ptolemy-II-Philadelphus. Accessed 2 Feb. 2018.
[163] "Philo of Alexandria > By Individual Philosopher > Philosophy." http://www.philosophybasics.com/philosophers_philo.html. Accessed 2 Feb. 2018.
[164] "Hellenism - Jewish Virtual Library." http://www.jewishvirtuallibrary.org/hellenism-2. Accessed 5 Feb. 2018.
[165] "The Influence of Platonism on Jewish Philosophy | Angelo Nasios ...." http://www.academia.edu/4115125/The_Influence_of_Platonism_on_Jewish_Philosophy. Accessed 5 Feb. 2018.
[166] "Macedonian Wars | ancient history | Britannica.com." https://www.britannica.com/event/Macedonian-Wars. Accessed 5 Feb. 2018.
[167] "Flavius Josephus | The Online Books Page." http://onlinebooks.library.upenn.edu/webbin/book/lookupname?key=Josephus%2C%20Flavius. Accessed 2 Feb. 2018.

civil war between the Roman Generals Pompey, Mark Anthony, and Julius Caesar.[168] This instability in Judea had come to an end when Herod the Great was declared 'King of the Jews' by the Roman senate.[169]

King Herod, in conjunction with the Roman army, helped re-capture the entire land of Judea from a multitude of Jewish-Hasmonean rebels (as well as others who were branded as Jewish bandits).

During his rule, Herod had executed all Hasmonean pretenders to the Judean throne . . . including his own wife and her sons. Although Herod is described as being a very cruel King, his rule had been accompanied by unprecedented prosperity and grand building endeavours --- including a huge expansion of the Temple mount in Jerusalem.

The Romans, at this stage, seemed to have prioritized maintaining their presence in Judea; as it had been a frontier between the Roman Empire, and the emerging Parthian Empire. Judaea had become a buffer zone between the Parthian Empire and Egypt (which had become the 'breadbasket of Rome'). In Egypt, Jews had been instrumental in the economic development, and had enjoyed great liberties and tax exemptions from the Romans.

The large Jewish-Egyptian population had been supportive of the Roman Empire's conquest of Egypt over the Ptolemaic Greeks. Judea itself, as well as Syria, had been Roman territories which became the backbones of the Roman Empire's frontier against the Parthian Empire to the East. Judea had also been the land corridor to the grain producing lands of Egypt and North-Africa. Trade and the Jewish population had swelled and spread all over the Roman Empire --- especially in: Egypt; Cyrene (modern-day Eastern Libya); Judea; Western Syria (modern-day Lebanon and northern Syria), and Cyprus. Judaism had been recognised as a respected and legitimate religion within the Roman Empire.

Jews, at that time, had been polygamous. This is a noteworthy observation, as it had been a religious deed of utmost importance in Judaism to breed and multiply. During relatively peaceful times, this would create 'Jewish population explosion pressures'; which drove Jews to seek opportunities for a better life in the neighbouring communities of Greeks, Romans and other nations throughout the Roman Empire --- spanning as far as Spain and North-Africa.

This rapid rise in the amount of followers of Judaism --- as well as the prosperity of the Jews --- would have also created multiple streams and sects of disenfranchised, or partly disenfranchised, Jewish populations.

A relatively large, sufficiently literate, and religiously educated population --- which is impoverished --- has the potential to become a recipe for disaster; as it would create various religious factions with different messianic views.

These factions began to wage war on each other, as well as upon the Roman Empire. Pharisees, Sadducees, Essenes and Zealots, had been the main sects documented by the Jewish/Roman historian, Josephus Flavius. The Sicarii are also mentioned as being a small group similar in their ideology to the Zealots.[170] The writings of Josephus Flavius is the sole source of the following brief review of history. This review may save readers who are interested in history, a lot of time:

---

[168] "Roman Civil War | 49–46 bc | Britannica.com." https://www.britannica.com/event/Roman-Civil-War. Accessed 2 Feb. 2018.
[169] "Herod | Biography & Facts | Britannica.com." 19 Jan. 2018, https://www.britannica.com/biography/Herod-king-of-Judaea. Accessed 2 Feb. 2018.
[170] "Flavius Josephus THE WARS OF THE JEWS OR HISTORY OF THE ...." http://www.documentacatholicaomnia.eu/03d/0037-0103,_Flavius_Josephus,_De_Bello_Judaico,_EN.pdf. Accessed 2 Feb. 2018.

The Zealots and Sicarii had been heinous murderers who targeted Romans and Greeks with the goal of ending Roman rule by force. The Sicarii had also targeted Jews who they considered to be apostates, as well as Jews who they believed had collaborated with the Romans. The Zealots are also mentioned in the Babylonian Talmud, which accounts for their burning of decades worth of food and firewood stored in the besieged city of Jerusalem during the 'Great Jewish Revolt' against the Roman Empire --- they had done this in order to force their fellow Jews to fight the Romans out of desperation.

According to Josephus Flavius, the 'Great Jewish Revolt' began in the year 66 CE in Caesarea (following some tension between various populations). Romans, Greeks and Hellenistic Jews on one side, versus the various traditional religious mainstream Jewish populations.

It is important to realise that although the Judean population had largely been comprised of ethnic-Jews; a multitude of Greeks, Romans, and Hellenistic Jews, were of significant numbers and power within many areas in and around Judea. The pro-Roman Jewish King, King Agrippa II, and his sister Bernice had been intimately involved with the Roman Flavian family. Bernice had even been General Titus' female companion; and had vested substantial amounts of her wealth in Titus' father, General Vespasian, in order to help him achieve his campaign to become Rome's new Emperor.

For generations, General Titus has been begrudgingly remembered by Jews around the world as the Roman General who had eventually destroyed the holy Jewish Temple in Jerusalem.

The Jewish rebels --- whom had been comprised of all the above mentioned sects --- were in constant war with each other. This added to the already complicated state of affairs. Each sect had strived to dominate the rebellion against the Romans --- the final result being the brutal defeat of all said Jewish sects; with hundreds of thousands of casualties, and possibly just over one million dead. The city of Jerusalem, and the Temple, had been burnt to the ground by general Titus.

Of all the Jewish sects that had participated in this rebellion, only the Pharisees had remained. The Pharisees --- who, during the rebellion, had been the group most willing to negotiate with the Romans. In turn, the Romans had spared them. As mentioned above, one of the most famous Pharisees' leaders, Yosef ben Matityahu (who had surrendered to the Romans) gained the favour of the Flavian family, is the historian . . . Josephus Flavius.

Flavius had been transferred to Rome, and granted a stipend for life to write the historical accounts of this revolt (as well as other Jewish histories preceding it). Most current day knowledge of that era consists of his writings.

The enslavement of around 97000 Jews had been another repercussion of the Great Jewish Revolt. Most of these slaves had been sold to rich Jewish families and communities around the Roman-Empire, who were under religious obligation to buy the freedom of their fellow Jews. Scores of Jews had fled to the neighbouring territories of: Egypt; Assyria; Cyprus, and Mesopotamia. Mesopotamia (Babylonia) had still been under Parthian rule.

The Pharisees,[171] who had survived this war with the Romans, became the origin population of modern-day mainstream Judaism. With the demise of the Temple in Jerusalem, rabbinical Judaism had begun to emerge as the leading form of Judaism in Judea. Rabbi Yohanan ben Zakkai had been permitted by Roman emperor Vespasian to establish a Judaic school at

---

[171] "Who Were the Pharisees? Bible Definition and Meaning."
https://www.biblestudytools.com/dictionary/pharisees/. Accessed 2 Feb. 2018.

Yavneh (about 30 km south of the modern city of Tel-Aviv), which later became a major center for Talmudic studies.

Though the troubles in Judea had been debilitating to Judean Jews, the growth and success of the Jewish populations in the neighbouring countries had remained unabated. In: Cyrene; Egypt; Coastal Assyria; and Cyprus, Jewish populations had grown to comprise as much as 50% of the inhabitants in that region.

Again, this mixture of highly successful Jews within a large mass of religiously indoctrinated Jewish fanatics would eventually --- inevitably --- lead to a second eruption against the existing powers within the Roman Empire. Jewish populations who were neighbouring the Greco-Roman populations in the large cities had sparked a colossal war known as 'The Kitos War', or --- the Jewish rebellion of the diaspora.[172]

The Jewish rebellion of the diaspora was mainly documented by the Roman historian Eusebius of Caesarea.[173] According to his accounts, the revolt had begun in Cyrene (Cyrenaica/modern-day Eastern Libya) while the Roman Emperor Trajan's[174] legions had fought (and defeated) their arch-enemy in the North-Eastern front --- the Parthian Empire.[175]

Jewish rebels had attacked the small Roman garrisons left behind, and initiated the war by massacring many of the Greek and Roman inhabitants and destroying their numerous polytheistic Temples.

The devastation had been so great that in Cyrene and Cyprus, the Greek and Roman populations were nearly wiped out completely. In Alexandria, the Egyptian Temples and the tomb of Pompey had also been destroyed; all this had happened while the remaining Greek and Roman populations, and the small army forces, fled the city.

The revolt had spread to Mesopotamia; where large populations of Jews, combined with Parthian Empire inhabitants, had clashed with the conquering Roman forces. A Jewish revolt had also taken place in Judea just 40 years earlier --- the Jews had joined the widespread revolt.

The situation had been quite menacing from a Roman perspective. So much so that Emperor Trajan[176] had quickly crowned a Parthian royal family member as King of Parthia so as to quell the rebellions in Mesopotamia; enabling Trajan to return with his troops and engage the revolting Jews in: Judea; Egypt; Cyrene, and Cyprus.

On his way to Judea, Emperor Trajan had died from a stroke in 117 CE. It was his successor, Emperor Hadrian,[177] who managed to quash the Jewish rebellion. First by abandoning all territorial gains that had been captured from the Parthians; then by concentrating on vanquishing the Jewish rebels.

The aftermath of this rebellion had devastated Jewish communities. Most Jews in the Middle-East had been annihilated; rendering the territories of Cyrene and Cyprus

---

[172] "The Jewish Roman Wars - How has Judaism survived for 4000 years." http://www.jewishwikipedia.info/romanwars.html. Accessed 2 Feb. 2018.
[173] "Eusebius of Caesarea | Biography, Writings, & History | Britannica.com." https://www.britannica.com/biography/Eusebius-of-Caesarea. Accessed 2 Feb. 2018.
[174] "Trajan | Roman emperor | Britannica.com." https://www.britannica.com/biography/Trajan. Accessed 2 Feb. 2018.
[175] "Parthia | ancient region, Iran | Britannica.com." https://www.britannica.com/place/Parthia. Accessed 4 Feb. 2018.
[176] "Trajan - Ancient History Encyclopedia." 25 May. 2013, https://www.ancient.eu/trajan/. Accessed 4 Feb. 2018.
[177] "Hadrian | Roman emperor | Britannica.com." https://www.britannica.com/biography/Hadrian. Accessed 2 Feb. 2018.

unpopulated. This arose the need to transpose people from other parts of the Roman Empire to settle in Cyrene and Cyprus.

An order had been made; declaring that no Jewish foot may ever step in Cyprus and Cyrene. Execution had been the punishment for any Jew that would even mistakenly set foot there.

Hadrian had also decided to rebuild Jerusalem as a new city named Aelia Capitolina; so as to erase any memory of Jewish linkage to the city. No Jew had been permitted entrance into the city.[178] The Roman Empire's anger towards this Jewish rebellion had clearly been intense, and deep-rooted.

Another major act by Hadrian had been the renaming of Judea as Palestina.[179] This act of re-naming Judea into Palestine has carried political ramifications with it throughout the ages, and up to modern times. Judea and Palestine are interchangeable, confused, and contested with regards to disputes about ownership. This conflict exists between Jews who claim that the area is part of the modern state of Israel, and Arabs who declare themselves as Palestinians and rightful owners of the land.

This re-naming had also given rise to historical injustices within many historical documents; as a number of historians --- including many Jewish and Christian historians who write about Judea's history before Emperor Hadrian's reign --- have been naming Judea as Palestine. Early Christians, and definitely Jesus if he ever existed, would have neither heard nor known of the name 'Palestine'. Perhaps history books should be corrected in order to highlight this historical injustice. The area should be named Palestine from the beginning of the second century --- not from the theoretical time period in which Jesus had lived.

After the Kitos Rebellion, the harsh measures taken by the Romans to destroy Jewish populations had instigated yet another extremely violent Jewish revolt in 132 CE known as the Bar Kokhba revolt.[180] The result of this revolt being the death of most of the Jewish population in Judea, as well as a ban imposed upon the Jewish religion throughout the Roman Empire. This ban had been ordered by Caesar Hadrian, and was only lifted once he had died in 138 CE[181].

From that time onwards, Jews had become a minority in each and every country that had existed within the Roman Empire. Judea had lost its name, and had become Palestina. The future for Jews within the Roman Empire turned bleak.[182]

Outside the Roman Empire --- within the Parthian Empire of Mesopotamia and especially within the cities --- there had still remained a large number of Jews who had been instrumental in advancing Jewish life and Jewish studies.

Although, back then, Judaism had produced religious fanaticism --- which, as shown above, is a complicated matter that once established can lead to divisions, extremism, and deadly consequence --- there may also be indications of another recurring pattern within ancient

---

[178] "Hadrian's Curse - The Invention of Palestine - Think-Israel." http://www.think-israel.org/ronen.hadriancurse.html. Accessed 2 Feb. 2018.
[179] ibid
[180] "History Crash Course #37: Bar Kochba Revolt - Aish.com." 18 Aug. 2007, http://www.aish.com/jl/h/cc/48944706.html. Accessed 2 Feb. 2018. (This reference is from a Jewish religious point of view)
[181] "Hadrian returns to Jerusalem - Opinion - Jerusalem Post." 15 Feb. 2016, http://www.jpost.com/Opinion/Hadrian-returns-to-Jerusalem-444995. Accessed 2 Feb. 2018.
[182] "The Bar-Kokhba Revolt 132-135 CE - Jewish Virtual Library." http://www.jewishvirtuallibrary.org/the-bar-kokhba-revolt-132-135-ce. Accessed 2 Feb. 2018.

Jewish history . . . the creation of individuals on the other side of the spectrum. Open-minded realists.

The Jewish religion produces a somewhat high number of literate and brainy populations. Parts of these populations then venture into the world with traits that allow them to compete with, and in-fact surpass, the general non-Jewish population (when it comes to trade and business). This then leads to Jewish domination over the economy, which in turn leads to jealousy and hate from the non-Jewish population.

This hate is magnified when said jealous non-Jewish population compares economically dominating Jews to their poor Jewish brethren who invest their time solely into religious studies. Comparisons between successful Jews, and other Jews who become religious fanatics also magnifies the non-Jewish population's hate for Jews. This hate is therefore exacerbated through confusion as to why the Jewish culture produces such extremely contradictory individuals that, when juxtaposed, are impossible to reconcile due to their inconsistency (especially during those ancient periods in history).

The fact that rich upper-class assimilated Jews had originated from a fanatic and despised group of religious hard-heads had been too surreal for the Greek and Roman populations to accept and comprehend (not to say that Romans who had practiced human slavery and performed ruthless massacres and genocides had been such a good example of human conduct when compared to fanatic Jews).

Over history --- as will be shown --- many: Hellenised; Romanised; Spaniarised; Germanized, or nowadays Americanised Jews become assimilated Jews and rise to the top of the economic elite. Given the opportunity, they also rise to the top of the political elite. This had simply been too bothersome for non-Jewish populations (especially in Europe where Jews had always been perceived as outsiders, foreigners, and somewhat temporary guests --- at times, even unwanted guests).

The overwhelming and mind-boggling riddle of success that is the Jewish culture leads to all kinds of conspiracy theories and explanations mired in prejudice. The strange and illogical behaviour of people is always followed by their perceived illogicality and strangeness of the situation they are faced with. This illogical behaviour is another pan of anti-Semitism that has been present over the centuries.

At the time of the Roman Empire's rule, the non-Jewish population's hate towards Jews had also been fueled by their fear of the fast growing numbers of religious fanatic Jews who had proved to be a volatile, unpredictable mob that became murderous to the Greeks and Romans. Fear produces hate --- and hate is one of the fuels of anti-Semitism.

The Greeks and Romans who had exerted vast amounts of cruelty themselves could not comprehend why one Jew would kill his 'progressive' Hellenized/Romanized ethnic brother in the name of an imaginary God. Why some Jews would embark on what seemed to be a suicide war in the name of this imaginary God remained another mystery to the Greeks and Romans. The religious Jewish zealot had been beyond their comprehension. Hate and fear of the Jew had been common.

The fear was real. The writings of Eusebius of Caesarea and Apion demonstrate the intense anti-Semitism that had existed throughout the history of the Roman Empire. Caesar Hadrian's acts against Jews demonstrate the hate and fear that had been felt toward them.

Concluding Remarks

This general historical overview in the last few chapters has presented what the probable origins of Judaism, and Jews, had been (from an archaeological and historic perspective). It has demonstrated that the Bible, and especially the Torah, had been cleverly designed; and made for the sole purpose of rebuilding a nation on the premise that the Jewish people had been the 'chosen nation' --- chosen by an almighty omnipotent God.

The Judeans' defiant and aggressive personalities, as well as their innovative capabilities, have been discovered through scrutiny of their shared past as Canaanites. From creating a new sophisticated alphabet, to actively pursuing knowledge and truth; all innovations had culminated into marvelous literature --- literature that, at the time, had been new and innovative. Within a historical context, one would be valid in claiming that the Torah had been a marvel for its time.

This literature, namely the Bible, had been way ahead of its time in its philosophical outlook on humanity; as well as its quest to determine the desired behaviour of civilization. Many values, such as civil liberties and freedom from slavery, had been propagated --- values which form the basis of our modern-day societies.

The trade routes that had been established through the land of Canaan, as well as the Mediterranean Sea, further demonstrate the expansive character of this nation. This also explains, and provides proof of, its dispersion throughout the Mediterranean region; and later, into the European continent. The uncompromising belief in, and drive to preserve, its unique ethnic make-up --- combined with physical geographical dispersion --- had probably been the keys to the survival of this nation.

The strengths and benefits of literacy and wisdom (gained from consistent religious studies) were shown to have been the factors responsible for determining Jewish success. In contrast to these benefits, said religious studies had also brewed the obsessive, fanatical, and unrealistic beliefs which highlight the past weaknesses of the Jewish religion. This is also true to varying degrees in all religions throughout history, and is still prevalent in religious based societies existing in this modern-day and age.

Said religious weaknesses have always resulted in, and will always result in, civil wars and destruction. This had been demonstrated during the Greek and Roman Empires' rule in Judea; and is even demonstrated in world conflicts taking place today (such as inside the Muslim world between Sunni and Shia in Syria and Iraq, as well as within other Muslim countries such as Yemen). It has also manifested in the deep inherent conflict between the Western American-dominated civilization, and a large section within the Islamic world.

Some other causes of the historical seeds of anti-Semitism had also been revealed in this chapter. These spiteful feelings had brewed as a result of the non-Jewish population witnessing the success of the hated Jewish minority; breeding further jealousy, fear, and hate in the hearts of the surrounding non-Jewish populations.

The difficulty in reconciling this economic success on the one hand, and the feelings of contempt on the other hand, also magnifies this hate for Jews. Such jealousy and hate can drive even a normal person insane --- let alone religious personalities that preach their religion and culture to be better than Judaism, and are then faced with the difficult task of explaining the reality of the Jews' prosperity; as well as the Jews' ability to exhibit a more successful image.

This theme of Jewish success --- and resultant hate from others --- will be apparent in the following chapters regarding old continental European Christianity, as well as with regard to Islam within the Middle-East and North Africa.

Since the quest of this book is to discover the reasons for the phenomenal intellectual and economic success of some Jewish people, the questions that still remain unanswered are of formidable difficulty to resolve.

Questions such as: 'What are the traits that Jews develop in order to enable them to rise to the helm of intellectual and business pursuits?', and 'How had they acquired those traits?' ; as well as 'What happens to all the other Jews that do not rise to elevated levels of success?'

To answer those questions, we will have to delve further into the numerous character traits of the Jews that have not yet been discussed. Character traits that had undoubtedly been shaped by the Jewish culture that had been developed over a prolonged period of time (since Judaism and Jewish people have changed, and are still changing, in a long historical process).

Chapter 5

From Torah studies to Talmudic studies, and beyond.

Summary: This chapter will expand on the Torah and the social tools it provides. It will explain the reasons for the development of the Talmud, as well as the impact the Talmud had on the development of further intellectual skills --- skills that have provided Jewish people with an intellectual advantage over others in the field of law. The importance of Jewish deeds and their impact on modern family law will also be laid out in this chapter. It will also demonstrate how Jewish education is at the root of Western education.

In previous chapters, it was argued that Judaic people of antiquity had been instrumental in the creation of the modern alphabet. It was also shown that Judaism had most probably been shaped into a monotheistic religion in Babylonia; during the Persian Empire's rule.

The creation of Judaism as a monotheistic religion had enabled the Semitic Judaic minority population to become a prominent nation in the Middle-East. This is evident from Roman historical records stating that just before the Great Jewish Rebellion against the Roman-Empire, the majority of the population in Judea --- as well as nearly 50% of the population in the surrounding territories --- had consisted of Jews. There had also been a substantial amount of large Jewish populations in the big cities of Mesopotamia.

It had already been a known fact back then that the Bible, and the Torah within it, had become the heart and soul of the Jewish nation.

The skills and tools that had been developed in order to continue the building of this nation are of interest. Let us examine what exactly these skills and tools are, and how they have been beneficial in the generation of intellectual and economic wealth.

Building a nation on spiritual pursuits

In the previous chapter, it was mentioned that in antiquity, it could be assumed that many Judaic people had possessed literacy skills that had exceeded their surrounding non-Jewish populations' literacy skills. This was due to the fact that it had been a religious duty for every Jew to write a Torah scroll at least once in their lifetime. To validate this assumption, one needs to turn yet again to circumstantial evidence (combined with what is known today about Judaism).

First, it has been noted that the Torah specifically, and the Bible in general, had become the heart and soul of this Jewish nation; the most important deed being to learn and know the Torah (which had been depicted as God's own words delivered unto the Jewish people by his chosen prophet Moses). Achieving this would require an individual to possess the ability to read in Babylonian Aramaic, and also understand Hebrew.

Secondly, it has been documented throughout historical records that Jewish people had mostly been a minority within the Empires they had lived under. Whether it had been the: Babylonian; Persian; Greek, or Roman-Empires --- managing day-to-day life under these Empires would have require one to learn their respective languages. This requirement must have resulted in the creation of Jewish populations that had been bilingual, and at times maybe even trilingual. Surely there are intellectual benefits to bilingualism and multilingualism.[183] If nothing else, it would've increased brain activity and processing capacity among individuals within these Jewish populations.

So, while the occupier --- be them: Persian; Greek; or Roman, had gradually imposed their language upon the occupied populations (one of which being the Jewish population); the occupied must have learnt said languages as fast as possible in order to interact efficiently with the occupier. At times, the quick learner may have received benefits (such as being appointed as a translator, or being given other necessary work which involves language). Said quick learner would have also most likely benefited from some empathetic emotions felt towards them from the conqueror. This would have been due to the fact that every person feels most comfortable when conversing in their mother-tongue language; and that the efforts of the Jewish learner to grasp the new language would have been appreciated by the conqueror. These empathetic emotions may have eventually developed into trust --- assigning Jews to supervisory positions, and providing them with economic benefits. It is only natural for humans to enjoy the fruits of their labour.

Therefore, rapid learning had become a survival need for the Jew --- not just a religious duty. It had still, nevertheless, been first and foremost strongly embedded as a strict spiritual religious deed. The deed to know the word of God, and live by it wholeheartedly.

The onerous deed of studying 'God's word' via the 'holy language' of Hebrew required reading and understanding the Torah, down to its smallest detail. The problem with this was that not every law written in the Torah had been clear. In fact, there had been many passages in the Torah that were quite confusing. This confusion had prompted some interpretations by people who could articulate the Torah's writings and philosophy on an expert level. This need for clarity would eventually result in the creation of the Talmud.[184]

The Talmud had enhanced the benefits of Judaism even further, as it had generated advanced life skills --- skills that would have been applicable to all facets of life, be them moral, legal, or economical skills. Through interpretation of the written life stories in the Torah, issues had been raised. A written debate was then ensued, whereby different opinions of various esteemed Rabbis had been put forward; and, after deliberations, a conclusion was reached. This conclusion had usually been the invention of a good practical guide for human conduct; otherwise known as a 'mitzvah' ('deed' in Hebrew).

The importance of Jewish deeds

Built upon the studies of the Torah and the Talmud, a whole system of deeds had been devised. Considered within the context of Jewish history as one of the most important philosophers of the Jewish religion, Rabbi Moshe ben Maimon (1135-1204 CE, widely known as the Rambam) had compiled an entire set of 613 deeds --- derived from the Torah and the Talmud --- in his most famous work 'Mishneh Torah'.[185] Said deeds have become the cornerstone of what Judaism is all about in the real world. The life of the Rambam and his general philosophical outlook is outlined in chapter 7.

---

[183] "7 Powerful Benefits of Being Bilingual That'll Change Your Life ...." https://www.fluentu.com/blog/benefits-of-being-bilingual/. Accessed 20 Feb. 2018.
[184] "The Talmud | ReformJudaism.org." https://reformjudaism.org/talmud. Accessed 5 Feb. 2018.
[185] "Halakhah, Mishneh Torah | Sefaria." https://www.sefaria.org/texts/Halakhah/Mishneh%20Torah. Accessed 5 Feb. 2018.

It is not in the scope of this book to outline all the deeds and their derivatives; however, in order to understand the Jewish religion --- and some of its associated rituals --- some integral deeds will be discussed. The reader is able to explore the link below for in-depth information about all 613 deeds.[186] There is no specific order in which these deeds are outlined, but a common classification is normally used as follows:

The first crucial deed is all about the belief in a single God --- an eternal, omnipotent deity that should be loved and feared. A God that should not be blasphemed or tested, and whose name shall not be profaned. A God who's good ways should be imitated.

The second deed deals with the Torah. This deed promotes the learning and teaching of said Torah, in order to ensure that no detraction or addition of any commandment is made. Each person shall write a scroll of a Torah for themself --- a deed that promotes literacy.

The deeds about God and the Torah are inseparable; since in the Jewish monotheistic religion, the Torah is considered to be the word of God.

Then come the deeds which are written in the Torah that exist because God willed them to be so; starting with the physical rituals of male circumcision,[187] and the unique Jewish clothing of tallit (as well as specific prayers to be performed).

Much has been written about circumcision in recent years. The exact origin of circumcision is attributed to the Egyptian Pharaonic Kingdom.[188] The Greek historian Herodotus had written of it at around 400 BCE on his visit to Egypt. As we know from one of the previous chapters, chapter 2, Canaanites had been ruled by the Pharaonic Kingdom for approximately 350 years. It is therefore quite plausible that Judaic people had already been practicing male circumcision while in Babylon --- hence before the Torah had even been written.

Although Christianity had largely eliminated this practice, the Egyptian Coptic Church --- as well as Ethiopian and Eritrean Christians --- still practices male-infant circumcision (in almost the exact same way Judaism has been practicing it). While the Egyptian Coptic Church is one of the earliest Christian churches, the Ethiopian royal family --- which had practiced Judaism --- is documented to have been christianized at around 350 CE.[189]

The modern legal debate about this practice is ongoing --- between the moral issues of mutilating a baby without their consent, versus the baby's right to be a part of his community and their traditions. The 'elephant in the room' of the debate against circumcision lies with female circumcision;[190] which is still widely practiced in countries like Egypt and Sudan under Islamic law (which is prevalent in these countries). Female circumcision is not practiced in Islamic-Iraq, Saudi-Arabia, and the other Islamic states of the Middle-East --- a fact that may point to the non-Islamic origins of female circumcision.

Female circumcision has been proven to be a very dangerous practice, which can lead to death due to bacterial contamination. Also worrying are the long-term effects of this practice on the psyche of both men and women during adult sexual life.

---

[186] "Judaism 101: A List of the 613 Mitzvot ...." http://www.jewfaq.org/613.htm. Accessed 5 Feb. 2018.
[187] "Circumcision - History and Recent Trends - CircInfo.net."
http://www.circinfo.net/history_and_recent_trends.html. Accessed 5 Feb. 2018.
[188] "Nip Tuck: circumcision in ancient Egypt | Ancient Near East: Just the ...." 31 Oct. 2014, https://ancientneareast.org/2014/10/31/nip-tuck-circumcision-in-ancient-egypt/. Accessed 20 Feb. 2018.
[189] "Ezana Facts - Biography - YourDictionary." http://biography.yourdictionary.com/ezana. Accessed 20 Feb. 2018.
[190] "Female genital mutilation (FGM) frequently asked questions | UNFPA ...."
http://www.unfpa.org/resources/female-genital-mutilation-fgm-frequently-asked-questions. Accessed 5 Feb. 2018.

Women cannot enjoy their sexual life, and are in-fact hurt during sex; resulting in them despising partaking in sexual acts due to the pain. Apart from the fact that such a situation is undesirable from the female perspective; it is also terrible for the male partner, as he cannot satisfy a woman's physiological and psychological need for sex.

These last three paragraphs are able to provide a perspective on the Jewish and Islamic practice of male circumcision, and the debate on its effects. Apart from its unsavoury impression on people who do not practice it, there is nothing to suggest that it is extremely harmful.

Then there are the deeds that are of most interest for the purpose of this book. These are the laws specified in the Torah regarding relationships between humans; be them family and friends, or strangers. Mainly in the books of Leviticus and Deuteronomy.

The Torah is the first book in the Western world to demonstrate how human relationships should be conducted. The basis is kindness. It begins with commandments about loving Jews and strangers --- giving charity to the poor and needy, and not doing others wrong in speech or business. Other specifics are commandments that insist on restraint from: taking revenge upon others; bearing grudges; shaming others; cursing others; hating others, as well as avoiding any other harmful acts that could be done unto a fellow human being.

All these ideals --- which originate from Judaism --- went on to become ideals of: the Christian religion; the Islamic religion; and later on, the ideals of the modern secular world. But, in order to battle anti-Semitism, it is incredibly important for everyone (be them: Christian, Muslim, or a modern secular person) to remember which nation had been the first to implement and document these ideals . . . the Jewish nation.

We are all aware of how many of these moral ideals are compromised due to mankind's biological nature and strong self-interest (which can often develop into greed). Nevertheless, all societies have adopted these as benchmark deeds; and always strive to implement them.

The next important deeds to investigate are family laws within the Torah. These include marriage laws which forbid incest, as well as laws which advocate respect and honour for one's parents and one's spouse. Most of these laws are applied today within legal systems around the world. The further one reads into the 613 deeds, the more apparent it becomes that the basis of modern society's moral values and legal substantive content originates from Judaism.

There are negative commandments in the Torah that have been abolished in modern Western societies, such as: laws forbidding one to marry out of their faith; laws regarding illegitimate children; cruel ways of punishing criminal offenders, and laws instigating the genocide of idol worshippers. Through rabbinical orders for over two millennia, these unsavoury deeds had been watered down; and became irrelevant within the Judaic diaspora. In some Islamic countries, however, these unsavoury deeds remain practiced. This includes the gruesome stoning of homosexual individuals --- as well as adulterers --- until death. The horrific decapitations performed by the Islamic state (ISIL) that we have all witnessed in recent years over the internet had also been the fate of idol worshippers in antiquity.

As has been highlighted above, the study and replication of the Torah is an educational type of deed. The reality of the Jewish life quest of retaining and preserving their Torah under the Empires that had ruled over them resulted in the creation of an interesting education system. This education system can be compared to other education systems at the time. This can further enhance one's understanding about Judaism's educational development and its advantages.

Jewish education and its impact on the individual and community

Scant information remains regarding education in antiquity (as with every historical subject we have investigated). Nevertheless, some records may help the reader grasp an understanding about Jewish education post-Babylonian exile; and allow for easier comparisons between Jewish education, and education within the surrounding nations.

The first thing known from Jewish scriptures is that a Jewish father bears the religious duty of teaching his children the truth, and laws, of the Torah. The father had also been responsible for teaching his children: a trade; morals; manners; rituals; the use of weaponry, and how to solve practical day-to-day problems. The mother had also educated her children --- mainly by teaching them house duties, as well as religious rites and rituals. The mother also had the responsibility of maintaining a Jewish ethos within family. Some Talmudic stories highlight the importance of education within the Jewish culture.[191]

Related to education are the Sabbath laws and customs. As it turns out, the Sabbath laws and the synagogue --- which seem mundane today --- had been remarkable innovations from a historical perspective. They had turned out to be formidable tools with which to instruct and educate the Jewish community on the Torah. A kind of 'weekend school' with a fixed and rigid timetable. Every Sabbath had its own chapter in the Bible called 'the weekly Torah portion'. This portion of the Torah had been discussed, and lessons regarding the issues raised within the story were learned.[192]

Religious scholars have discussed a great deal on the topic of the Jewish Sabbath. Over many centuries --- until the rise of Christianity --- the Sabbath had been viewed by many Gentiles as a form of laziness.[193] Everyone else had worked at any time of the week as was needed; while the Jews had halted work altogether on the Sabbath. Jews had used this day to sharpen their knowledge of the Torah --- first by rituals, and thereafter by instruction.

The origins of the Sabbath are largely surrounded by mystery; however, it is documented that the Babylonians had not been permitted to conduct certain activities every seven days --- and on the fourth cycle (after 28 days), they had been forbidden to conduct any work whatsoever. This had been a day of rest for the Babylonians.[194] We have already established that Jews had adopted the Babylonian calendar, as well as the Babylonian myth that God had created the world in the six days. Therefore, it is reasonable to assume that the Jews living in Babylon had adopted and modified Babylonian customs to suit the religious Jewish way of life; the most important result being the dedication of an entire day of the week to mental and spiritual pursuits --- consequently expanding brain capacity. Synagogue attendance had been compulsory, in order to assure guaranteed execution of the deed of the Sabbath (it had also promoted discipline). The Sabbath, in effect, had become another day of compulsory education for the individual; and the community.

As is well known, the Sabbath (day of rest) had been modified by Christianity and Islam, to take place on a Sunday and Friday, respectively. In our modern Western world, it has been

---

[191] "Tzedakah And Jewish Education | My Jewish Learning." https://www.myjewishlearning.com/article/tzedakah-and-jewish-education/. Accessed 5 Feb. 2018.
[192] "Parashah | Define Parashah at Dictionary.com." http://www.dictionary.com/browse/parashah. Accessed 5 Feb. 2018.
[193] "Antisemitism (2) - Livius." 16 Dec. 2016, http://www.livius.org/articles/concept/antisemitism/antisemitism/. Accessed 5 Feb. 2018.
[194] "Archeology and the Sabbath - Ministry Magazine." https://www.ministrymagazine.org/archive/1980/08/archeology-and-the-sabbath. Accessed 5 Feb. 2018.

expanded to the weekend (which includes Saturday and Sunday). There is no need to explain why the weekend is a gift to humanity. Most people enjoy the weekend for leisure, reading, and family time (among other things) and would never give it up. This gift should therefore also be accredited to the nation who had kept this day, religiously. Perhaps it should be viewed as another gift of Judaic philosophy unto the world.

The deeds had promoted education in various ways; but the Jewish education system of antiquity can also enlighten us about the development of the Jewish culture. The education of Jews in antiquity can only be compared to the Greeks' education (which is historically documented). Greek education was mainly physical --- literacy education had been the domain of privileged individuals such as royalty and aristocracy. Normally, the pupil would begin their literary education at the age of 13 years. The teacher would usually be a literate, educated slave. Well-off families would send their children to a known paid teacher.[195]

For Jewish children, education had been compulsory by a decree from Rabbi Joshua ben Gamla (died 64 CE). Study of the Torah had been a requirement for every Jewish child; beginning from the age of 6 or 7 years[196] --- a practice that had been unprecedented within the ruling Empires.

Many years later within Jewish ghettos, during the Middle-Ages, Jewish children had entered into studies from the tender age of 4 years. In today's modern world, we know that young children's brains hold a great capacity for learning. It seems as though this had not been so obvious thousands of years --- or even a few hundred years --- before our modern era.

Up to 150 years ago, education had not even been compulsory within the general population; and illiteracy was common.[197] While the Jewish population had a very high level of literacy, their surrounding neighbours had largely been illiterate. It is needless to expand upon the ill fate of illiterate populations. This can still be seen nowadays in underdeveloped countries in Africa, South-America, and some Asian countries. Countries which suffer: economic underdevelopment; poverty; crime, and disease.

Following the excellent literacy of Jewish populations over the years, as well as their mastery in a few languages (namely Hebrew, Aramaic, and the local diasporic languages --- be them: German; French; Russian; English, and mixed hybrid Jewish languages such as yiddish[198] and Ladino[199]), Jews had been used by the Kings and rulers of Europe and Islamic countries in advisory capacities; as well as for various public administration purposes (including tax collections, and at times, on diplomatic missions).[200]

Since Jews had also possessed numerical skills --- and had been prohibited from pursuing many professions due to anti-Jewish laws in Europe --- money lending (and eventually

---

[195] "The History of Education - History-world.org." http://history-world.org/history_of_education.htm. Accessed 5 Feb. 2018.
[196] "Full text of "History Of Jewish Education From 515 B C E To 220 C E"." http://www.archive.org/stream/historyofjewishe027853mbp/historyofjewishe027853mbp_djvu.txt. Accessed 5 Feb. 2018.
[197] "The 1870 Education Act - UK Parliament." http://www.parliament.uk/about/living-heritage/transformingsociety/livinglearning/school/overview/1870educationact/. Accessed 5 Feb. 2018.
[198] "Yiddish alphabet, pronunciation and language - Omniglot." https://www.omniglot.com/writing/yiddish.htm. Accessed 6 Feb. 2018.
[199] "Ladino, the Sephardic Language - Judeo-Spanish Judeo-Espagnol." http://www.sephardicstudies.org/quickladino.html. Accessed 6 Feb. 2018.
[200] "TAX-GATHERERS - Jewish Encyclopedia." http://www.jewishencyclopedia.com/articles/14273-tax-gatherers. Accessed 6 Feb. 2018.

banking) had become a Jewish occupation. At times, when the only computer around was the human brain, Jews had a massive advantage over the non-Jewish population. Said advantage had been compounded over many generations through the Jewish education system. Many ethnic-Jews are still, to this day, prominent in the fields of accounting and risk management.

Although establishing a habit of studying had been a great achievement for the Jewish population at the time; the content of these studies had been of paramount importance as well. The content on which individuals are educated, as well as the method of teaching employed within their community setting, undoubtedly greatly influences the individual --- shaping and moulding their character well into adulthood. It is therefore important to note that a community's characteristics are largely determined by the individuals it is comprised of.

The substantive content of Jewish education

Torah stories form the basis of Jewish education. Over the years, studies and interpretations of the Torah had first resulted with the Mishnah; then with the Gemara (which interprets the Mishnah). The Talmud is comprised of both the Mishnah and the Gemara. The Torah is therefore the basic structure of Jewish education. It is comprised of all the fundamental Jewish laws which, according to tradition, had been given to Moses on mount Sinai by God himself. Since the Torah is not always comprehensible to ordinary folk, it had to be interpreted by Jewish Sages. Said Sages had provided a clear understanding and guidance of the laws. This represented the first level of deep analysis and understanding of the Torah. However, since the Sages' interpretation had not always been clear or sufficient, said interpretations had been further interpreted by wise and esteemed Rabbis --- providing a further, second level of deep understanding.

Since there had been two large centers of Jewish life in antiquity (in Judea and in Babylonia), there had been two Talmuds --- the Jerusalem Talmud, and the Babylonian Talmud. Both had contained the same Mishnah, which had been published by Judah (the president at around 200 CE). They differ in the Gemara, as the one had mainly been composed by Babylonian Rabbis; while the other by Rabbis living in Judea (which had eventually been renamed 'Palestine' by Roman rulers, as was previously discussed).

Following the expansion of Christianity during the beginning of the first millennia (at around 400 CE), Jewish life had been drastically downsized in Palestine. Babylonian-Judaism had survived for almost 850 years afterwards. The Babylonian Talmud --- which contains the Babylonian Gemara and had been compiled at around 500 CE --- is therefore the one mainly used today by religious Jews around the world. 500 CE had been around 200 years before the Arab occupation of Babylonia.

Apart from the Talmud, which contains around 6200 pages, mainstream Rabbinical literature contains thousands of other writings by famous Rabbis written over many centuries --- culminating into many more tens of thousands of pages.

The studies within the Gemara are argumentative and debative in nature. The debates and arguments revolve around the meaning of words and sentences, and the logic of these sentences in expressing Judaic laws derived from the Torah (much like the studies of modern-day Law). Throughout history, the Jewish learner had been required to study a vast amount of educational material; and had therefore undoubtedly utilized and developed their verbal skills (as well as their logic and abstract thinking) considerably.

So --- for thousands of years, Jews have been conducting their religious studies in patterns similar to modern-day law. What can this tell us about their inherent abilities within Legal studies?

Fast forward to the present day --- one can observe how the most respected and quoted Jurisprudence (philosophy of law) professors around the world are of ethnic-Jewish origins. Dworkin[201], Hart,[202] and Raz[203] --- all secular ethnic-Jews of American, British, and Israeli origins (respectively). Further than this, a substantial amount of lawyers in the United States are of ethnic-Jewish origins (as well as some very famous lawyers from European countries).

Rene` Cassin,[204] a secular French-Jewish professor of law, is considered to be the co-architect and finaliser of the United Nations Charter of Human Rights; as well as the founder of European justice laws. Other famous legal Jewish personalities are mentioned in chapter 11 (which discusses the role Jewish people had played in fighting for Human Rights throughout recent history).

Whether the affinity for Jewish excellence in law is genetically inherited --- or due to traditional behavioural patterns of Talmud studies that have been carried through generations within the Jewish culture --- it does not seem to be co-incidental that a strong link exists between generations of Jews studying Law, and the excellence of their secular Jewish descendants in the Legal profession around the world. Chapter 11 will reveal more (regarding Jewish people's affinity with Law and justice).

The Torah as a basic guide to life

In order to study the Torah, one had first been required to be literate (preferably literate in Hebrew). Even though, over the years, the Torah has been studied in other languages such as Greek --- especially within the faith of Christianity --- it is not the same experience as studying the Torah in its original language. Moreover, studies of the Talmud had required knowledge in Eastern and Western Aramaic languages; as those had been the languages used by the Babylonian-Jewish authors to write the Talmud. Said Aramaic languages are related to ancient Hebrew.

Even though Western-European alphabets, such as English and French, are derived from the Hebrew/Phoenician alphabet --- as had been shown earlier --- the characters of said Western-European alphabets are mainly used for their phonetic value. This is not the case in Hebrew. Through some of my own observations, I have found Hebrew to be a somewhat philosophical language. A language that, in its own unique way, describes life. The following analysis of the Hebrew language may demonstrate its uniqueness.

---

[201] "Professor Ronald Dworkin: Legal philosopher acclaimed as the finest ...." 15 Feb. 2013, http://www.independent.co.uk/news/obituaries/professor-ronald-dworkin-legal-philosopher-acclaimed-as-the-finest-of-his-generation-8497540.html. Accessed 6 Feb. 2018.
[202] "H. L. A. Hart - Wikipedia." https://en.wikipedia.org/wiki/H._L._A._Hart. Accessed 6 Feb. 2018.
[203] "Legal Philosopher Joseph Raz: An Engaging and Demanding Thinker ...." http://www.law.columbia.edu/media_inquiries/news_events/2012/january2012/joseph-raz-legal-philosopher. Accessed 6 Feb. 2018.
[204] "René Cassin - Biographical." https://www.nobelprize.org/nobel_prizes/peace/laureates/1968/cassin-bio.html. Accessed 6 Feb. 2018.

Every letter in ancient Hebrew had been designed to symbolize an important aspect of life (such as: domesticated animals for food: work; transport; construction objects such as a house, as well as human body parts such as: the eyes; the head; the legs, and the hands.)

The ancient 'Aleph' ⚹ (which is the first letter of the Hebrew alphabet) has been turned upside-down to become the English letter 'A'. This ancient Hebrew letter Illustrates an ox or oryx horns (which symbolize food --- the first basic need of a human being). It may have also been an ancient symbol of a God (the golden calf story in the Bible). The 'Beit' ⊐ (the second letter of the Hebrew alphabet) had been drawn as a house (a square) and pronounced "bait" (the word for a house in Hebrew). The 'Gimel' (the third word of the Hebrew alphabet) is drawn as a camel; and means "gamal" (the name for camel in Hebrew). These first 3 letters already describe food, shelter, and transport --- people's basic primary needs. An internet search on the origins of the Proto-Sinaitic alphabet will describe these features of the alphabet in a clear manner.[205]

The letters of the Hebrew alphabet had also been assigned numerical values. The 'Aleph' is 1, 'Beit' 2, and so on and so forth --- until the Hebrew letter 'yod', which becomes the number 10. The letters thereafter the letter 'yod' are assigned values of 20, 30, 40 . . . continuing to 100. The remaining letters of the alphabet receive the values of 200, 300, and 400. This had provided a sufficient numerical system, which the alphabet had deployed.[206]

This system could have allowed Judeans, Israelites, and Phoenicians to practice a simple form of accounting in their trading endeavours. What is most striking about the ancient Hebrew language is the derivation of its words. It is as though the language itself had been engineered according to some philosophical patterns --- both phonetically, and numerically.

The following example is based on my own observation, and can demonstrate the beauty of the Hebrew language's construction:

In English, the words: 'earth'; 'Man'; and 'blood', have no grammatical, phonetic, or symbolic connection whatsoever. However, the corresponding Hebrew words: "ADAMA" (אדמה); "ADAM" (אדמ); and "DAM" (דמ) are both grammatically and phonetically connected. It is as though they had been derived from each other; whereby the shortest three-letter word, which means 'blood', is within the four-letter word which means 'Man' --- and both are within the five-letter word which means earth. It also corresponds with the Biblical philosophical saying, "from earth you came and to the earth you shall return". The word "ADOM" (אדומ) describes the red colour of blood, and is also a kind of derivation from said previous words relating to Man. This construction is fascinating by any means.

Another example is the construction of the words 'Man' and 'Woman' in conjunction with the words 'fire' and 'God'. Phonetically; 'Eish' (אֵשׁ) is 'fire', 'Ish' (איש) is 'Man', and 'Isha' (אשה) is 'Woman'. In Hebrew, however, 'fire' is a two-letter word. By adding the first letter of God's name in-between the two letters of the word 'fire', one gets the word for a Man. Furthermore, adding the second letter of God's name to the word 'fire' results in the creation of the word for a Woman. This corresponds to Biblical stories of God's creation of Woman from Man, and Man from fire and soil.

Another example is the Hebrew word for the color Green, which is synonymous with vegetables that are mostly Green in nature --- 'Yarok' (ירוק) (Green), 'Yerek' (יֶרֶק) (vegetable). When directly translated, the Hebrew word for the sun is "there fire". One can interpret this

---

[205] "Proto-Sinaitic script - Wikipedia." https://en.wikipedia.org/wiki/Proto-Sinaitic_script. Accessed 6 Feb. 2018.
[206] "Judaism 101: Hebrew Alphabet." http://www.jewfaq.org/alephbet.htm. Accessed 6 Feb. 2018.

word as being the reaction of a person attempting to comprehend the sun's existence --- "There is fire up there!" (in the sky). 'Sham' (שם) ('there' in Hebrew), combined with 'Eish' (אֵש) ('fire' in Hebrew) yielding 'Sham-Eish' (שמאֶש) ('The Sun' in Hebrew). When translated, the Hebrew words that describe the sky combine to form "there water". Combined together, Sham (שם) ("there" in Hebrew), and 'My-im' (מים) ('water' in Hebrew) form 'Sham-My-im' (שמים) --- since the sky is blue in color, just like water (and water also falls from the sky when it rains). This verbal link is quite logical. In order to truly appreciate all these complex and fascinating Hebrew language combinations, the English reader must learn Hebrew. I would think that this is not such a bad idea for religious Christian populations who consider Hebrew to be a holy language.

The numerical values assigned to the words are also fascinating. For instance, the Hebrew word for 'God' --- (יהוה) ('yehova'/Jehova) --- consists of four letters which summate to the number 26. Some combinations of words that philosophically describe a relationship with God will also have a sum of 26. 'One love' (אהבה אחת) is such a combination whereby the word 'one' (אחת) sums up to the numerical value of 13, and 'love' (אהבה) also 13, giving a total of 26. There are many such examples which will appear in books that deal with Hebrew Gematria.[207]

The construction of the Torah itself has been found to contain a hidden order in which letters and sentences are composed. This hidden order being based on the number seven. The first sentence of The Book of Genesis is a seven word sentence, consisting of 28 letters [28 being a multiple of seven (7x4)]. Every 49 letters, a word will begin with a letter taken from the name for God (יהוה) ('yehova'/Jehova) in its corresponding order. This all hints to careful planning, writing, and editing done by meticulous individuals.

The Hebrew language itself is very orderly, and has been constructed in a precise and logical manner (far better than any Western-European language). Once mastered, it requires less words than other languages to generate a descriptive sentence. As an example, in Hebrew the first sentence in Genesis is described using only seven words; while in an English translation, it takes eight words to fully construct the sentence. This is because some singular Hebrew words will convey the meaning of two --- or at times even three --- English words (an example being the Hebrew word 'Bereishit' (בְּרֵאשִׁית), translating to 'In the beginning' in English). I have found that many sentences in Hebrew will use up to 20% less words than their equivalent sentence in English.

This efficiency is substantial; as in the Hebrew language, many words are derived from others --- making it much easier, and quicker, to communicate. This is in contrast to the cumbersome English language --- the combination of a multitude of words originating from: Latin; Greek; Celtic, and Scandinavian languages . . . adding unnecessary difficulty to the English language.

There has not been enough research done on the impact that various languages have on the human brain; so it is better to stay clear of any comparisons. However, it can be validly said that Hebrew had been developed as a thoughtful language with philosophical ideas behind it. It was back then, and is today, an extremely useful medium of organising and conveying ideas.

Before trying to quantify the legacy that Jewish education has imprinted on the world; it should be noted that over the years, many powerful nations have left their own tremendous influences upon world education in various fields. The ancient Greeks are known for their

---

[207] "Introduction to Gematria – Hebrew Numerology – GalEinai ...." 11 Feb. 2014, http://www.inner.org/gematria/gematria.htm. Accessed 6 Feb. 2018.

philosophical and mathematical influences, and I am convinced that many of my readers are all too familiar with Pythagoras' theorem and Archimedes' laws (as well as the philosophical legacies of personalities such as Plato, Aristotle, and Socrates).

Nevertheless, I would think that Jewish education has profoundly influenced our modern world. The following sub-chapter should demonstrate this influence.

The influence of Jewish education on our modern world

After all the above analysis about Jewish education, a simple question should be asked: What influences has Jewish education imparted onto the world?

The first thing that should be noted is that around the year 64 CE, Rabbi Joshua ben Gamla had decreed that education be compulsory for every Jewish child from the age of six. Nowadays, in most parts of the world, it is a given that children are to be enrolled into school from the age of six years old. Jewish children have been subject to compulsory studying from that age for millennia. It is also important to note that illiteracy within Jewish quarters had hardly been heard of.

Compulsory education is now Common Law, and is practiced in many countries around the world. It has had a tremendous influence on many individuals and communities around the world.

It had already been mentioned that the field of modern law has been saturated with personalities of ethnic-Jewish origins. These personalities have influenced the world's Legal systems in many countries. In one of the upcoming chapters (chapter 11 entitled 'In the legal profession --- fighting for human rights') these influences are brought to the fore. What about popular literature and common screenplay media content? This may be an interesting field to examine.

Long before Harry Potter, Lord Of The Rings, or any comic-book (such as Superman or Batman); the Bible had been the best-selling story-book. Serving many human generations, the fascinating stories of the Torah and the Bible had satisfied the curiosities and imaginative desires of both children --- and adults --- of all religious denominations. Even the Islamic Quran is mainly based on the Torah and the Bible (modified by some Jewish Talmudic interpretations). It is of no secret that Islam believes Mohammed himself had titled the Jews, 'The People of The Book'.[208] As will be shown in chapter 6, many of the first pieces of Islamic literature had come from Babylonia (whereby large Jewish communities had probably been Islamised).

It is not far-fetched to argue that many modern stories and heroes had either been consciously, or subconsciously, derived from Biblical stories (with no surprise from Jewish-American producers). In many biblical stories, God's behaviour is akin to that of Superman's. The Hulk, who receives his strength from nuclear energy, can be equated to Samson receiving power from the Sun. Batman can be equated to the stealthy winged-angel of God hovering over the night sky --- causing havoc and death upon the Assyrian army that had besieged Jerusalem.

Far more important than these stories are the morals embedded within them --- morals that deal with the struggles of life due to natural or man-made obstacles; lessons which are very

---

[208] "Ahl al-Kitāb | Islam | Britannica.com." https://www.britannica.com/topic/Ahl-al-Kitab. Accessed 6 Feb. 2018.

relatable to the human being and his/her experience in life. The aim of these stories had been to guide the Jewish people to conduct themselves with certain moral standards during times of struggle; by remaining faithful to the collective Jewish cause in order to overcome difficulties together, and reach a favourable outcome. These stories had taught young individuals the correct way in which to conduct their lives (that being in a dignified manner with good morals, so as to achieve betterment for themselves, their family, and the community).

These stories are of abundance in the Torah and the Bible. They had, according to tradition, accompanied all the forefathers of Judaism; and had continued through to Moses' reception of the Torah. Teaching the Bible is not the aim of this book; however, the following Biblical stories are able to demonstrate the valuable lessons a child is taught when they read and study the Torah.

The stories of Abraham describe his righteousness in times of peace and war. This is highlighted in his uncompromising belief in a God that favours good, moral conduct; as well as in his refusal to loot the enemy after a just victory. The way he had welcomed and treated the angels (who had been disguised as foreign guests) into his tent; and his largesse treatment of his nephew, 'Lot', regarding limited grazing for them both (as well as the equitable way in which he had negotiated a sale of property with Ephron the Hittite) also depict Abraham's said righteousness.

The story of Jacob reveals the various ills of human nature, and demonstrates the consequences of personal failings. These issues are displayed in Jacob's story, when he tricks his brother Esau and steals his father's blessing. Jacob then repents for his sins --- after many years --- by showering gifts upon his brother Esau. Furthermore, this story illustrates the values of maintaining a healthy work ethic; as Jacob had toiled for 7 years in service of his uncle, 'Lavan', in order to receive Lavan's permission to marry his youngest daughter Rachel --- only to be tricked into marrying Lavan's older daughter Leah (yet still dedicating an additional 7 years of labour to eventually attain his goal of marrying his true love, Rachel).

The story of Joseph promotes the belief that one should never, even in the worst of times, lose hope; and how wisdom will eventually triumph and change one's life. It also covertly preaches that once one is in a powerful position, one should never take revenge.

There is no doubt that Biblical stories have influenced the lives of many people around the world for thousands of years by directing their: way of life; business; careers; families, and many more aspects of life . . . similar to the way in which hollywood cartoon superheros such as Batman and Superman influence the lives of the public.

It is of great plausibility that the father of psychoanalysis, Dr. Sigmund Freud, had developed his psychoanalytical interpretation of dreams due to his inspiration from the Biblical stories of Joseph's interpretation of Pharaoh's dreams (as well as the prophet Daniel's interpretation of King Nebuchadnezzar's dreams). Freud had studied the Torah in a Jewish 'Cheder' (Torah study room) from the tender age of 4 years. His pure fascination of these Biblical stories had most likely been his incentive to research and develop techniques that improved humanities' understanding of the human psyche. This may have then, in turn, skyrocketed his career; leading to him becoming one of the few individuals who had changed humanity forever.

Other Biblical stories (such as 'Boaz and Ruth' whereby 10% of the crops in a field had been allocated to poor people) may have influenced other celebrated thinkers such as Karl Marx who had developed the theory of socialism --- a theory which has become the foundation of various socialistic European states such as: Germany; England; France; Sweden, as well as some Scandinavian countries.

Then there is the story of Moses, and the Jewish people's exodus from Egypt --- an epic story of liberation and exploration, in search of another land to call 'home'. A timeless classic that has never been forgotten. A story that had even inspired and guided the first British settlers of America on their voyage with the Mayflower ship. The Mayflower compact is a testimony to how the story of the Jewish exodus had influenced America's founding fathers thousands of years later. Transposed into a new 'exodus out of England and into America, The Land of Freedom' . . . the re-incarnated land of 'milk and honey'.

It is important to note that many ideas propagated in modern times had originally been conceptualized in the Bible, in some way or another. Most of these Biblical ideas have somewhat been the basis for modern ideas. Creativity among many modern personalities has some Biblical foundation --- whether said personalities like it or not.

The Bible itself has not been the only source of Jewish intellectual influence over the centuries. There are many idioms circulating within different societies around the Western world --- meantime, the vast majority of the people who use said idioms haven't a clue that they are derived from Judaic sources. The following few idioms are among many that come from the Talmud:

'Join the company of lions rather than assume the lead among foxes'[209]

'A good name is better than the sweetest oil'

'The owner of the hundred (money) is the owner of the opinion (decision maker)'.

Some of these quotes appear in secular quote websites.[210]

Conclusion and modern day implications of education

This chapter has demonstrated how the Torah and the Talmud --- which are important facets of Judaism --- have been instrumental in the creation of modern civilization's morals and ideals as we know them today. Therefore proving, once again, how valuable Judaism truly is to the world.

Being the first monotheistic religion to cement said morals in a written document had far reaching consequences --- not only for Jews over the centuries, but also for the way in which education had advanced around the world.

Unfortunately, the mentality of Judaism 'being first' has had --- and still has --- anti-Semitic ramifications. The monotheistic religions that had followed --- namely Christianity and Islam --- have been adopting said morals and values (to the benefit of humanity); but, at the same time, belittling and demonizing the true and original inventors . . . only to glorify *themselves* as the inventors of these social values.

The problem with this is that the nation that had actually invented these social values --- although badly battered over millennia --- is still alive and well. This makes it very difficult to lay claims to originality.

This domination of religion, and the endless quest to rewrite history, will be discussed further in chapter 13 regarding the inherent conflict of religions; as well as in the chapter on anti-

---

[209] "The Talmud Quotes." https://www.quotes.net/authors/The+Talmud. Accessed 6 Feb. 2018.
[210] ibid

Semitism, chapter 14. When Christian scriptures are read, the deep hatred towards Jews is overt and easily noticed; while reading Islamic scriptures will reveal hatred towards Christians and Jews altogether.

Every religion that had come after Judaism desired to claim responsibility for inventing morality; and for possessing a consciousness of the world. Doing this is not easy while members of the preceding religion are still alive and also claim responsibility.

The claims in this book may provide the reader with an idea about some of the causes for anti-Semitism (which are deep-rooted within individuals). Anti-Semitism, like racism, is a natural human condition. The act of 'murder and inheritance' had already been described in the Bible. Recently, a United Nations resolution which aimed to sever the link between Jerusalem and the Jewish people was to be passed in an attempt to further de-legitimize the Jewish State of Israel.

This state of affairs may give the reader an idea as to why the Israeli-Arab conflict is an insurmountable task to solve --- Palestinian-Arabs and Jewish nationalists will never see eye-to-eye, as this conflict is more about ideals than anything else.

The Israeli-Arab conflict is not solely based on the tiny piece of contested land in the Middle-East. It is mostly a war between ideologies --- Islam, or Judaism. Only a change of mind on a global scale may bring lasting peace to this area in the Middle-East, as well as other conflicts around the world. Conflicts such as the Muslim-Hindu conflict in India and Pakistan, the Muslim-Buddhist conflict in Thailand and Myanmar, and the Muslim-Catholic conflict in the Philippines. Education of the right kind may be the only source for redemption.

This chapter, which had dealt with education, has demonstrated the priority that Jews have given to education and literacy; as well as the incredible value of educating the community. The correct, substantive education is key to human survival and can be used as an effective tool to change an individual's mind. It is the key to unlocking creativity, and is essential in developing any intellectual and business pursuits. Education is the only tool that may be effective in resolving human conflicts in the long run of history.

This shift in the collective mindset can only be achieved through exposure to the right kind of education. Education which restores respect for 'the other' nation/religion. Education which gradually reduces, and eventually eliminates, hate; and in doing so, unwinds religious prejudices that have been built over centuries.

The task is not an easy one, as inherent resistance to change is subconscious and very strong. I hope that my book may be a step towards this goal.

In this chapter, it has also been demonstrated that the Hebrew alphabet --- and the Hebrew language --- had been produced in a philosophical, logical, and sophisticated manner. Said Hebrew language had been used to construct Biblical stories, as well as some of the Talmud --- literature that has inspired Jews, and non-Jews alike. This religious literature has been amalgamated and modified by the larger Abrahamic religions of Christianity and Islam, to form the basis of many of today's morals and laws.

This chapter has also claimed that, simply based on empirical observation, due to the excellence in literacy required for an individual (such as a Rabbi) to interpret the complexities of religious literature written by advanced Jewish scholars; as well as the intricate numerical skills developed over generations --- brain activity within the average Jew would have been excited (which, in turn, may have expanded the capabilities of the future Jewish generations in the fields of literacy and numeracy).

This chapter had also instigated speculation into the possibility of Talmudic studies contributing to the field of modern Law; as the most influential jurisprudence philosophers are secular descendants of religious ethnic-Jews who had engaged with Talmud and Biblical studies --- as well as Jewish philosophy ---- some time in their lifetime.

Above all, this chapter has demonstrated how important education has been to Jewish people over 2 millenia. The amount of effort and resources Jews have invested in the education of their children is phenomenal.

Even today, in many Jewish communities around the world, you will find many highly educated ethnic-Jews. Their parents will do the utmost to provide their children with a higher education. These educated individuals eventually become the army of intellectuals and businessman who, in turn, create wealth for themselves; and for the world (whether it be medicinal, technological, or humanitarian wealth).

The 'proof is in the pudding'. The Jewish population produces the highest numbers of innovators, nobel prize winners, and technological businessman --- as well as doctors, lawyers, and accountants --- in the world (in relation to the overall size of the Jewish population).

Education has become a major trait of the Jewish culture, and a fundamental tool for wealth creation. A tool that has also aided them in surviving previously hostile environments (within the Christian and Muslim worlds).

Chapter 6

The Rise of Christianity and Islam, and their impact on Judaism

Summary: This chapter will first deal with the formation of Christianity as a possible offshoot from the pacifist stream of Rabbinical Judaism. It will be shown how Christianity became the Roman Empire's principal religion (and how being such had almost completely decimated Judaism in the Middle-East, as well as restricted Judaism throughout the Roman Empire). The highlights of this chapter will become apparent when the rise of Islam is analysed. The multiple linguistic and religious customs of Judaism, and their role in the formation of Islam, will be discussed. An analysis of the Arabic language --- and Islamic customs --- will bring to the fore many surprises that may astound Jews and Muslims alike. The chapter will end with an assessment of the impact that Christianity and Islam had on the Jewish people.

'What is history but a fable agreed upon?' --- **Napoleon Bonaparte**

It is well known today that throughout history, leaders who had risen to power aimed to censor and dictate the knowledge available to the population under their control in such a way that had benefited their own reign of power. By propping up their nation or ethnic legacy, they had strived to influence their subjects to remain steadfast to their rule. This, naturally, also served to enhance their descendants' well-being as the undisputed heirs of their rule.

Throughout history, religion --- coupled with a strong ethnic identity --- has proven itself to be a most powerful tool for leaders to control and direct mass populations. Empirically observing the believers in the: Jewish Bible; Christian New Testament; and Islamic Quran, will reveal that a recorded scripture installed in the memory of the masses as holy, true, and irreplaceable can become a formidable mechanism for the leaders of a religion to control their followers --- a tool used to control their conduct.

The heart and soul of all Abrahamic religions lies in their scriptures (the Jewish Bible, the Christian New Testament, and the Islamic Quran). These scriptures are sanctified in such a way that the believer should never question them. They are propagated as being the truthful word of God --- written by either God himself, or by people who had been inspired by God (Moses, Jesus, and Muhammed). The scriptures are presented as being true historical chains of events. For better or for worse, the believer and his descendants are captured for eternity within the agenda of the scriptures' creator. For many centuries, disobedience or doubting the scriptures had been punishable by death --- a punishment that is still carried out upon Atheists, Agnostics, and apostates in some Islamic countries.[211]

Napoleon Bonaparte --- who is credited for possessing an extremely high intelligence --- had realised that history is full of twists, and harbours many lies. His above quote is self-explanatory.

The absolute truth of history can never be revealed. It is however possible to find clues within known historical facts that may guide us to a possible truth. It is also possible to ascertain the agenda of scriptures (when taking into account the general state of affairs that

---

[211] "There Are 13 Countries Where Atheism Is Punishable by Death - The ...." 10 Dec. 2013, https://www.theatlantic.com/international/archive/2013/12/13-countries-where-atheism-punishable-death/355961/. Accessed 7 Feb. 2018.

had occured at the time of writing). These techniques can lead to other more logical, or plausible, explanations of the actual historical chain of events. Understanding human history may enhance our understanding of human nature; which can, in turn, assist us in accurately understanding the conflicting and competitive world we live in today. Based on this premise, I would like to investigate the historical rise of the Christian and Muslim religions; and evaluate their true relation to Judaism.

It is well documented that (historically) the Christian religion --- which had begun after Judaism --- rose to prominence at around 312 CE[212]; eventually dominating the Western world. About 350 years thereafter, the Christian hegemony in the Middle-East and North-Africa had been lost due to the formation and rise of a new Abrahamic religion --- the Islamic religion. How this happened, and its impact on Judaism --- as well as the re-moulding of the Jewish people following the rise of Christianity and Islam --- is of interest to this book.

The following statement, which comes from the Jewish Bible, teaches another lesson in life regarding human societies --- a lesson addressing the enemy from within . . . each and every society will give rise to people who rebel or want to change the old order.

'Your sons have hastened; those who destroy you and those who lay you waste shall go forth from you' --- Isaiah 50:17

This statement is also relevant to anti-Semitic conduct. During the long course of history, some Jews --- as well as some assimilated Jews --- had exhibited the highest level of anti-Semitism against their own ethnic-Jewish origins; some of whom are mentioned in this book. Some religious Christian literature openly exhibits this type of anti-Semitism.

I have an assumption that the assimilation of Jewish people had been a real enhancing factor regarding the development of anti-Semitism (within a historical perspective). Assimilation of Jews in the past had mainly been the result of ruthless regimes demanding a demonstration of absolute loyalty from the assimilated --- whether that regime had been Christianity or Islam. This demand would have most probably driven assimilated individuals, or communities, to take extreme action against their own brethren (this had been prompted by the establishment of the new religions of Christianity and Islam). How this had happened, however, is unclear. I would like to offer my views regarding this process.

Christianity and Judaism

As Judaism had been banned from --- and destroyed in --- Judea by the Roman Caesar Hadrian; another religion, based on the similar premise of a single omnipotent God, arose --- the Christian revelation religion.[213]

The problem with analysing this new revelation is the same problem we had encountered with the Torah and the Biblical stories of Judaism --- a lack of proper historical or archeological evidence to confirm the religious claims of the new religion, as well as a lack of reliable descriptions of the historical chain of events that had led to the creation of the religion.

---

[212] "BBC - History - Ancient History in depth: Christianity and the Roman ...." http://www.bbc.co.uk/history/ancient/romans/christianityromanempire_article_01.shtml. Accessed 7 Feb. 2018.
[213] "Revelation | religion | Britannica.com." https://www.britannica.com/topic/revelation. Accessed 7 Feb. 2018.

The Christian New Testament is composed of various Gospels supposedly written by apostles and important figures such as Peter, and Paul of Tarsus (who wrote about the life of a Jewish scholar who had been proclaimed to be Jesus --- the messiah). The problem is, none of the apostles (including the proclaimed Jesus himself) are historically or archaeologically documented at the time of their supposed existence.[214]

The first fragmented inscriptions of the Gospels are from late 1st century, to early 2nd century CE. Nearly 90 to 120 years after the events regarding Jesus had supposedly occurred.[215]

Roman historians, such as Tacitus[216] and Pliny the younger,[217] indicate that Christians had been present as a persecuted religious movement within the Roman Empire. Within Tacitus' extensive work of 30 books; in the Annals --- which is estimated to have been written at around 116 CE --- there is a small passage about Nero Caesar blaming Christians for The Great Fire of Rome (which had taken place in 64 CE).[218] The account determines that Nero himself had ignited the fire, so as to evacuate land for his building ambitions. It describes how the shameful Christians who had believed in Christus were blamed, and punished in cruel ways.

Quite a few scholars today believe that this 15th century document of Tacitus' Annals writing had been a Christian church interpolation (in order to backdate the creation of Christianity, and support the idea that the Christian religion's formation and establishment had occurred *before* 64 CE) --- cementing a belief of the existence of Apostle Paul and his execution by no other than the Nero Caesar himself in Rome in 64 CE.[219]

Based on Pliny the younger's letter to Trajan Caesar (estimated at 112 CE), and the first confirmed fragmented Gospel inscriptions found; Christianity had probably been formed sometime during the late 1st Century, to early 2nd Century CE . . . at the height of ongoing Jewish rebellions against the Romans. Perhaps this had been a direct result of the Jewish rebellions; as creating a new religion, offered alternative ways of dealing with the Roman-Empire. It may have even acted as a refuge out of Judaism, since Judaism had been in a bitter war with the Roman-Empire --- a war that meant death to many peaceful Jews who had not been part of the rebellion.

There is no doubt that as a new religious movement, Christianity was up against three of the biggest religions at the time --- namely Greco-Roman paganism, the Jewish religion within the Roman Empire, and the Parthian Zoroastrian religion. Judaism had also been well entrenched in the form of Babylonian-Judaism within the Parthian Empire's territories of Mesopotamia.

In order to understand how Christianity rose to prominence, it may be of value to examine its writings. Examining the political and religious situation at the time raises the question as to

---

[214] "Archaeological Finds from the Jesus Era - National Geographic Channel." 27 Feb. 2015, http://channel.nationalgeographic.com/killing-jesus/articles/archaeological-finds-from-the-jesus-era/. Accessed 7 Feb. 2018.
[215] "Mummy Mask May Reveal Oldest Known Gospel - Live Science." 18 Jan. 2015, https://www.livescience.com/49489-oldest-known-gospel-mummy-mask.html. Accessed 7 Feb. 2018.
[216] "Tacitus | Roman historian | Britannica.com." 8 Jan. 2018, https://www.britannica.com/biography/Tacitus-Roman-historian. Accessed 7 Feb. 2018.
[217] "Pliny the Younger | Roman author | Britannica.com." https://www.britannica.com/biography/Pliny-the-Younger. Accessed 7 Feb. 2018.
[218] "Tacitus on the Christians - Livius." 29 Nov. 2015, http://www.livius.org/sources/content/tacitus/tacitus-on-the-christians/. Accessed 7 Feb. 2018.
[219] "Interpolation in Josephus on Jesus." http://www.skeptically.org/bible/id12.html. Accessed 7 Feb. 2018.

which populations Christian writings had addressed, and what message said Christian writings had attempted to convey?

The political and religious situation at the time had already been examined in Chapter 4 of this book. The growing Jewish population in the Roman Empire had clashed with Rome between 66 CE, and 132 CE. The Eastern-Roman Empire consisted of a multitude of ethnic and religious groups. Pagan Romans and Greco-Roman populations, Greek populations, and various types of: Greek speaking; Aramaic speaking; and assimilated Hellenistic, Jewish populations. Romans had held the political and military ruling power over all other populations. There had been much infighting and suspicion between the various populations. Jews who had often rebelled and fought the other groups, also had various sects fighting between themselves in Judea --- making that period in history a horrendous time to be identified as a war mongering Jew . . . but a great time to be identified as a Christian pacifist.

One of the most important factors to consider when analysing the rise of Christianity is the language used in the Gospels of the New Testament. The Greek Koine language had been used to write the Gospels.[220] There is no real evidence that either: Roman; Aramaic; or Hebrew, had been used.[221] This Greek Koine language had been used in all the former Alexandrian territories, including: Greece; Asia minor; Syria; Western-Mesopotamia, and Egypt. Greek Koine had been used to a large extent by Hellenistic Jews in Judea and Syria. This fact can point to the very high probability that the people who wrote the Gospels would have belonged to Greek-Jewish --- or mixed Greek-Jewish --- populations. The fact that the Gospels are written in a style that resembles the Old Jewish Testament (a style characterized by prophecies, revelations, and miracles) may be a stronger indicator that Hellenized Jews --- or mixed assimilated Greek-Jews such as Paul of Tarsus[222] --- had written the Gospels. They would have been proficient enough in the Old Hebrew Bible to devise a 'New Testament' in the Greek language.

There is a wide consensus within the academia of history that the main promotion and marketing of the new Christian religion had been done through Paul of Tarsus' writings.[223] This by no means validates the existence of Paul of Tarsus; nor does it disprove that said writings may have been composed by a different individual.

Tarsus had been a large city located on the South-Eastern Mediterranean shores of Asia minor (modern-day Turkey). It had been the home of many pagan, Greek-speaking inhabitants (as well as substantial numbers of Greek-speaking Jewish populations). The letters of Paul in the New Testament also indicate as to which populations the letters had targeted, as well as the message that the letters had attempted to convey.

The New Testament describes Paul as originally being a Jew named Saul; who had been born a Roman citizen. In his writings, he had professed to being an observant Pharisee Jew. A student of Rabbi Gamliel (an esteemed Rabbi in Jerusalem); and the grandson of Rabbi

---

[220] "The Language of the Gospel – Zola Levitt Ministries." https://www.levitt.com/essays/language. Accessed 7 Feb. 2018.
[221] "Were any of the Gospels written in Christ's own language? | Catholic ...." 4 Aug. 2011, https://www.catholic.com/qa/were-any-of-the-gospels-written-in-christs-own-language. Accessed 7 Feb. 2018.
[222] "Saint Paul, the Apostle | Biography & Facts | Britannica.com." 15 Dec. 2017, https://www.britannica.com/biography/Saint-Paul-the-Apostle. Accessed 7 Feb. 2018.
[223] "BBC - Religions - Christianity: Paul." 21 Jun. 2011, http://www.bbc.co.uk/religion/religions/christianity/history/paul_1.shtml. Accessed 7 Feb. 2018.

Hillel. Rabbi Hillel had been a Jewish sage of the Mishnah, and had established the Beit Hillel Judaic Philosophy.[224]

The Greek-speaking Jewish populations --- who are addressed by Paul/Saul --- must have been very familiar with the stories, philosophy, and status regarding Rabbi Gamliel and Rabbi Hillel's legacies. According to the Talmud, the 'House of Hillel' (which had held a lenient approach to some of the harsh ancient Judaic laws) had been the prevailing doctrine within the Jewish world at the time.[225]

In Jewish Talmudic tradition, it is said that Rabbi Hillel was asked to define the Torah. His response being: 'What is hateful to you, do not do to your neighbour[226] that is the whole Torah, the rest is commentary, go and learn'. Another important saying of Rabbi Hillel's had been: 'If I am not for myself who is for me? And just being for myself, what am I? And if not now, when?'[227] --- a phrase which should shake a person of a passive lifestyle, as well as prompt immediate action to improve oneself (while at the same time rejecting egoism and contributing to other fellows in the community). 'Love of Man' had been the kernel of Judaism according to Rabbi Hillel.

This type of philosophy is what Paul's letters attempt to promote as Christianity's new foundational philosophy. A philosophy based on: peace; compassion; free love, and help to your fellow human beings. A matching and corresponding philosophy to the Beit Hillel philosophy. At least some respectable Christian scholars acknowledge this.[228]

Paul's perceived mastery in Greek and Hebrew had enabled him to approach Greeks and Jews alike in promoting this newly founded religion. It is as though this religion was made to bridge Judaic and Greek philosophy. It had been unchaining itself from Greek polytheistic traditions which had waned in popularity under the Roman Empire; while at the same time letting go of the need to be Jewish by birth and customs (one of many Jewish laws that had influenced large populations of assimilated Jews to convert to Christianity). This is similar to the problem facing millions of assimilated American reformed Jews today when dealing with strict and conservative Orthodox Judaism.

All that was needed to become a Christian had been a quick and painless conversion by baptism; and a change of heart. There had been no need for non-Jewish converts to perform any painful circumcision, nor give up their way of life in order to adopt many onerous Jewish customs (such as the prohibition of consuming pork and certain seafoods). The Jewish converts had been saved the duty of painfully observing many of their religious Jewish duties; and could attempt living a harmonious life with their newly accepting Greek and Roman Christian neighbours (who seemed to have also become willing converts).

Christianity had removed what was considered by the Greeks and Romans as repulsive aspects of Judaism --- introducing the Beit Hillel Judaic Philosophy of: free love; compassion; peace, and the aid of others . . . pacifism at its best. A real substitute to the repressive Roman

---

[224] "Epistle to the Hebrews - Wikipedia." https://en.wikipedia.org/wiki/Epistle_to_the_Hebrews. Accessed 7 Feb. 2018.
[225] "Beit Hillel - Wikipedia." https://en.wikipedia.org/wiki/Beit_Hillel. Accessed 7 Feb. 2018.
[226] "Chapter 7: Hillel and Rabbi Akiva - (Adapted from Likkutei Sichos, Vol ...." http://www.chabad.org/library/article_cdo/aid/2312343/jewish/Chapter-7-Hillel-and-Rabbi-Akiva.htm. Accessed 7 Feb. 2018.
[227] ""If I am not for myself, who will be for me?" A ... - Hillel International." 28 Feb. 2017, http://www.hillel.org/about/news-views/news-views---blog/news-and-views/2017/02/28/-if-i-am-not-for-myself-who-will-be-for-me-a-discussion-for-developing-a-practice-of-self-care. Accessed 7 Feb. 2018.
[228] "The House of Hillel, and Paul - Christian Doctrine from Bible Theology ...." 5 Jan. 2015, http://www.christiandoctrine.com/christian-doctrine/history/1153-the-house-of-hillel-and-paul. Accessed 7 Feb. 2018.

rule of persecution and crucifixion, as well as the fanatical Judaic religious zealots and their rebellious and terroristic way of life.

There are other theories regarding the birth and rise of Christianity. Some scholars even suggest a conspiracy theory that the Gospels had been written by the Roman Flavian family as propaganda against the Jews --- a kind of literary warfare that would have weakened Jewish resistance, and promoted the Roman Empire's rule.[229] Some of their claims are quite startling. Some correct facts regarding the writings of the Gospels --- such as the 'hindsight prophecies' about the precise way Jerusalem would be destroyed --- point to the fact that these Gospels had either been written during, or after, the Flavian family's rule of Rome. The writing style and parallel events to the Old Testament (such as the miracles performed by Jesus) may suggest that the people who wrote the Gospels had been proficient in Hebrew, and well conversed in Jewish literature. The remarkable similarities of the Gospels to events taken from Josephus Flavius' books about the Jewish rebellion (an example being the crucifiction of Jesus compared with Flavius' story about the crucifiction of certain Jews) indicate that the writers of the Gospels had also been very familiar with Flavius' writings about the Roman-Jewish wars.

In my opinion, the above conspiracy theory contains one major flaw which becomes apparent when examining the course of history --- that is, it is difficult to imagine Romans commissioning the Gospels (literature that had fundamentally undermined their own pagan religion, traditions, and culture). Greeks, and Greek-Jews in Asia minor, were more likely the ones to have initiated a movement that would have eventually undermined the Roman pagan religion; Since both Greeks and Jews had been oppressed by the Romans for a few centuries, and would have been happy to gain control and establish a new ruling order.

Without any concrete historical evidence, the exact and precise development of Christianity (alongside Rabbinical Judaism) will always remain obscure and elusive. What is definitely a fact, however, is that following the Roman-Jewish wars and the rise of Christianity; there had been a drastic decline of Jewish populations in Judea (and throughout the Roman-Empire). For hundreds of years after the rise of Christianity as the Roman Empire's official religion, there are but very few and insignificant records of Jews.

Whether it had been because of: Jews being convinced that Jesus was the messiah; the convenience of joining a growing new mainstream religion of the Roman Empire; or even simply wanting to discard the burden of the onerous Jewish religion --- Jews must have converted to Christianity en masse. Jewish communities which had comprised about 10% of the Roman-Empire before the rise of Christianity, had shrunk into small and insignificant communities.

The new Christian religion had been gathering momentum throughout the Roman-Empire. It had even spilled over its borders into Parthian territories as far as India in the East (and later on through the Arabian-Peninsula into the African-Ethiopian Aksumite Empire in the South).[230]

By 250 CE, the edict of Roman Emperor Decius --- which had attempted to force Christians to perform sacrifices to Roman Gods --- consequently initiated the death of refusing Christians.[231] This edict indicates that by the middle of the 3rd century, Christianity had become a major problem to pagan Romans. The huge decline in Jewish populations

---

[229] https://www.youtube.com/watch?v=SNtF1-Y-JJM (accessed 22/04/17)
[230] "History of Christianity - New World Encyclopedia." 10 Jan. 2018, http://www.newworldencyclopedia.org/entry/History_of_Christianity. Accessed 7 Feb. 2018.
[231] "Decius | Roman emperor | Britannica.com." https://www.britannica.com/biography/Decius. Accessed 7 Feb. 2018.

throughout the Roman Empire may also suggest that many Jews, at that time, had converted to this new powerful anti-pagan religion --- a process which had accelerated assimilation into the fast growing Christian religion.

By 313 CE, the edict of Milan --- ordering Romans to cease Christian persecution --- had been issued by Constantine the Great (who had been the first Christian-Roman Emperor).[232] Christianity's popularity had overflowed past the Roman Empire's borders --- all the way into far territories such as India and Ethiopia. Christian Assyrians --- through their Assyrian Orthodox church --- had been the most successful missionaries in this unprecedented new religious expansion.[233]

By the 4th century CE, Judaism had become a tiny minority in its ancestral land --- a persecuted religion in the Eastern-Roman Empire. Many Greek-speaking Jews had probably converted to Christianity. Judea had become a Christian land (which had embraced the Roman's renaming of it as Palestine).

Jews --- who had become an insignificant minority --- had been prohibited from setting foot in Jerusalem's ancient Jewish holy areas. Jerusalem had been named Aelia Capitolina, and became a Christian Holy Land.

The only place in the world where Judaism had remained strong was Southern-Mesopotamia /Babylonia. Some significant communities had also been present in North-Africa, Spain, and Gallic lands. Some Jewish minorities had wandered into Germanic and Northern-European lands; where Christianity had not been as strong yet, and religious persecution had not posed an imminent threat.

What *is* documented in Jewish history, is that the remaining world Jewry had now relied upon Babylonia as the center of Jewish studies (since the former Judea had become Christian Palestine). The Babylonian Talmud had been finalized at this time; and became the authority for all Jews around the world. Jerusalem, and its Jewish studies institutions, had ceased to exist. The Jewish population in Palestine would remain a tiny minority for the next 1600 years.

A remaining group of hardcore, 'die-hard' Jews within Palestine --- who had refused to convert to Christianity --- had been the result of the Christianization of the Roman-Empire. Said hardcore Jews had been thoroughly and intimately involved with Jewish life and Jewish studies. Who were they, and why would they cling to their religion so fiercely?

For more than 500 years until the rise of Islam, those Jews had to endure a constant pressure from Christianity (whose drive had been to convert everyone to the Christian religion). This physical and mental pressure on communities and individuals must have had some character building effects on Jews. Some characteristics that come into mind would be extreme faith, stubbornness, and mental endurance --- a passive-aggressive resistance that may have included a huge drive to demonstrate some kind of 'faith superiority' over the oppressors. Perhaps mental superiority --- a type of superiority that would have justified Jews' unrelenting faith in Judaism, and their unwavering refusal to convert to Christianity.

---

[232] "Constantine I - General, Religious Figure, Emperor - Biography." 1 Apr. 2014, https://www.biography.com/people/constantine-i-39496. Accessed 7 Feb. 2018.
[233] "ASSYRIAN MISSIONARIES AND KERALA CHRISTIANS. | Abraham ...."
http://www.academia.edu/14908649/ASSYRIAN_MISSIONARIES_AND_KERALA_CHRISTIANS. Accessed 7 Feb. 2018.

Islam and Judaism

The sudden rise of Islam had briefly changed the fortunes of Jews in the Middle-East, North-Africa, and Spain. Islam --- as another Abrahamic revelation type religion --- once again presents great difficulties with regard to attempting an assessment of its origins. The name 'Islam' --- as well as its supposed creator and first leader Muhammad --- has no reliable historical documentation; and completely lacks archeological evidence.

Esteemed Scholars like Butler[234] state that the entire period of Islamic occupation, between the early 7th century to 9th century, is covered in almost complete darkness. Most of the information comes from religious Islamic theologians from the mid 9th century onwards.

Amongst thousands of desert rock inscriptions on trade routes from the Middle-East to Arabia, there are many inscriptions regarding Kingdoms, Kings, and important personalities. Said inscriptions are in Nabatean writings. None of those inscriptions mention: Islam; The Quran; Muhammad; the Hebrew Bible, or even the religiously proclaimed fathers of: the Arabs; Abraham; Ishmael; Ishaq Esau, and Yaqub.[235]

Archeological evidence in the form of Islamic coins are allegedly first minted by the 9th Umayyad Caliph Abd al-Malik ibn Marwan in Damascus; and are estimated at 690 CE[236] --- at least Sixty years after Muhammad's proclaimed death in Islamic religious literature (caution must also be taken of all those estimations, due to religious bias of backdating the time period in order to validate religious stories).

It is unfathomable that simply based on inscriptions on the coins (which are the same as the inscriptions on The Dome of The Rock in Jerusalem) academics have determined that these coins were minted by the Umayyad Caliph Abd Al-Malik --- despite the fact that his name does not even appear on the coin. As will be shown below, there is archeological evidence that the true builder of The Dome of The Rock had been the Abbasid Caliph Al-Mamun.

Archeologists have always twisted archeological findings and evidence to suit religious narratives (whether said narratives be Islamic, Christian, or Judaic). In order to ascertain Islam's origins, it is therefore important to analyse the historical information and archeological findings that exist about the religion.

The first piece of information about Islam and its origins comes from Arab-Muslim theologist Abu Muhammad Abd Al Malik Ibn Hisham[237] from Basra; who probably died around 830 CE (that is, if he even existed; and if his writings had not actually been composed by others at a later stage). He claimed to have edited the work of Muhammad Ibn Ishaq from Baghdad, born in Medina 704-770 CE (caution must also be applied to this claim due to religious bias of backdating) in order to finalise the biography of the Prophet Muhammed --- nearly 200 years after the theoretical death of Muhammad in 632 CE.

Muhammad Ibn Ishaq's works --- as testified by Ibn Hisham --- are proclaimed to be the collected oral traditions over the years of his life. Those orals are, in essence, a third degree

---

[234] Butler, Alfred (1902). *The Arab Conquest of Egypt and the Last Thirty Years of the Roman Dominion*. Oxford: Clarendon Press
[235] "Crossroads to Islam: The Origins of the Arab Religion and the Arab ...."
https://www.amazon.com/Crossroads-Islam-Origins-Religion-Islamic/dp/1591020832. Accessed 7 Feb. 2018.
[236] "The British Museum, London :: Islamic Coins."
https://depts.washington.edu/silkroad/museums/bm/bmislamiccoins.html. Accessed 8 Feb. 2018.
[237] "Ibn Hisham, Abu Muhammad Abd al-Malik - Oxford Islamic Studies ...."
http://www.oxfordislamicstudies.com/article/opr/t125/e942. Accessed 8 Feb. 2018.

source of evidence. The fact that the Islamic writers themselves admit to having relied upon oral sources that span nearly 200 years, should raise an alarm. All those stories must be treated with extreme caution.

The other pieces of writing considered to be most reliable by Sunni Muslims are in the Hadith collection, 'Sahih Al-Bukhari' by the Imam Al-Bukhari[238] (810-870 CE from Samarkand Uzbekistan). Said samples of writing being, again, third or fourth sources from around 220 years after the religiously proclaimed Muhammad era (571-632 CE).

The writings of the Muslim theologians mentioned above form the basis of the Quran and Hadith stories about Muhammad and the formation of Islam. Based on these stories, generations of scholars have written up numerous books and academic works attempting to explain the rise of Islam. As a result: books; articles; and the internet, are all full of information which is of a very dubious nature. At times, due to the bias of its religious origins, this information exceeds the imaginary possible.

It is suggested that in order to arrive at the most plausible conclusion regarding the formation and rise of Islam, the evidence (writings) must be scrutinized in a process similar to Legal analysis and reasoning. This process involves steps that will consider various aspects of the circumstances that had taken place during the time of the writings (such as: who the rulers had been at the time of the composition of these writings; what the ruler's conduct had been like; what message had they attempted to convey to the public at the time?; are there any reliable external sources that can corroborate or contradict these writings?; are there any other clues such as geographical, demographic, ethnic, or linguistic factors that are able to shed some light on the circumstances surrounding this evidence?)

As per Legal reasoning techniques, the meaning of words and terms is important; and 'hearsay' evidence will be considered null and void (that is, unless it corroborates with facts). In this case --- exactly like my analysis of the Jewish Torah in previous chapters --- only carefully scrutinized archaeological or historical evidence will be entertained.

Islamic literature surfaces during what is considered the 'Islamic golden age' under the Abbasid Caliphate.[239] According to the writings, the Abbasids had overthrown the Umayyads from power; as the latter had lost their right to rule following the murder of the Imam Ali (who had been the closest living relative to the prophet Muhammad).

Obviously, the reason this religious story had been created was to give credit to the Abbasids' rule over the Islamic world as the followers of Muhammad. The Abbasids are described as having a direct lineage to the prophet Muhammad's male ancestry via his youngest uncle . . . to continue with this 'thrilling' story would be falling into the trap of generations of religious and academic scholars since the time of the Abbasid Caliphate. The main point is that the names invented all indicate to the intentions of the storytellers --- names such as the Abbasids ('Abb' meaning fathers, and 'Assids' meaning lions) translating to 'fathers of the lions'; and the Umayyads ('Um' meaning mother, and 'Ayyads' meaning blessed) translating to 'the blessed mothers'. The Umayyads' predecessors had been the Rashidun (the pious).

---

[238] "Imam al Bukhari: a lesson to be learned from the life of Bukhari." 2 Sep. 2015, https://islamhashtag.com/imam-al-bukhari-greatest-scholar-of-islam/. Accessed 8 Feb. 2018.
[239] "The golden age of Islam (article) | Khan Academy." https://www.khanacademy.org/humanities/world-history/medieval-times/cross-cultural-diffusion-of-knowledge/a/the-golden-age-of-islam. Accessed 8 Feb. 2018.

One can interpret the Abbasids' coup against the Umayyads rule as being 'the fathers of the lions of Islam' taking over from 'the known mother of Islam'; who had previously taken over from the Rashidun (the pious of Islam).

It is of no secret that amongst Arabs, and within the Islamic religion itself, the father had a far more important status than the mother --- much like amongst Jews and within Judaism at that time (since they had been a patriarchal society). Therefore, the Abbasids would portray themselves as the 'fathers' of Islam, in order to claim superiority over the mothers of Islam (the Umayyads).

The Abbasids claim that they are the fathers of Islam. Then comes the prolonged justification story of why they possess the right of being the ruling fathers. The rest of the story will remain as such, and its components can never be confirmed.

What *is* certain is that the Abbasids begin ruling from the mid 8th century til the 13th century --- a time in history considered as being 'the Islamic golden age'. The Abbasids are the first to preach the Islamic religion. This had all taken place within where modern South-Central-Iraq is situated today (in the city of Kufa, close to Najaf). Their stories are the basis of the Quran and Hadith.

While propagating the stories of Islam, the authors also present auxiliary information about themselves and their circumstances. Said information is also of a dubious nature, and may have been included by the authors as an attempt to give credibility to their stories.

Having considered all of the above, it is still beneficial at times to sift through the stories; as some stories may contain clues as to the conditions of the time (as well as other circumstantial evidence which is crucial in revealing the Abbasids' hidden agendas). It is also reasonable to believe that the closer the story is, chronologically, to the physical Abbasids rule; the more likely it is of some accuracy.

The further one goes back in time (into the Umayyads and Rashidun periods), the more likely the stories become grossly inaccurate due to a lack of historical evidence (but more so due to the hidden agenda of the Abbasids, as they had desired to determine Islamic history in order to glorify themselves and denounce their predecessors [the Umayyads]).

It is therefore necessary to turn to other external clues regarding the circumstances of the formation of Islam. The two most crucial pieces of information which have to be investigated are: first, the geographical location of the Abbasids base of operations; and second, archeological or historical clues from this geographical base.

The Abbasids had claimed that they had begun operating from the Iraqi city of Kufa (which had previously been the Umayyads' base of operations). A bit of research will reveal that Kufa is a city in the Southern parts of Iraq (around 150 km south of Baghdad). The Abbasids had taken control over this city from the Umayyads. Kufa holds the oldest Mosque in Iraq . . . most probably the oldest Mosque in the world. What is most miraculous and surprising is its unnervingly close proximity to the Jewish Talmudic academy of Sura (which had been a major center of Babylonian-Judaism for nearly a thousand years before Muhammad's era).

Why would the first Ishmaelites in Iraq (refraining from using the term 'Muslims' as yet for reasons that will be revealed below), the Umayyads (if this had been their real name) position their main city of Kufa in close proximity to a major Jewish study centre that had been there for many hundreds of years? Why are the verses of the Quran called 'Sura' . . .? Could it be connected to the Jewish Sura academy, since it is adjacent to the city of Kufa?

In his testimony of his voyages around 1170 from Spain to the Abbasid Caliphate (in what is today Iraq and Iran); Benjamin of Tudela[240] had visited Jewish centres in old Babylonia, and

---

[240] https://www.gutenberg.org/files/14981/14981-h/14981-h.htm (accessed 03/04/2016)

stated that there had been around a mere 7000 Jews remaining in the city of Kufa. All these areas along the Euphrates had once been inhabited by Jewish settlements --- that is, until the arrival of the Arabs. Before the rise of Islam, the Jewish population in Mesopotamia had been estimated at nearly 1 000 000. Sura, Pumbedita, and Nehardea[241] had been the most famous Jewish Talmudic academy centres at the time --- they all feature in the Jewish Babylonian Talmud; hundreds of years before the appearance of Muhammad in Palestine and the Arab conquests in the Middle-East (but they all disappear sometime between 650 CE --- 750 CE)

According to Islamic writings, shortly after the Abbasids take over from the Umayyads; their leader, Abu al Abbas Abdullah As-Saffah[242] moves his capital to Anbar. Anbar is situated at a very short distance from another Jewish Talmudic academy . . . the academy of Pumbedita (present day Fallujah).

As-Saffah's brother and successor, Al Mansur(754-775 CE),[243] is credited for establishing Arabic as the official language of the Caliphate; as well as for the construction and establishment of Baghdad as the center of the Islamic Caliphate.

Some four hundred years later, when Benjamin of Tudela visits the area; his reports and descriptions about the Caliph and his Caliphate are detailed, and can provide the reader with a sense of the Caliphate during its heydays (in what is termed by historians as the 'Islamic Golden Age').

Baghdad is described as being a rich and splendid city. The Jews are about 40 000 in number, within 28 Synagogues; and some Jews hold high positions within the Caliphate. The exilarch (Jewish leader) visits the Caliph every 5 days, and is received in great honour. The Caliph is tremendously well-educated, and even knows Hebrew; as well as the laws of Israel. The Caliph is a Hafiz (knows the Quran wholeheartedly) and also knows many other languages such as Greek.

These descriptions of the Islamic Caliphate and its relationship with its Jewish populations portray a good era for Jews at that time in history --- a period that has been termed 'the Islamic Golden Age'. This indicates that there may have been times of good relations between Jews, and the conquering Arabs (earlier in history).

Given the striking similarities between Islam and Judaism; for many generations within Jewish communities there had been legends about Muhammad learning from Jews, and basing his religion on Jewish values and customs. These legends can never be proven; however, as will be revealed below, it is possible to expose the extremely strong links between Islam and Judaism --- links that may change people's views of how exactly Islam had been formed. It may, hopefully, bring more understanding and tolerance to modern-day Jewish-Muslim relations.

A review of the end of 7th Century to 9th Century CE can reveal interesting clues regarding the formation of Islam --- clues stemming from the language and writings used, as well as other clues from non-Islamic sources which are also enlightening. The geographical cradle of Islam's origins, its development, and its population composition at the time; as well as the language used and the stories featured in the Hadith and Quran relating to that time, may also reveal hidden clues. The first religious structures in the area, and the names of the

---

[241] "Talmudic Academies in Babylonia - Wikipedia." https://en.wikipedia.org/wiki/Talmudic_Academies_in_Babylonia. Accessed 8 Feb. 2018.
[242] "Abū al-ʿAbbās as-Saffāḥ | ʿAbbāsid caliph | Britannica.com." https://www.britannica.com/biography/Abu-al-Abbas-al-Saffah. Accessed 8 Feb. 2018.
[243] "Al-Manṣūr | ʿAbbāsid caliph | Britannica.com." https://www.britannica.com/biography/al-Mansur-Abbasid-caliph. Accessed 8 Feb. 2018.

personalities featuring in key positions during the time of Islamic writings, can also be of some significance.

The first thing I chose to concentrate on was the Arab language. The Arab language used in Islam is the closest language to Hebrew you can get. It had probably been even closer to Babylonian-Jewish Aramaic; which utilized a hybrid of ancient Hebrew, and Southern-Babylonian Aramaic. Hundreds of words are easily identifiable. 'Allah' (in Arabic) is 'Aloah' (in Hebrew) --- meaning 'God'. 'Bayt' (بيت) is 'Bayit' (בית) meaning 'House'. 'Ras' (رأس) is 'Ros' (ראש) meaning 'Head'. 'Shams' (شمس) is 'Shemesh' (שמש) meaning sun. 'Sahar' (فجر) is 'Shachar' (שחר) meaning 'Dawn'. Even 'Kalb' (كلب) is 'Kaleb' (כלב) meaning 'Dog', and 'Gaml' (جمل) is 'Gamal' (גמל) meaning 'Camel'. 'Ana' (أنا) is 'Ani' (אני) meaning 'Me', and 'Anta' (أنت) is 'Ata' (אתה) meaning 'You'. 'Nachna' (نحن) is 'Anachnu' (אנחנו) meaning 'Us'. 'Yaum' (يوم) is 'Yom' (יום) meaning 'Day'; and 'Sana' (سنة) is 'Shana' (שנה) meaning year. 'Bab' (باب) in Arabic and 'Baba' (בָּבָה) in Talmudic Hebrew both mean 'Gate'. What about numbers, names of the months, and names of the days in the week? Aside from Friday --- which had been changed from 'Yom Shishi' in Hebrew, to 'Jummah' (gathering) in Arabic --- all other days are equivalent. There can be hundreds, if not thousands, of these word similarity examples.

These similar words between Arabic and Hebrew, and many similar customs --- between Islam and Judaism --- leave no doubt that Arabic and Hebrew, Islam and Judaism have shared some strong relationship in the past.

'When had this relationship been prevalent?', is the big question. Had it been intertwined with ancient Biblical religious connections (such as the stories of Abraham and Ishmael as religions want people to believe)?; or perhaps it had begun during the formation of the Arabic writings and Islam during the 7th to the 9th century CE.

Analysing terms used in the Arab language to describe Islam can give some indications about Islam itself. The word 'Islam' most probably comes from 'Salaam' which is equivalent to the ancient Hebrew word 'Salem' (whole) of which in modern Hebrew (under Ashkenazi influence) is pronounced Shalem.

The famous Hebrew word 'Shalom' and Arabic word 'Salaam' are derivations of 'Salem' meaning, within a broader sense, 'I am whole'. If one is physically and emotionally whole it means that one is within a peaceful state of existence. The Arabic term 'Salaam Alaikum' (السلام عليك), as in ancient Hebrew 'Shalom Aleikhem' (שלום עליך), meaning 'peace on you'; with the intention that no harm will befall on you.

The word 'Muslim' itself would correspond to the Hebrew word 'Mushlam' (מושלם). This word had most probably been pronounced 'Muslam' or 'Muslem' by Babylonian-Jews. The Hebrew meaning of the word is 'perfect' or 'complete'. The religious intention for Islam had most probably been that a Muslim is the metamorphosis of the flawed human being into divine perfection itself.

How many Muslims have any idea about this simple and most descriptive word? None that I have encountered. I have asked Muslim friends, and other Muslim people that I have encountered, "what does the word Muslim mean?". The answer I had always received was some description that the meaning is a man who serves God, by praying and obeying God's instructions as per religious scriptures; or a man that performs the Islamic faith --- that is, according to Islamic tradition. They had quite a surprise when I told them the Jewish meaning of the word --- especially Israeli-Arabs and Palestinian-Arabs who know modern Hebrew but can still not clearly recognise the similarities due to Eastern European accent influences on modern Hebrew.

Discovering the meaning of the word 'Muslim' had even been difficult for me, as the modern Hebrew pronunciation is different than the old Babylonian Jewish pronunciation of words.

'Mushlam' vs. 'Muslam' or 'Muslem'. Aside from old-aged Yemenite Jews' pronunciation --- which is probably similar to ancient Hebrew and Babylonian Jewish Aramaic --- no one today pronounces in old Babylonian Jewish Aramaic. Quite a bit of phonetic imagination is needed to overcome the Eastern-European ashkenazi influence on modern Hebrew and discover the fine link with Arabic. Other words, which will be used below will, also demonstrate this observation.

What about words which are used to describe religious structures or acts? Mosque is Masgad in Arabic ('Misgad' in Hebrew derived from the word 'Sagad'-worship), the Islamic religious academy is Madrasa in Arabic ('Midrash in Hebrew), the Quran ('Qriaa' in Hebrew means 'reading'), 'Sunan' ('Shinun' in Hebrew meaning 'reciting through the teeth'), 'Hadith' ('Hidud' in Hebrew meaning 'sharpening and understanding of the verse'). This is exactly the process that has been used throughout generations of Talmud studies in Judaism: read the sentence; recite the sentence; sharpen the understanding of the sentence by interpretation. Is that not also the Islamic practice?

Then we can start analysing other terms of Islam:

Caliph ('Chalif' [תַחֲלִיף] in Hebrew meaning replacement);

Imam ('Im ha am' [עִם הָעָם] in Hebrew meaning 'with the people'), Isn't that the duty of the Imam? To be with the people of the community?;

Sadaqah ('Tsedakah' [צְדָקָה] in Hebrew meaning the just deed of giving charity to the poor); being considered as one of the pillars of both Jewish faith and Islamic faith,

Ramadan ('Ram ha dan' or 'Ram ha zan' in Judaism means 'God the judge' or 'God the feeder'). Isn't Ramadan (or Ramazan as it is pronounced in some Muslim countries) about God's judgement of his subjects? And fasting so as to thank God for providing food, in the hope that his judgement will be merciful --- the same as the holiest day in Judaism . . . Yom Kippur.

Ahl al bayt ('Ohel ha bayit' [אוהל הבית] meaning 'tent of the home'). Sana ('Shana' [שנה] meaning 'year'), Yaum ('Yom' [יוֹם] meaning 'day'). Hijrah ('Hagirah' [הֲגִירָה] meaning 'immigration') Taher ('Tahor' [טהור] meaning 'pure'). Al Mubarak ('El Mevorakh' meaning 'God blessed') --- a term that had been used by Iraqi-Jews to describe the day of 'hakippurim'; the holiest day in Judaism.

The term that had initially puzzled me the most, however, was 'Abu'. This term is used in a seemingly illogical manner, by renaming a person as 'the father of' his first son's name. However, some imagination will reveal a connection to the ancient Hebrew word 'Abi' which means 'father'. Names like 'Abichai' and 'Abimelech' can trace this tradition back to ancient Judaism. Therefore, 'Abu Muhammad' would have originally been used as 'the father of Muhammad' in a traditional way based on the man's first born son; and as a title of respect, by showing that the man has produced a son. Sons were considered as being very important assets for tribes who constantly needed males to fight other tribes.

What about Muslim people's names? Ali, Omar, Bakr (Eli, Omri, Bachar are all Biblical Jewish names). Others like Hasan ('Hason' (חסון) in Hebrew meaning 'strong') Huseyn ('Hasin' in Hebrew meaning impenetrable). Banu Hashim ('Bnei Hashem') meaning 'sons of Hashem'. Many more names such as: Musa; Ibrahim; Ishaq; Esau; Yaacub; Galeb; Dawud; Salman (which is even spelled 'Zalman' in Ashkenazi-Judaism, or 'Sulaiman' in Turkish); Zachariah, and Ayyub --- in Hebrew: Mose (Moshe in modern Hebrew); Abraham; Itzchak; Esav; Yaakov; Kaleb; Dawid (David); Solomon; Zechariah, and Iyov are all Biblical Jewish names and are easily recognizable. All these names --- and many more that are not listed here --- could only have survived following the adoption of Jewish Biblical names handed down over generations (they would unlikely be names from bedouin populations from Arabia).

A multitude of Islamic words or names will have a Jewish/Hebrew equivalent that will be of a similar phonetic sound, and hold the same --- or close --- meaning. In fact, Hebrew words will at times explain Islamic terms better than Islamist Professors in London providing explanatory English words ever could. Over the years, Muslims may have lost the true meaning of the words (due to vast expansion into many different linguistic populations within many territories). Hebrew translations can serve far better than English translations (which at times are out of context and grossly misleading).

The name 'Muhammad' only appears four times in the Quran, and is probably more of a title than a name. English translators determine that the name Muhammad means 'the worthy one' or 'the blessed one' or 'praised worthy'[244]. Most other references in Islamic writings are of The Messenger of God 'Rasul Allah' or the Prophet 'Nabi' ('Navi' נביא) in Hebrew meaning 'Prophet').

The name Muhammad also has Hebrew equivalents, which are rooted in the number One (numeric 1, 'Echad' (אחד) in Hebrew, 'Wahad' (واحد) in Arabic). 'Chemed' (محبوب) means delightful or desirable, and 'Mechmad' (מחמד) is used often to describe 'the desirable/delightful' --- therefore, 'Muhammad' could easily mean 'the delightful' or 'the desirable'. The Turkish pronunciation 'Mechmet' almost sounds like the Hebrew pronunciation. Another Hebrew derivation is 'Meyuchad'; which means 'unique'. 'The unique' is also derived from the number one --- 'the one and only'. The meaning of these words are like an attribute or a title, rather than a name. Could there have been more than one Muhammad? In early Islam, the name had been given to many Muslims as a first expressive term before their actual name.

What about Arabic writing? Are Arabic writings able to provide further interesting clues as to the origins of Islam? When and where are the first Arabic writings documented? Some research into this question has been conducted, and can provide us with a pretty good idea/understanding of the source of Arabic writing.[245]

Sifting through the religious bias of the above referenced article will reveal that the first Arab writings termed 'Arabic Jazm' may have originated from the settlement of Al-Hirah. Where had this settlement been located? Surprisingly, it had been situated in very close proximity to the city of Kufa, in Iraq. The scant and dubious Arabic writings that appear in Saudi-Arabia in the 7th century (questionable dating and origin) are already classified by experts as Kufic-Iraqi styled writings --- a classification which heavily hints to their origin.

When reading the above referenced article written by an obviously well-educated and intelligent Muslim author; it is somewhat disheartening to realize that most people are so indoctrinated from childhood --- and probably so pressured by their environment --- that they desperately attempt to manipulate their exceptional findings in order to make them fit within 'traditional religious truths'. Older generation Christian and Jewish archaeologists --- that had been mentioned in the initial chapters of book --- do the same.

The original diacritic system of Kufic Arabic and its similarities to Torah Hebrew diacritics, should also be examined by scholars. Diacritics seem to be used much more in Hebrew and Arabic than in any other known languages in the world. Further than this, no research has ever been done comparing Arabic writing to Judeo-Aramaic cursive writing. Quite a few letters look like alterations of Hebrew cursive letters --- either by: dropping the right part of the letter

---

[244] "Behind the Name: Meaning, origin and history of the name Muhammad."
https://www.behindthename.com/name/muhammad. Accessed 8 Feb. 2018.
[245] http://arabetics.com/public/html/more/History%20of%20the%20Arabic%20Script_article.htm (accessed 04/04/2016)

such as the Hebrew Aleph ('Alif' in Arabic); trimming slightly, and turning the letter 180 degrees such as the Beit ('Ba'a' in Arabic); or adding a diacritic dot in the middle of the letter, as with Gimmel ('Giim' in Arabic). Careful scrutiny will reveal connections between most of the letters in the Hebrew and Arabic alphabets. At face value, it looks to me as though the Arabic alphabet is some kind of Nabatean and Jewish Babylonian-Aramaic hybrid.[246]

What about historical sources other than Islamic sources at the time of Islam's creation? Can they reveal interesting facts regarding the formation of Islam? There are a few other Christian historical sources of the era that may be more reliable than the much later Islamic sources of the Abbasid Caliphate. These pre-date the Abbasid Caliphate by 100 --- 150 years. One such source is the Christian Doctrina Jacobi[247] text, as well as the Armenian Chronicle 661 written by Sebeos.[248] Said writings provide further clues as to what may have transpired in Palestine in the early 7th century.

The Sebeos writings indicate a good relationship between Jews and Saracens (the Christian name for Arab desert-dwellers of the Middle-East) in their efforts to dominate Christian Palestine and Jerusalem. In those writings, Jews are described as being full of joy; claiming that a Messiah had appeared among the Saracens. The governor of Jerusalem --- after the Saracens' had taken control of Palestine from the Christians --- is reported to have been a Jew appointed by the Saracens. It should be noticed that the terms: 'Arabs'; 'Muslims'; and 'Islam', are missing from all those writings.[249] It should also be noted that the year 661 CE is 31 years after the death of Muhammad (according to Islamic religious writings) --- which hints to the strong possibility that even Muhammad's life and death had been backdated (either deliberately or out of lack of information).

Interesting is the claim in this Christian writing, that the Saracens had become jealous of the Jews' Temple of worship in Jerusalem; and eventually repossessed it as their own Temple (It is currently well-known that The Dome of The Rock is constructed on top of this old Jewish Temple).[250]

Then there are the extensive writings of the very credible scribe St. John of Damascus; about heretics of Christianity.[251] These writings are dated at 746 CE --- a very important year in Islamic history. 746 CE had been the year of the Abbasids' rebellion against the Umayyads (which began in the city of Kufa . . . thousands of kilometers in travelling distance away from Jerusalem). St. John of Damascus' writings list over 100 various cults and religions that --- according to him --- had been heretics. This list includes: Judaism; Hellenism; Samaritans, and many others. Ironically, listed at no.101 are 'The Ruling Ishmaelites of Palestine' --- a long and detailed piece of writing about the Ishmaelites, their beliefs, and their scriptures. The most important detail to be noticed from these writings is that, again, there is no mention of: Arabs; the Quran; Islam, or Muslims. There is only mention of Muhammad, Ishmaelites, and Saracens. Another important detail is that the Ishmaelites were already worshipping the Kaaba (as per the details around his arguments against the holiness of the Kaaba). There is,

---

[246] "Aramaic alphabet - Wikipedia." https://en.wikipedia.org/wiki/Aramaic_alphabet. Accessed 8 Feb. 2018.
[247] "Muhammad - Livius." 21 May. 2017, http://www.livius.org/articles/religion/messiah/messianic-claimant-20-muhammad/. Accessed 8 Feb. 2018.
[248] "Non-Muslim Source speaks of Muhammad (661 AD) - Free Minds." 23 Mar. 2013, https://freeminds.org/forum/index.php?topic=9605183.0. Accessed 8 Feb. 2018.
[249] http://www.livius.org/articles/religion/messiah/messianic-claimant-20-muhammad/ (accessed 05/05/2017)
[250] ibid
[251] http://orthodoxinfo.com/general/stjohn_islam.aspx (accessed 27/04/2017)

however, no mention of where this Kaaba is situated. Not even a hint of Mecca, Medina, or Arabia for that matter.

It is not the goal of this book to debate religious arguments; but an interesting detail about the origins and source of the word 'Khabar', and the term 'A-khabar', can be entertained. St. John of Damascus maintains that the Ishmaelites worshipped Khabar (the morning star, Venus) before they became monotheistic. Bear in mind that 'Khabar' as a word, also has an ancient Hebrew equivalent. In Hebrew 'Khabir' means 'Great' --- whether or not it relates to the morning star (Venus) as St. John of Damascus wants Christians to believe, is another issue. Perhaps since Venus is the largest visual star, it had been named 'The Great'. So . . . 'Allah Hu Akbar' (God Is Great), may have had a different meaning before Islam was established as a monotheistic religion.

Some Jewish literature regarding the beginnings of Islam can also shed some light on Islam's formation. The Babylonian-Jewish Haggadah of Bustanai ben Haninai portrays a strong relationship with Caliph Umar (co-operation against the Persian King with the Caliph which results in rewards, and appointment as the exilarch --- the leader of Babylonian-Jews). Umar supposedly gave Bustanai ben Haninai one of the daughters of the vanquished Persian King, for a wife; while taking her sister for himself. The story might just be a legend; however, it does point to the fact that Jews --- at some point early in the Arab occupation of Babylonia --- had considered themselves to be in a very good relationship with the Arabs.

Islamic and Judaic: scriptures; beliefs; religious conduct, and customs can also highlight the incredible similarities between the two. Islam's greatest scripture --- the equivalent to the Jewish Torah --- is the Quran. The Quran consists of most of the Biblical stories of the Torah, with the addition of the book of Isa (Jesus) and Muhammad. Muhammad is hailed as the last prophet sent by God to correct humanity's ways. If it were to be judged today according to intellectual property criteria, whole parts of the Quran might have been considered as plagiarism of Jewish Biblical and Talmudic writings.

The writings of the Islamic religion repeat and stress that Muhammad's revelations and arrival is to correct the ways of the people; namely Christians and Jews. In many passages within the Hadith and Quran, there are instructions to tolerate the people of God; while there is a strict order to kill pagans on the spot.[252]

Although slightly modified, the customs and religious duties of Islam are extremely close to Judaism's. Examples of this similarity are: the prohibition of eating pork; the laws of slaughtering animals (Kashrut and Halal); circumcision of males at age of 13 In Islam (the Jewish Bar Mitzvah age), while in Judaism male circumcision occurs 8 days after birth; daily prayers to God (which had been expanded from 3 times a day in Judaism, to 5 times a day in Islam); polygyny, which had been limited to four wives (polygyny had been abolished in Judaism in Europe by Rabbinical order at around 1000 CE), and the day of prayers and rest --- which had been altered to Friday in Islam (Jews had already claimed Saturday, and Christians Sunday).

The pillars of the Islamic religion are also extremely close to Judaism. Instead of 3 pillars in Judaism --- which include: the study of Torah (which is God's word); working for God (which includes prayer); and Gemilut Hasadim (which includes Tzedakah) --- Islam has 5 pillars. The first of the 3 pillars is equivalent to Judaism with regards to an unequivocal faith in God (only in Islam, the Prophet Muhammad is added). The second pillar, within those 3 pillars, is about work for God (which includes prayer). The third is Sadaqah (which is equivalent to

---

[252] "Verse (9:5) - The Quranic Arabic Corpus - Translation." http://corpus.quran.com/translation.jsp?chapter=9&verse=5. Accessed 8 Feb. 2018.

Jewish Tzedakah). The additional 2 pillars are: fasting during the month of Ramadan; and pilgrimage to Mecca. In Judaism, fasting is conducted on Yom kippur and other religious occasions. Pilgrimage to Jerusalem had also been common amongst Babylonian-Jews in antiquity. However, fasting and pilgrimage are not considered to be pillars of Judaism. It is clear that Islam puts more onerous physical duties on its believers than Judaism does on Jews.

Islam seems to have been created through the alteration of ancient Judaism. It had most probably been a religion that the common Jew at the time could easily identify with, and convert to. Many Jews of Babylonia, and assimilated Jews, had probably converted to Islam ---- possibly because they had been convinced that it would be the true continuation of Judaism. Overall, it was an exciting time. The Persian/Parthian Zoroastrian rulers had finally been defeated by an uncompromising religion that would 'return the days of glory to the sons of Abraham, and hasten the arrival of the true Messiah' (then named 'The Mahdi'). In the followers' eyes, Islam had also proved the falsehood of Christianity --- something that the Jews must have rejoiced upon.

Further significant evidence that Islam had been created by altering ancient Judaism is Islam's retention of Jewish names. Many Islamic names are of ancient Jewish origin. Especially Islamic writers' names such as Ibn Ishaq (Ben Itzhak), and Ibn Dawud (Ben David). Other names of importance are Al-Mamoun (Maimon, meaning 'fortune' in both Hebrew and Arabic), as well as many of the important Quranic leaders (as will be demonstrated below).

It is as though there had been a conscious effort to preserve Jewish names, alongside adding a few new Arabic names. This might also point to the familial origins of the first literate people of Islam.

Another interesting retention of a Jewish name can still be found In Afghanistan, which had been isolated from world politics for many years (that is, until the arrival of Al-Qaeda into the country). Until recently, the name 'Israel' had been very common --- and highly respected --- amongst the dominant Islamic Pashtun tribe. Perhaps it had also been common in other Islamic countries until the establishment and independence of the state of Israel in 1948. Muslims in Arab countries have since discontinued the use of the name 'Israel' (for obvious reasons).

The process of forming a new religion has already been discussed in Chapter 2. The theme repeats itself throughout history. In essence, it is the creation of a shared historical legacy; which then prompts people to amalgamate over a common vision. This group of people then become a nation which: works towards; fights for; and advances into, a common future.

What could have been more compelling to an Arab desert-dweller than a sophisticated civilization that could present him with the Torah --- written proof of his origins as a descendant of Abraham and Ishmael (who had also been desert-dwellers). He would have been even more compelled to adopt the Jewish Torah when liberated Palestinian-Jews had hailed him as a Messiah; and had presented him with written proof of his credentials as said Messiah (Muhammad) that had liberated the Holy Temple.

It is quite logical to assume that the Old Testament would have more likely been adopted and revered by Muhammad and his followers, than the New Testament (which had no room for another holy figure after Jesus; who, according to Christianity, is also the undisputed future messiah to come).

Most Islamic sources themselves maintain that Muhammad had neither read nor written; but instead possessed unique visionary skills that enabled him to convey the word of God to his followers.[253] Given these accounts regarding the leader of the Ishmaelites, one can only imagine what the literacy rate of Muhammad's Ishmaelite followers had been.

Through its interesting architectural structure --- as well as written phrases within the structure that are described as the 'big daddy' of archeological Islamic writing[254] --- The Dome of The Rock (Al-Aqsa Mosque) can provide clues regarding the formation of Islam.

What is interesting about The Dome of The Rock is the manipulation of the most important clue as to what the origins of Islam had been. This manipulation is not of mal-intention, as whoever did so had simply been exposed to generations of accepted religiously biased information.

The unique octagonal structure of The Dome of The Rock has yet to be found in any other Mosques around the Arab world. The Dome of The Rock is more of a Temple than a Mosque, pointing to the use of circumambulation while worshiping (an ancient Jewish religious custom). Among Arab words with a connection to Hebrew is 'Al-aqsa Mosque' (also known in Arabic as 'Bayt Al-Maqdas' --- 'Beit Hamikdash' being the Hebrew term used to describe the Temple Mount).

The phrases inscribed on The Dome of The Rock can indicate to the message that is being conveyed, as well as to whom said message addresses. Aside from praising God and his prophet Muhammad numerous times, the inscriptions continually stress that 'God has no son' --- probably meaning that God does not share his status with any human being. 'The blessed Jesus son of Mary is but God's messenger' is another inscription. Can there be any doubt that this message is intended to strengthen and encourage Christian conversion into Islam? Probably --- since Christians had been the overwhelming majority of the population in Palestine, at this time in history.

I would think that the most important clues within the inscriptions of this fabulous structure are: the reference to the builder of the Mosque --- the 'Caliph Imam Al Ma'mun[255] in the year 72'; as well as the fact that all the inscriptions are in Arabic Monumental Kufic-style writing.[256]

The composers of the above referenced website immediately came to the conclusion that it is obvious that Caliph Al Ma'mun (God's treasure) had inserted his name (according to their belief of Qur'anic accounts and Al Bukhari's writings). According to Bukhari's writings, the counting should start from approximately 620 CE (Islamic Hijrah story of Muhammad) --- which means that according to the religious Islamic timeline, the Dome had been constructed in 692 CE. This conclusion has been reached by many scholars: Jews; Christians; Muslims, and Atheists alike. Why. . .? Because everyone consumes the available traditional religious knowledge without questioning it too much.

Well then, what if the original counting years of Islam began at 750 CE --- precisely when the Abbasids overthrew (whom they had eventually named) the Umayyads?

The Abbasids' first Imam had also been named Muhammad; and according to some Christian legends of Bahira at the time,[257] Islamic counting had to have begun from the time when Caliphs had directly descended from Muhammad. The Islamic stories regarding Caliph

---

[253] "Claim of Muhammad's illiteracy | Submission.org - Your best source for ...."
http://submission.org/Claim_of_Muhammads_illiteracy.html. Accessed 8 Feb. 2018.
[254] http://www.islamic-awareness.org/History/Islam/Inscriptions/DoTR.html (accessed 04/04/2016)
[255] "Al-Maʾmūn | ʿAbbāsid caliph | Britannica.com." 10 Dec. 2017,
https://www.britannica.com/biography/al-Mamun. Accessed 8 Feb. 2018.
[256] "Kufic - Wikipedia." https://en.wikipedia.org/wiki/Kufic. Accessed 8 Feb. 2018.
[257] "Muhammad and the Monk: The Making of the Christian Bahira Legend ...."
http://www.academia.edu/2940939/Muhammad_and_the_Monk_The_Making_of_the_Christian_Bahira_Legend. Accessed 8 Feb. 2018.

Al Ma'mun portray his open-minded policies, and his continuation of his father's (Harun al Rashid) 'Mu'tazilah'[258] philosophy --- an Islamic philosophy that had claimed the Quran to be a man made, not a God created, book; and could therefore be changed and modified according to reason and logic. If this had been the Abbasids' declared philosophy under Caliph Al Ma'mun, would it be reasonable to assume that they may have changed older Ishmaelite scriptures into the first Islamic scriptures? Had the Quran been modified, and re-modified, a few times from: the time of the Umayyads; to the time of the Abbasids, and through the rule of the Abbasids up to a certain point? Was the Quran, alongside the Hadith, perhaps finalized during Al-Bukhari's prime under the Caliph Al-Mutawakkil (who is recorded to have scrapped the Al-Ma'mun Mu'tazila philosophy during the mid 9th century). Al-Mutawakkil is also known for having abolished the 'House of Wisdom' and all foreign influences; as well as reinstating 'Dimmi' laws on the Jews of the Caliphate, and forcing them to wear a yellow badge on their cloths so as to be identified as Jews.

If the original counting years of Islam had indeed begun from 750 CE, the date of the construction of The Dome of The Rock would be 822 CE --- exactly nine years into the reign of Caliph Al-Ma'mun (which is recorded between the years 813-833 CE). Caliph Al-Ma'mun has been credited for many advancements of the Islamic Caliphate during the beginning of the Islamic Golden Age. These advancements include: translating a vast amount of important literary work, from around the world, in the fields of science and the humanities into arabic; cartography; revamping the 'House of Wisdom' ('Bayt El Chikma' --- 'Beit Ha Chochma' in Hebrew), and acquiring more power and wealth by expanding the Islamic Caliphate. Such achievements would have provided Al-Ma'mun with the means of building such a monumental construction. The Kufic-style Arabic writing inscribed on the Dome suggests that the origins of the construction had been under the Abbasids' rule, and not under the obscure era of Abd al-Malik --- as Malik would have ruled over the areas of Syria, Palestine, and Egypt. Said areas would have had different architectural styles to that of the Kufic style with which The Dome of The Rock had been built. Archeology suggests Arabic writing had probably not even existed during Al-Malik's time.

Had Caliph Imam Al-Ma'mun begun constructing The Dome of the Rock in the beginning of the 9th century (as is inscribed on the Dome's walls)? This being almost 130 years after the religious story of Abd al-Malik? Is there a need to adjust history books or scholarly work?

Further obscurity occurs when questioning why the verses on the Dome are not identical to any known Quranic verses. Many are in the spirit of the Quran --- but not identical. Such an important religious monument should surely have Quranic verses inscribed on it. Is it possible that the final version of the Quran had still been in progress in the year 822 CE? Had Caliph Al Ma'mun been instrumental in initiating the writing the Quran? Islamic religious writers are prominent just shortly after Al-Ma'mun's rule --- the same time when: Islam; Mecca; Medina, and other Islamic terms start becoming part of history.

The first blessing inscribed on The Dome can again demonstrate the strong Judaic similarities between Arabic and Hebrew. 'Assalamu alaikum wa rahmatullahi wa barakatuh' (In Hebrew --- 'Shalom aleichem ve rahmat elohim ve birkato'), meaning 'Peace on you and mercy of God and his blessings upon you' --- may this written blessing lay upon all humanity in its quest for truth, wisdom, and reconciliation.

---

[258] "Mu'tazilah | Islam | Britannica.com." https://www.britannica.com/topic/Mutazilah. Accessed 8 Feb. 2018.

The general debates on some of the oldest Mosques in the Islamic world may also provide clues about the development of Islam. No one doubts that the Kufa Mosque[259] in Iraq is one of the oldest in the Islamic world --- built sometime in the 7th century. This Mosque may have existed earlier than the Medina mosque in Saudi-Arabia. Based on its architecture, the Medina Quba Mosque is closer to the Egyptian Fatimid architectural style of the 10th century.[260] All written references to the Medina Mosque come from Persian-Muslim writers of the Islamic Golden Age (again a major chronological contradiction between archeology and religious writings).

Some scholars claim that the qibla on some of the older Mosques in Iraq --- such as the one in Kufa --- had pointed to a closer destination than Mecca; and possibly Jerusalem or even Petra[261] (located in Southern-Jordan), and that at some stage it had been changed to point to Mecca. If this is true, it may further indicate to the efforts of the Islamic religion to differentiate itself from its Jewish roots --- creating a new legacy for the Arab and Islamic nation in the far away Arabian-Peninsula.

Another major clue can be found within Islamic scriptures themselves. There are extensive justifications for the reasons Caliph Ali had in changing his capital from: Medina --- which is proclaimed to be the deathbed of Muhammad --- to the city of Kufa in Babylonia.[262] Medina and Kufa are thousands of kilometers apart . . . such an extreme and far-distanced move seems extremely unlikely and illogical.

No one has ever questioned all these religious writings and justifications as being a cover up for the great possibility that Kufa --- with its first historical Arabic inscriptions --- had been the true capital of Islam; and where Islam had *actually* been formed.

So --- why had Medina and Mecca been chosen as the cradles of Islam? Perhaps because they had been the only places in the vicinity of the Middle-East that: Christianity; Judaism; and the Zoroastrian religion, were non-existent --- the only territories in the area that Islam, as a monotheistic religion, could cleanse from idol worshippers and thereafter claim its origins from. An area that had been roamed and settled by bedouins that shared some customs and aspects of the Arab culture of the Caliphs in Kufa, as well as some aspects of language. As a powerful caliphate with the new powerful Islamic formation, they could now mould: Mecca; Medina; and the Arabian-Peninsula, as they had desired.

'Where had the Quran been written?' is a question that haunts historians and theologians. Islamic writings state that at some stage, Caliph Uthman had re-assembled the true God-given Quran; and burnt all other Qur'anic material.[263] This might indicate to a possible 'backdating' by the Abbasids (possibly Caliph Al-Mutawakkil) who took action in modifying the Quran to suit their agenda, and spread a story that the Quran had been written during the Rashidun Caliphate times. This would bestow credibility unto their new modified Quran, as well as demean Al-Ma'mun's (and his father Harun Al-Rashid) 'Mu'tazilah' Islamic philosophy (The philosophy that claims the Quran, as well as all other religious writings, to be man made, and

---

[259] "Great Mosque of Kufa - Wikipedia." https://en.wikipedia.org/wiki/Great_Mosque_of_Kufa. Accessed 8 Feb. 2018.
[260] "The Evolution of Mosque Architecture - Omrania." 24 Apr. 2017, https://omrania.com/inspiration/evolution-mosque-architecture/. Accessed 8 Feb. 2018.
[261] "When Did the Qibla Change? - The Sacred City." http://thesacredcity.ca/When%20Did%20the%20Qibla%20Change.pdf. Accessed 8 Feb. 2018.
[262] https://www.al-islam.org/restatement-history-islam-and-muslims-sayyid-ali-ashgar-razwy/change-capital-medina-kufa (accessed 27/04/2017)
[263] http://www.harvardhouse.com/quran_purity.htm (accessed 28/04/2017)

not God created). This would have been within the best interests of Islam and, of course, the Caliphate's best interests.

Based on some of the above facts regarding the Abbasid Caliphate's dominance and use of propaganda, it can be assumed that perhaps the entire origins of Islam being within the Arabian-Peninsula is but a myth --- similar to Judaism's origins beginning in *Egypt* most probably being a myth (as well as the probable myth of Christianity originating in Jerusalem by Jesus, and not in the Syrian city of Tarsus by Apostle Paul).

Islam and the Quran are far more likely to have been conceptualized in the city of Kufa in Babylonia (modern-day Iraq) by the very same people who had invented Arabic writing; and finalized in Samarkand by Al-Bukhaari and Al-Mutawakkil. The individuals who had conceptualized Islam and the Quran had probably either been ethnic-Jewish Talmudic scholars, or their mixed-assimilated 'Islamised descendants' (perhaps there had even been other Arabs who were taught, and inspired by, Judaic scriptures --- all under Arab leadership). They had been the ones to create Islam and convert other: Jews; Christians; and vanquished Zoroaster-Parsi, to the new religion. They had also been the individuals who had created a new written Islamic culture, with a new language and new scriptures that would differentiate them from older monotheistic religions that had existed in that area at the time.

To test these assumptions further is not an easy task. Questions such as: who had formed and established Islam? ; when had it been established? ; and why? Need to be answered.

Considering the great possibility that the cradle of Islam was in the city of Kufa (situated within what had been known as Mesopotamia the time) will require additional clues, as follows:

One such clue is that the names of scholars and writers such as 'ibn Ishaq' and 'ibn Dawud' are of Jewish origin. It is very unlikely that Jewish scholars had hailed from the distant settlements of Medina and Mecca. As was demonstrated above, they had lived in Mesopotamia for many years before. Their Talmudic Sura academy had literally been a two-to-three-hour walk from Kufa.

This geographical proximity clue can also be used to eliminate the possibility that the Arab rulers at the time had arrived from the extremely distant areas of Medina and Mecca. The most probable possibility that remains is that these Arabs had been Bedouin tribes (named, by Christian writers, as Ishmaelites) that --- sometime during the 7th century --- had invaded old Babylonian urban centres, as well as the areas of Syria and Palestine. This is corroborated by Christian historical testimony at the time (mentioned above).

The possibility is elevated considerably when taking into account the fact that these arid places border ancient urban Babylonian cities; as well as the fact that even today, the Bedouin population in the arid areas of: Southern-Iraq; Jordan; and Saudi-Arabia, are of substantial size --- amounting up to nearly 5 million people within those geographical areas.

Some of the Islamic orders and descriptions point to their Bedouin origins. One of the orders and descriptions regard the Bedouin tribes. They are described as the spine (back bone) of the Arab nation. Never to be hurt and always respected.

Archeological evidence of thousands of years before the 7th century generally points to the dominance of city dwellers over the desert-dwellers. Some archeological records reveal the attempts of: Assyrians; Babylonians; and Romans, to invade the desertous Arabian-Peninsula --- however, these invasions usually ended in miserable failure (most probably due to the harsh conditions of the desert). Armies back then were not built for such extreme conditions --- conditions that are prohibitive to big armies that need to sustain themselves by utilizing the environment, or human settlements, during their occupational expeditions.

Desert conditions only suit smaller scale caravan mobility --- fewer people with many camels, and ample supplies of food and water. These same conditions had always kept the population in the Arabian-Peninsula small. No serious Empire ever had its capital city in the desert.

To stop small-scale invasions from the desert during the Roman and Parthian-Empire wars, both Empires had employed Bedouin tribal people in their Southern borders. The Ghassanids[264] and Lakhmids[265] are historically recorded. Those tribes primary function had been to stop other Bedouin tribes from harassing the Roman and Parthian Empire citizens. At times they would fight with each other as proxies of the dominant Empires. No large-scale invasion from the Arabian desert has ever been recorded.

It is therefore hard to imagine the religious stories of large and equipped Arab armies storming through thousands of Kilometres in the unforgiving desert to unbelievable conquests and gains in extremely short periods of time.

A quick invasion is possible if there are external factors that tip the balance of favour from urban conditions towards Bedouin-style living conditions. For instance, climate change and desertification of large areas may reduce the urban populations dramatically (due to drought and famine) and provide a greater opportunity for desert-dwellers to survive under these extreme conditions and terrains.

Bedouins under desert conditions are very mobile and maneuverable, allowing them to exploit the terrain and make a living out of scarce, scattered resources throughout the desert.

Historical records of Michael the Syrian[266] account for severe climate change in the Middle-East around the beginning of the 7th century. This could have brought about the possibility that Bedouins had invaded Palestine.

Michael's accounts speak of a situation in the year 622 CE, where half of the sun is covered; and from October to June, the days are in a state of darkness. People feared that this had become a permanent situation.

If these accounts are true, it may be that a lack of sunlight had caused desertification, famine, and disease --- perfect conditions for Bedouin raids on severely weakened urban areas. Moreover, the timing corresponds well with the estimated time of the Arab occupation of Palestine; as well as with incidental evidence in the Quran regarding great famine and disease in the area at approximately the same time.

In the beginning of the book, Mark Twain's voyage to the Holy Land in the year 1865 had been described. His observations had been that the area was a harsh desert --- a desolate place full of danger from Bedouins. The city of Jerusalem is described as being a very small-scale city, consisting of around 4000 Jewish/Arab households, surrounded by a harsh desert. Very few small-scale settlements like Safed and Nazareth were mainly inhabited by Jews and Christians. The rest of the country had been a desolate desert whereby you could have travelled for days without seeing a soul. It was such a turn-off for Mr. Twain, that he admits he was glad to get out of there. This had only been about 152 years ago! Then there are further historical records compiled which portray the dire straits of the population living in the area hundreds of years prior to Twain's visit.[267] Records that may even help explain the Israeli-Arab Palestinian conflict today.

---

[264] "Ghassān | ancient kingdom, Arabia | Britannica.com." https://www.britannica.com/place/Ghassan. Accessed 8 Feb. 2018.

[265] "Lakhmid Dynasty | Arabian dynasty | Britannica.com." https://www.britannica.com/topic/Lakhmid-dynasty. Accessed 8 Feb. 2018.

[266] "Michael the Syrian - Wikipedia." https://en.wikipedia.org/wiki/Michael_the_Syrian. Accessed 8 Feb. 2018.

[267] "Habitation of Palestine - Arabs Speak Frankly." https://www.arabsspeakfrankly.co.uk/pdfs/5-habitation-of-palestine.pdf. Accessed 8 Feb. 2018.

Through the excitement of doing research, as well as revealing and exposing meanings of words in Hebrew and Arabic, I had ventured to discover the source, and meaning, of the term 'ARAB'. To my surprise, I found that there is hardly any reliable account for the origin of this word. Historical use of this word before the rise of Islam is almost non-existent. As was mentioned above, the occupiers of Jerusalem were named Saracens, Hagarenes, or Ishmaelites --- not Arabs or Muslims --- in the Christian Doctrina Jacobi text and the Armenian Chronicle 661 written by Sebeos and St. John of Damascus writings.

The first time the word is properly described in history is when the Roman Emperor, Philip the Arab, is named after his birthplace which had been located in the Roman province of Arabia. This province included modern Jordan and Southern-Syria --- nothing at all to do with the new Saudi-Arabia territories. The name most probably originates from The Bible's description of the Arabah desert, which stretches South of the Sea of Galilee; through the Dead Sea, and down to the Red Sea Gulf of Aqabah --- an area that is shared today by Israel and Jordan.

This fact can further enhance the argument --- mentioned in previous chapters --- that the Jewish Bible had been written in Babylon, as the root of the word 'Arabah' is derived from the Hebrew word 'ereb' or 'arab' ('ערב' meaning 'evening' or 'where dusk falls') . . . and dusk falls West of Babylonia in exactly the Arabah desert. Roman historical accounts mention that the Saracens and Tayei had lived in that area.

What the above paragraph tries to suggest is that the new invaders into Palestine, and later the city of Kufa in Babylonia, had originated from 'The Arabah' --- a particular area falling between Palestine and Babylonia where the Bedouins had lived for eons. Yathrib; Mecca; Medina --- or any other cities that are nowadays identified with: the Arabian-Peninsula; Islam; and the Arabs in Saudi-Arabia --- are simply stories propagated by the Abbasid Caliphate.

If it is accepted that Bedouin tribes had been the first Arabs, and were responsible for the creation of Islam within Jewish-Babylonian Talmudic centers; further questions with regard to understanding Islam's legacy arise --- questions about: the choices made in creating this legacy; the reason behind choosing what is now Saudi-Arabia as the place of Islam's origin; the timing of Islam's creation, and what the pressing issues needed to build the legacy of Islam had been.

To answer such questions, other possible scenarios could be eliminated by some simple logic. Would Bedouins, who had incorporated the ancient Jewish religion philosophy and laws into their culture (in order to to create a new religious legacy), point to Jerusalem as their origin? Would the small area of TransJordan, the former Roman-Arabia province, suffice as their origins? Would they even indicate to the formation of Islam being in Iraq; in-and-amongst old Jewish-Babylonian study centres?

All of those options do not offer great promise considering the large populations of Christians and Persians that had been conquered and expected to convert and live under the new Islamic occupation.

Moreover, would the Abbasids --- who had overthrown the Umayyads in 750 CE and had faced war against the bigger cities of Parthia --- point to the close proximity of Kufa or Al-Hirah as their base? Or even: Jerusalem; Damascus; or Petra, as their stronghold and legacy? How about Palestine's small cities that had been populated with Christians? All of these options do not suffice.

Where in the Middle-East --- without casting doubt on their newly formed Caliphate and human resources --- could the Abbasids have pointed to where Arabic had been spoken? Where could they have pointed to, in order to backup their invincibility in the eyes of their new converts and the anxious Persian enemy? The vast area of nowadays Saudi-Arabia had been a far and safe option. No danger could have emanated from these areas. On the contrary, it had been very easy to control it via the Bedouins (whom had a stake in Babylonia and the Middle-East). It is the vast unknown that instills fear into the hearts of the enemy --- especially if a good propaganda campaign is disseminated.

Who can be the best suspects for such a literary propaganda war? Who had been the best writers and storytellers in the Parthian Empire who could create, fuel, and disseminate these propaganda stories and install fear at the heart of their Persian enemies. The answer . . . Talmudic Jews who had possessed the knowledge and skills to devise and write stories --- and it just so happens that big Jewish communities had been spread in each and every large Parthian city. Jews had lived in Parthia for just over a thousand years.

Disseminating those stories via the multiple Jewish communities within the Persian Empire at the time, could have worked well. Said Jews could have also spied on the Persians from within. Not such a far-fetched assumption given the fact that large Jewish populations had been under Persian/Parthian rule for more than a thousand years.

Many times, wars are won on psychological grounds. Choosing Mecca and Medina to be the origins of Islam would offer some respect and credibility to the Arabs --- telling their people about God's will and the stories of the armies of Islam that can never be defeated (stories about Jihad, and afterlife benefits would have instilled motivation within their armies; and fear among their Parthian enemies).

Praising a Jewish connection had not been a good idea; as Jews had been a minority at the time, and were engaged in a bitter struggle with the ruling Christian majority in Judea. They had also been under the Persian/Parthian mighty rule in Babylonia for hundreds of years.

In the wake of the creation of a new nation based on Jewish customs, many Jews had probably become Muslims; and the new Arabs had proven to be formidable forces --- leading to the conquering of the whole of Babylonia and Persia from the Zoroastrian Parthians. Later, converting the Persians/Parthians to Islam (leading up to the historically famous Islamic Golden Age).

The converting of Persians to Islam must have been a very harsh affair. Following executions and forced conversions, the Zoroastrian religion had not been treated by the new Muslims as Christianity or Judaism were (since it had not shared Abrahamic and Biblical traditions). Zoroastrians had to flee Persia all together, and landed up as a minority religion in Northern-India. It is nowadays a tiny religion of around 70,000 members in Mumbai and Gujarat.[268]

Unlike Jews and Christians, the Zoroastrian religion had been regarded by the new Islam as Idol and fire worship; and was viciously attacked and driven out of Persia. This treatment can also be explained on grounds of ethnicity, as the Persians had been a different ethnic group than the Semitic Arabs and Jews (including the largely Semitic Christian population of the Middle-East). They had become an obvious target of hate for the Arab-Muslims --- a situation that had eventually lead to the formation of the Persian Shia Islam[269] (which is mostly comprised of ethnic-Persians). These historical rifts are evident today in Iraq and the Middle-East; where Shia-Muslims lead by Iran, are fighting Sunni-Muslims led by the Arab countries --- proving, once again, that ethnicity is stronger than religion; and that religion will always be modified to suit its ethnic group.

---

[268] "Sanjan (Gujarat) - Wikipedia." https://en.wikipedia.org/wiki/Sanjan_(Gujarat). Accessed 8 Feb. 2018.

[269] "BBC - Religions - Islam: Sunni and Shi'a." http://www.bbc.co.uk/religion/religions/islam/subdivisions/sunnishia_1.shtml. Accessed 8 Feb. 2018.

Following the defeat of the Persians in wars that span around 150 years by the 8th century CE, we find that Islam is fairly established in Baghdad; and enters what is termed the 'Islamic Golden Era' led by the Caliph Harun al Rashid[270] (a name which could be 'Aron ha Hasid' in Hebrew . . . 'Hasid' meaning 'pious', as 'Rashid' does in Arabic). Al-Rashid had established the 'House of Wisdom' ('Bayt al-Hikma' --- the same meaning as 'Beit Ha Hochma' in Hebrew).

Islamic stories themselves are essentially further clues that point to the co-operation between Jews and Arabs in creating Islam. Most of said stories are similarly based on the goal of returning to the old glory of Biblical Judaism --- fantastic Quranic stories that are strikingly similar in their grandiose to ancient Biblical stories of victory.

Muhammad and Umar are invincible, and of an unbelievable nature --- just like King David and King Solomon. King David being a warrior who had vanquished many canaanite nations --- his son and follower being King Solomon; who had continued the expansion, but is credited for initiating monumental constructions as well as building the Temple.

Amazingly enough, Muhammad is also credited as being and supreme warrior; and his successor Umar has also been credited for building the Bayt Al-Maqdis (at exactly the same spot in Jerusalem that King Solomon had built it . . . what a co-incidence).

When reading the amazing Islamic stories regarding Umar, it is not of great difficulty to realize that many of these stories are impossible --- same as how a good amount of old Jewish Biblical stories are likewise, impossible.

Umar is portrayed as a 'superman' who had lived his life across three continents, been a champion martial-artist and supreme scholar, and fought and triumphed over his enemies everywhere. The most telling feature being his extreme wisdom --- much like Solomon's famous virtue, according to the Bible. Had Biblical King Solomon been the first 'Farook' as per Umar's legacy? An enlightened being possessing absolute knowledge of what is right, and what is wrong.

What is most striking about Umar's stories relating to the Jews is that on the one hand, he beats them mercilessly in the Arabian-Peninsula; while on the other hand, he hands them privileges regarding Jerusalem, and brings thousands of them to the city of Kufa (as if Jews had been absent in Babylonia --- their homeland for more than a 1000 years before Islam).

Another striking fact that can be gleaned from the Islamic stories is that, in Islamic sources, all the names of Jewish leaders and their tribes do not sound Jewish at all; rather, Bedouin. Quraish, Nadir, Badr, Marhab, Utba, Walid, Shaybah, Uqbah --- nowhere ever in history had Jews used such names. These Islamic stories about Jews are made for the sole purpose of discrediting the Jewish religion upon which Islam was founded.

The reason the Islamic authors could not have used proper Jewish names in their stories is because they themselves bore Jewish names, as was demonstrated above (Ibn Ishaq, Ibn Dawud and so forth). After all . . . no-one wants to 'demean' their own name.

One of the most fascinating contradictions is the Quranic story of Umar's Islamic victory over Kheibar Jews, and the complete expulsion of said Jews from the city --- even bringing some of them to the city of Kufa.

The diaries of Benjamin of Tudela testify a visit to Kheibar and Teima, at around 1170. Benjamin describes the strong Jewish city of Kheibar being inhabited by around 50,000 Jews; who had been shielded by a harsh desert and fortresses, and were renowned for their invincibility due to this topography. They had been surrounded by Bedouin tribes who co-

---

[270] "Hārūn al-Rashīd | 'Abbāsid caliph | Britannica.com." https://www.britannica.com/biography/Harun-al-Rashid. Accessed 8 Feb. 2018.

operate with them as brothers, and would never dare challenge them. Teima is described similarly, with an even greater Jewish population of 100 000 strong.

All this appears at around 540 years after the supposed Jewish defeat to Umar, and his Islamic Armies. Had Umar's story been an exaggeration in order to claim victory and superiority over Jews in their most impenetrable city in the area? Had this been an attempt at convincing Babylonian-Jews to convert to Islam?

The possibility that Benjamin's records are flawed is remote (considering his important mission of recording Jews around the known world; as well as his precise descriptions of Islamic Baghdad, and its glory and might). It is also highly unlikely that Benjamin had been familiar with the Quran's stories and Arabic script. Benjamin's records are of good quality considering his admiration to the Islamic Caliphate; as well as the reigning Caliph Emir al-Mu'minin al-Abbasi --- describing him on same footing as the Pope of the Christians.

Benjamin's records are also mild overall, and far better than the exaggerated Islamic religious stories (which are based on a few memories of already dead and non-existent third and fourth degree oral sources). The point being that the Kheibar story is exactly that . . . a story. Jews in Kheibar had probably been converted at a later stage in history (while facing the far more technologically advanced Ottoman army which had subjugated the entire Arabian-Peninsula under its Empire).

Then we must examine the Arabian-Peninsula itself as a possible origin of Islam. The strongest clue to the unimportance of Arabia, and its cities of Mecca and Medina, is the fact that there had not been any real interest in this area for nearly 700 years after its Quranic glorification.

After the fall of the Abbasid Caliphate to the Mongols --- and the tremendous military expansion of the Mongolian-Empire everywhere in the Middle-East --- it would have been expected that the Mongols would try to occupy these 'holy places' of Mecca and Medina. However, the Mongols had not ventured into the Arabian-Peninsula at all --- they had shown no interest whatsoever. They were well-aware that there had not been any treasure waiting for them in the Arabian-Peninsula (Hay for horses had been more valuable to them than crude and unrefined oil, at the time).

All clues lead to the inevitable conclusion that the likelihood of Islam's roots originating from the regions of: Mesopotamia; Palestine; Syria; and Babylonia (Iraq), is far greater than said roots originating from the Arabian-Peninsula (modern Saudi-Arabia) --- as the Quran claims. Before the Islamic 'Golden Age' in Babylonia --- and thereafter --- there had been little economic or cultural interest in the Arabian-Peninsula. The only interest had been a religious one (following the Quran, and the order that all Muslim believers should undergo pilgrimage to Mecca at least once in their lifetime).

The first time Arabia had become significant was under the Ottoman occupation of Selim I in 1517 --- nearly 700 years after the start of the Islamic 'Golden Age'. The Ottoman Empire had remained there until the Saud family managed to rebel, take over from them, and establish the Saudi-Arabian monarchy.

Aside from the physical pumping of oil to supply the modern Western world with energy, nothing of any great: intellectual; scientific; technological, or philosophical value has come from the vast deserts of the Arabian-Peninsula.

Unlike many archaeologically renowned ancient Empires that had built big cities and structures; there is almost no substantial archeology in Saudi-Arabia (save for Mosques that were most probably built by the Abbasid Caliphs of Baghdad in the 9th century).

Due to the vast revenues of oil money (petrodollars); new and large civil structures, and infrastructure, have been built in recent modern times. Even those structures had been designed and constructed by large international firms from outside Saudi-Arabia --- mainly American, British, and Australian firms.

The Arabian population had never been a knowledge-based society, and never experienced a true 'Golden Age'. Saudi-Arabia's potential has reached its maximum limit with the 'Black Gold' oil age in modern times. Today, under a new and daring leadership, things may change in the future.

The final clues about the origins of Islam come from the stories, and the names of the characters within those stories, of the Quran and Hadith. It was mentioned above that the very first complete and sealed Quran and Hadith were most probably composed during the Abbasid Caliphate reign. The Abbasids would have undoubtedly portrayed themselves in the best possible light, by proclaiming to be the Fathers of Islam ('Abb As' meaning 'father lion') --- having the same lion symbol as the symbol of ancient Judea and the House of David. Their predecessors could have not been ignored, and were portrayed as the 'Umayya' (probably meaning 'Holy Mother' if translated from Hebrew) who's symbol for holiness had been a Hawk. Long before Islam, the Hebrew term 'Ayya' had been adopted by the Greek Christian Orthodox Church i.e. 'Ayya Sophia' meaning 'Sophia the Holy'.

Tracing Abbas's and Muhammad's lineages is even more interesting. Muhammad and his uncle Abbas are traced back to 'Hashim' (meaning 'The Semite') --- a revered name from the Bible; while Muhammad's parents names are 'Aminah' meaning 'The Credible' (as in Hebrew 'Amina'), and his father's name is 'Abd-Allah' meaning 'The Worker of God' (as in Hebrew Ebed-Elloah) --- giving them credibility and monotheistic virtues.

In contrast, the full name of the Caliph 'Umayya' is 'Umayya ibn Abd el Shams' meaning 'The Holy Mother Hawk, Son Of The Worker Of The Sun' --- tainting him with some idol worshipping characteristics, and thus discrediting some of his lineage. Are these real names, or are they tailor made in order to suit the Abbasids' story that the Abbasids are the true continuation of Muhammad's legacy, and monotheism?

Further scrutiny of the names will reveal that Abbas's descendants are: his son, Abd-Allah (Worker Of God); Ali, his grandson; and the first Imam, Muhammad --- all pious and credible individuals who had belonged to the Abbasids' God-worshipping lineage.

The names of Umayya's descendants are, however, of mixed character. Their fabricated names testify to this. His one son is 'Harb' ('Chereb' in Hebrew) meaning 'sword' (symbolizing death); while his descendants are all mixed in good and bad character. Muawiyah (meaning 'howling fox') and Yazid ('Zid' meaning 'disobedient to God' in Hebrew) are the worst of Umayya's descendants; being accused of the murder of Hasan and Husayn --- the direct heirs of the prophet Muhammad. They are also portrayed as treacherous individuals who had held double standards.

Umayya's other son, Abu al-As (father of the lion) produces good children and grandchildren. Al-As's son, Al-Hakam 'the clever one', and his grandchildren Uthman and Osman (names which are most probably derivatives of 'Eitan' and 'Otsman' meaning 'mighty' and 'powerful'). Osman is portrayed as a very rich and powerful ruler.

All the names of the Islamic characters are derived from Hebrew adjectives that fit the character's behaviour and actions, as well as the general plot of the Islamic stories said characters occur in . . . strikingly similar to Biblical stories constructed by Jewish scribes in exactly the same geographical area 1000 years earlier.

During my research and reading, I had the feeling that --- sometime during my early childhood --- I had encountered the term 'Yazid' in the Bible (within some bad context). I painstakingly searched for it, and to my great surprise . . . I had indeed found it in the Torah. Discovering the meaning of the term was even more of a surprise. It is written: 'But if a man plots deliberately against his friend to slay him with cunning, even from my altar you shall take him to die' (Exodus 21:14).

This remarkable term perfectly describes the Islamic story of Yazid's plot to murder Muhammad's only male heir --- Imam Huseyn. 'Yazid' in the Hebrew Bible is an adjective used to describe a man who cunningly and deliberately plots to murder his friend. The severe punishment is an indication as to the seriousness of this offence. According to Islam, Yazid's reign was short lived, with him dying a horrific and inglorious death. Yazid's story is the theological basis for the Shia-Sunni Muslim split. But, as mentioned earlier, this split is most probably based on ethnic lines of Arab vs Persian; the theological story of Yazid murdering Muhammad's rightful heirs is just used as a justification for the split. There are other clues that can demonstrate that the people who wrote the Quran had some intimate knowledge of Biblical numerical philosophy.

Another clue which indicates to Islamic writers using Jewish numerical techniques is the use of Jewish numerical themes in the writing of the Quran. The manipulation of the holy Jewish number, seven, can be an indication. The name 'Quran' appears 70 times in the Quran (7x10). Muhammad's life span is 63 (7x9), and his name in Hebrew Gematria is 98 (7x7 + 7x7). These being similar to the Jewish Torah's uses of the number seven, and its multiplications. All done to inspire the holiness of the literature, and personas within it --- this cannot be co-incidental.

The historical glory of Islam's Golden Age in Iraq cannot be denied. It became one of the world's finest philosophy centres. A place where life-sciences, alongside humanities, advanced considerably; that is, until its destruction by successive Mongol invasions over 400 years. Said invasions, followed by invasions from Turkic tribes, eventually led to the Ottoman Empire. These Mongol and Turkic invasions also changed the character of Islam forever; from a relatively open-minded and advanced religion of the Abrahamic religions during the Islamic Golden Age, to a much harsher and aggressive proselytizing religion. Some of the newly Islamised Mongolian rulers had adhered to harsh policies towards Christians and Jews under their rule.

Towards the end of my exploration into Islam, I had read some more into Dan Gibson's[271] archeological research; and was pleased to find that some of my findings --- through the available historic literature and the use of my imagination --- correspond to some of his life-long research on Islam.[272] Especially the probability that Mecca and Medina were never the cradle of Islam, and that fundamental changes had been made to Islam sometime after 822 CE under the reign of Caliph Al-Ma'mun. Also that Petra is the starting point of the Ishmaelites and Arabs in their expansion during the days of Muhammad (which corresponds well to my assumption regarding the origins of the name 'Arab'). At some stage during my writing of this chapter, I had felt uneasy with all my assumptions and interpretations; but Mr. Gibson's findings came as a big surprise and relief to me.

This journey of exploring Islam and its connection to Judaism --- in what I believe to be the forgotten history of the role of Jews in the development of Islam and the 'Islamic Golden Age' --- had been a fascinating experience.

The arrival of Arabs into Ancient Babylonia had caused the Babylonian-Jewish population --- which had been estimated at approximately 1 000 000 --- to dwindle by 90% within a few

---

[271] "Dan Gibson (historian) - Wikipedia." https://en.wikipedia.org/wiki/Dan_Gibson_(historian). Accessed 8 Feb. 2018.
[272] "Petra: Holy City of Islam - Nabataea.net." http://nabataea.net/holycity.html. Accessed 8 Feb. 2018.

hundred years. Jews had been dwelling in Babylonia for more than a thousand years, developing a culture of study and intellectual engagement; as well as the Jewish Talmud --- which has served Jews for nearly two millennia. In its place, a substantial Muslim population had appeared in the same geographical area. This had happened without any record of any major calamity upon the Jewish population --- even though, throughout history, Jews have been known for excellently recording major calamities befalling on them .

Should Muslims reconsider their historical relationship with Jews? Should Jews be given any credit from Muslims regarding: their beliefs; the Quran; the Hadith, and the historic 'Islamic Golden Age' in general?

As a final word of caution, it is submitted that all the above possibilities are the product of my own perception and imaginative process. These perceptions are, however, logical and of high probability/plausibility. But, as with: the Torah; the Bible; the New Testament; Abraham; Moses; and Jesus, it seems as though the exact and truthful story of Islam's creation and the prophet Muhammad will forever remain illusive to every human being on this earth.

Modern-age thinkers can only weigh the advantages and disadvantages of religions, so as to perhaps promote relevant information that may benefit society as a whole; and, in doing so, bridge the gap between the religions themselves (as well as between the secular world and religious world) in order to create harmonious relationships.

After dealing with Judaism's influences on the two big Abrahamic religions of Christianity and Islam; attempting to understand how Judaism had coped with the rise and dominance of those religions, is of interest. How had it managed to preserve itself as a small and insignificant religion in comparison to those two proselytizing religions?

Judaism's survival of Christianity in the first centuries

The rise of Christianity and Islam, which are proselytizing monotheistic religions, had affected Judaism considerably. Every Jewish person could have easily, by their own will, convert to these religions at any time; without any severe ramifications.

In antiquity, Judaism had been unique in its monotheism (when compared with idol worship). With the appearance of Christianity and Islam as monotheistic-based religions, Judaism had lost its major differentiating aspect of being monotheistic. Since it had continued to be locked within its own strict ethnic rules, it could not recruit fresh populations like the new monotheistic religions had. Only people born to a Jewish mother would have been considered Jews.

Jews, who had always been connected as an ethnic group and many times defined themselves as the 'Jewish nation', were always alienated --- either by their own will, or, through the force of the neighbouring environment. Jews would, at all times, be subject to persecution; as well as pressure from the bigger religions of Christianity and Islam, to convert. Even though, at times, Jews had been forced to convert; most conversions had probably been a matter of convenience for many Jews. Frequent secularisation and assimilation in America today, is a vivid example of the historical Jewish pattern of conversion and assimilation.

A question that may be of interest is: why would some Jews stick to their religion, despite all the difficulty and hardship? As well as the question of: who were these die-hard Jews that had continued to cling onto their beliefs?

To answer this question, it is necessary to ascertain: who these Jews had been; what the source of their resilience had been; what Christianity and Islam could have possibly offered them so as to convince them of conversion, and what had been so attractive about Judaism that had enabled it to retain some Jews.

The general character of Jews had already been discussed in previous chapters (that character being sturdiness and steadfastness; people who stick to their beliefs and their identity). Whilst existing in an overwhelmingly Christian and Islamic environment, they had lived in closed communities. Said communities were often prosperous, organised, and stimulating. Apart from temporary alleviation from persecution, the Church had nothing of value to offer. Over time, the larger irresolute population of Jews had converted; and only strong-minded individuals had remained.

The warring traits of these strong-minded people had persisted (albeit in a passive-aggressive manner). The communities had become too small to stage an uprising or rebellion. Jews had resisted in other ways; such as possessing the will to die for refusing to eat pork or desecrate Shabbat. Jews had defined this form of death as 'Death for the holiness of God'. Many Jews in Christian lands had died in this way, despite rabbinical orders to submit in order to save their lives.

The love of these people to Jewish studies and way of life had probably been addictive. As was discussed earlier, Jewish studies had contained massive amounts of literature that had stimulated the reader's mind in the fields of law, philosophy, and general life-orientation. Neither Christianity nor Islam had offered this on the same scale as Judaism. Their literature had not been as vast as the Talmud, or many other Jewish writings such as the Kabbalah.

Christianity's intellectual stimulation had only been offered to clergy who were required to abandon real life. The priest could not have a family --- a very unnatural, distorted and celibate kind of a life (which had most probably been an unhealthy lifestyle).[273]

The priest was expected to devote his life to the Church, and Christ, by performing religious duties for the community. Most of the community had been treated like ignorant sheep that were to appear for religious ceremonies: sit; listen to the sermon; sing a bit, and donate money to the Church.

The most intelligent individuals were expected to enroll into the clergy, and were prohibited from having children. This practice prevented the passing of capabilities to future generations --- either genetically or behaviorally. The clergy had relied upon the community to continue providing young and capable individuals to serve in the Church. Once in the commited service of the Church, their genetic potential would be lost forever.

Rabbis on the other hand were expected to have as many children as they could afford. Rich and wealthy community members were honoured to wed their best daughters to Rabbis; as well as marry their sons to a Rabbi's daughter --- a practice that had enhanced a Rabbi's family life by marriage into wealth. The opportunity to produce as many children as could be afforded had usually resulted in an increase of intelligent individuals within the community.

Those children had also been personally instructed by their Rabbi, father, or older brother --- further enhancing the intellectual capability of the community. Even though Rabbis had been expected to devote their life to the pursuit of knowledge by studying the Torah and Talmud (as well as other Jewish studies), They were not restricted in seeking other occupations --- including conducting trade and business.

---

[273] "Is it even possible to live a celibate life? - BBC News." 5 Mar. 2013, http://www.bbc.co.uk/news/magazine-21654663. Accessed 9 Feb. 2018.

Judaism's survival of Islam

Historical records reveal that Islam had, at first, alleviated Jews from Parthian rule in Mesopotamia (as well as from Christian persecution in the Middle-East, North-Africa, and Spain). Later on, Islam had a far more profound impact on demolishing Judaism within Islamic countries.

At first, during Muhammad and the Ishmaelites' time, the Arab people had followed the instructions of their new-found faith (the old Jewish Torah) by leaving the people of God to convert out of their own free will. The larger Christian population, and the minor Jewish population, had lived in relative peace and safety under the Ishmaelites. At that time, Jews had been considered as 'people of the book' who were not to be harmed. It was even claimed that Muhammad's goal had been to correct those people's ways back into the old ways of the Torah.[274]

There were, however, strict restrictions of the 'Jizya tax' on non-Ishmaelites; as well as general 'Dhimmi' laws[275] ('Dam' meaning blood in Hebrew --- the goal of the Ishmaelites being to distinguish between Ishmaelite blood, and non-Ishmaelite blood) which included the prohibition of: marriage to an Arab woman; owning an Arab slave; testifying in court against an Arab, and holding a public office. There had been other, less severe, restrictions as well.
Once Islam had been established, all the above laws had been transposed onto Christians and Jews alike.

Based on historical records, it can be assumed that many Jews in Mesopotamia had indeed converted to Islam; as their numbers had dwindled considerably during the Islamic Golden Age from an estimate of more than 1 000 000 Jews who had lived in Mesopotamia before the rise of Islam, to around a meagre 100 000 (according to the records of Benjamin of Tudela). The Jewish population in Mesopotamia had therefore decreased by nearly 90% in just 400 years of Islamic rule.

As Islam became the dominant religion in the area, the need to preserve and increase this dominance had resulted in intermittent persecution of the other Abrahamic religions --- namely Christianity and Judaism. Depending on the ruler's view and interpretation of Islam, a tolerant --- or alternatively intolerant --- era would commence. At times, Christian and Jewish populations were forcefully Islamised. This had been particularly true during the Mongolian occupation,[276] and their rule over the Islamic Caliphate. When a Mongolian ruler would convert to Islam, he would usually try to force Islam on the other faiths under his rule.

After the fall of the Islamic Caliphate, the general condition of Jews in Islamic countries deteriorated. Aside from a brief period under the Ottoman-Empire during the expulsion of Jews from Spain, Sultan Bayezid II[277] is recorded to have accepted Jewish refugees from Spain (mostly settling in the Greek city of Salonica, as well as other major Turkish and Balkan cities within the Ottoman-Empire).

In the years leading up to the establishment of the State of Israel in 1948 --- and the ongoing fight between Jews and Arabs in Palestine --- pogroms against Jews had ensued in Islamic-

---

[274] "Corruption of the Tawraat (Torah) and Injeel (Gospel) - islamqa.info." 26 May. 1998, https://islamqa.info/en/2001. Accessed 8 Feb. 2018.
[275] "Dhimmi - New World Encyclopedia." http://www.newworldencyclopedia.org/entry/Dhimmi. Accessed 9 Feb. 2018.
[276] "Ilkhanate - Wikipedia." https://en.wikipedia.org/wiki/Ilkhanate. Accessed 9 Feb. 2018.
[277] "Bayezid II | Ottoman sultan | Britannica.com." https://www.britannica.com/biography/Bayezid-II. Accessed 9 Feb. 2018.

Arab countries.[278] The most notorious pogroms known as the 'Farhud' had taken place in Baghdad --- the capital city of Iraq.[279] In fear of extended Arab-Muslim retributions, an estimated total of 800 000 Jews from: Iraq; Egypt; Syria; Lebanon; Libya; Algeria;Tunisia; Morocco; and Yemen, had fled to Israel. Nearly 31 years later, another 100 000 Jews fled from Iran (shortly after the Islamic revolution of 1979).[280] Most of these Jews had fled to the United States.

Said hundreds of thousands of Jewish refugees had lost all of their possessions --- some who had been incredibly wealthy. Most settled in Israel; never to be recognized as refugees, and without any rights (unlike the Palestinian-Arab refugees of 1948, whom even their grandchildren are still recognized by the United Nations' agencies as refugees, and have received generous international aid for more than 70 years).

Many Moroccan and North-African Jews had moved to France, and now comprise most of France's post-World War II Jewish population --- the vast majority of France's original Ashkenazi-Jewish populations had been exterminated during the holocaust.

In most Arab countries today, no Jews remain. Even the Christian population has dwindled considerably, and has become a persecuted minority in all those Arab and Muslim countries. The inclination of the Jewish population in Palestine in the late 19th century, and the establishment of Israel in 1948, had created a small but formidable safe-haven for Jews within the Middle-East. Time alone will tell what the future holds for Jewish people in their ancestral land. Most of their neighbours are laden with hate and destructive ideologies --- Especially the Islamic Republic of Iran, who is currently attempting to establish hegemony in the Middle-East.

Judaism accredited

As a persecuted minority religion, Judaism has never been accredited by Christianity or Islam for leading to the twos' creations --- on the contrary, they have always attacked Judaism. This is not abnormal, since every new religion seeks to assume domination. In chapter 13 (the inherent conflict between religions), the reason new religions attack and demean old religions --- and vice-versa --- is explained.

One important purpose of this book is to show the cultural influence of Judaism on their surrounding neighbours --- whether they be the ancient polytheistic worshippers of the Middle-East, or the conquering desert-dwellers of Arabia. Some of this cultural influence (namely family laws and social justice) has been carried through by Christianity and Islam to vast areas of the world, and into the modern-era. By specifying the basics of this cultural influence, Judaism can be accredited.

First is the belief in a single eternal God --- whether that God be 'Allah' or 'Elohim' or a 'natural all-encompassing secular entity'. This belief has eliminated the worshipping of all kinds of Idols; as well as the massive energy and emotions wasted by humans on such Idols. This belief in a single God also forms the basis for modern agnosticism and atheism --- the progressive disbelief in many Gods had lead to the belief in only one God; which had then,

---

[278] "The Expulsion of Jews from Muslim Countries." http://jcpa.org/article/the-expulsion-of-the-jews-from-muslim-countries-1920-1970-a-history-of-ongoing-cruelty-and-discrimination/. Accessed 9 Feb. 2018.
[279] "Farhud - Wikipedia." https://en.wikipedia.org/wiki/Farhud. Accessed 9 Feb. 2018.
[280] "Jews of Iran - Jewish Virtual Library." http://www.jewishvirtuallibrary.org/jews-of-iran. Accessed 9 Feb. 2018.

with the help of science and technology, developed into the complete disbelief in the existence of any God.

Then there are the scriptures of the Abrahamic religions. No matter how illogical --- and at times defaming --- these scriptures are, they had still been composed through writing; not illiterate worship to statues or monuments. This scripture-based practice had promoted literacy around the world. Reading and writing --- the founding pillars of humanity. Whether said literature had been in: Hebrew; Aramaic; Greek; Latin; or Arabic --- it had expanded in societies over the millennia. One can only imagine what the world had been like before literacy was invented. Following literacy, numerical skills had also been developed (although, much ground had already been broken in ancient Greece regarding mathematics). In Europe, much had been accomplished with the help of literacy. The invention of Algebra[281] (which had formed the basis for modern mathematics); as well as the adoption and use of the Hindu-Arabic numeral (decimal) system --- which is used all over the world --- had been established under the literate Islamic Caliphate in Baghdad.[282]

Then come the morals of society. Even though Western moral conduct is widely considered as far more advanced than antiquated religious morals, the basis of Western morality had originated from the Abrahamic religions themselves. Those morals being: the prohibition of murder, incest, adultery or covet; extensive family laws, and the eventual abolition of slavery (to name a few). All having emanated from the Jewish Bible; running their course of changing world culture via Christianity and Islam.

The world still faces many obstacles with regard to infighting amongst religions; as well as the conflicts between religions and the secular world. But one must give credit where credit is due --- and credit is due to the Jewish religion that brought forth many modern-world concepts (including morals and values).

This entire chapter has demonstrated, once again, the importance of literacy and dedication to learning. It has again substantiated how literacy promotes creativity; and how Jews had been the initial driving force for the creation of new religions and a modified way of thinking. Said religions eventually went on to dominate the Western world, Middle-East, and vast areas of Asia.

Jewish philosophy had begun as the philosophy of a small nation in the heart of the Middle-East, but had evolved into a Global philosophy . . . an amazing story of human endeavour. An amazing story of wealth creation.

---

[281] "Islamic Mathematics - The Story of Mathematics."
http://www.storyofmathematics.com/islamic.html. Accessed 26 Feb. 2018.
[282] "Hindu-Arabic numerals | History & Facts | Britannica.com."
https://www.britannica.com/topic/Hindu-Arabic-numerals. Accessed 26 Feb. 2018.

Chapter 7

Between the Muslim and Christian worlds.

Summary: This chapter will examine Jews' experience as a minority between the clashing forces of Europe's Christianity, and North-Africa's Islam within the Iberian Peninsula. This chapter will also layout the facts and fiction surrounding the Jewish Kingdom of Khazaria.

'My heart is in the East and I am at the edge of the West.
Then how can I taste what I eat, how can I enjoy it?
How can I fulfill my vows and pledges while
Zion is in the domain of Edom, and I am in the bonds
Of Arabia?'

--- **Rabbi Judah Halevi (Muslim Spain 1075-1141)**

The Spanish golden era of Judaism

As Arabs had absorbed most of the Jews in Babylonia, and Islam had begun to form into the major religion in the Middle-East (expanding to the West, into North-Africa and the Spanish Iberian Peninsula) --- Judaism had gained a temporarily ally in its quest for survival in these Christian lands.

Judaic people had probably been allies of the Arab occupation in Spain, against the Christian oppressors. This is apparent even according to Islamic sources.

According to Islamic sources, it was Tariq ibn Ziyād[283] who crossed the straits of Gibraltar with 7000 new berber converts to Islam and eventually formed Andalucia (the Islamic name of modern day Spain). First in Cordoba --- whereby he appointed his Jewish allies to guard the city --- and then Toledo and other Spanish cities.[284]

As was apparent in the previous chapter, it is difficult to rely on Islamic sources, as they originate from the abbasid caliphate in Babylonia (modern day Iraq) which had been heavily biased towards its own rule and dominance in the Islamic world. What is of certainty are the Muslims fighting in order to establish dominance in the Spanish Iberian Peninsula. Over a period of just over 500 years (711-1236) Islamised Berber people (also Jews and Christians who had been converted into Islam) established the Emirate of Cordoba in most of the Iberian Peninsula. This Emirate later became the 'Caliphate of Cordoba' which had been a prosperous Islamic state --- that was, until its gradual demise by the Spanish-Christian re-occupation.[285]

---

[283] "Ṭāriq ibn Ziyād | Muslim general | Britannica.com." https://www.britannica.com/biography/Tariq-ibn-Ziyad. Accessed 9 Feb. 2018.
[284] "The Jews that opened the gates of Toledo | Judaism and Islam ...." 10 Oct. 2012, http://www.judaism-islam.com/jews-opene-the-gates-of-toledo/. Accessed 9 Feb. 2018.
[285] "CULTURAL FLOURISHING IN TENTH CENTURY MUSLIM SPAIN ...." 17 Dec. 2008, https://repository.library.georgetown.edu/bitstream/handle/10822/553279/allenmarilyn.pdf;sequence=1. Accessed 9 Feb. 2018.

During the ensuing wars with the Christians, the Muslims in Spain had eventually been left with a much smaller area in the South of Spain; this area being named 'The Emirate of Granada'.[286] This small emirate had eventually been completely destroyed by the Christians who forced the Muslims and Jews to either: convert; deport; or, die.

Over these periods, Jews had intermittent golden eras under both Christian and Muslim rule --- that was, until the final execution of the edict of expulsion of the Jews from Spain in the year 1492 by King Ferdinand and Queen Isabella.[287]

During these periods --- and until Judaism's final decline in the Iberian-Peninsula --- Jewish thought, and along with it the centre of Jewish philosophy in the world, had shifted from Babylonia to Spain (largely due to the fact that during the Abbasid Caliphate, Judaism had shrunk dramatically in Babylonia).

The life pattern for Jews in Spain had been typical of Diasporic Jewish life throughout history --- a cyclical period of Jewish prosperity and economic domination; eventually leading to: jealousy; animosity; anger, and retribution from the non-Jewish population. This was then followed by Jewish immigration to more tolerant environments. Jews had been moving between Muslim rulers, into the Christian world of Europe; and then back into Islamic areas within Spain (depending on the reigning rulers' level of tolerance toward Jews).

The most notable Jew who rose to prominence in Islamic Spain was Hasdai Ibn Shaprut[288] --- the physician and a minister of the 'Caliph', Abd ar-Rahman III (912-961 CE) and his son 'Caliph Al-Hakam II'. Another Jew by the name of Joseph Ibn Naghrela[289] had also become a vizier in the Emirate of Granada. His recorded crucifixion, as well as the massacre of Jews in Granada committed by a Muslim mob in the year 1066, is yet again a reminder of the Jewish people's cycle of economic success, followed by envy and anger from the non-Jewish population; ending in disaster.[290]

Gilbert[291] quotes historian Andrew Bostom's suggestion to cite the Muslim poet 'Abu Ishaq', who's poems justify the killing of Jews. Bernard Lewis[292] also quotes Abu Ishaq's poem, which describes the feelings that common Muslims felt toward the Jewish people's prosperity when juxtaposed with the Muslim populations' obscurity.

'Do not consider it a breach of faith to kill them, the breach of faith would be to let them carry on. They have violated our covenant with them, so how can you be held guilty against violators? How can we have any impact when we are obscure and they are prominent? Now we are humble, beside them, as if we were wrong and they were right! '[293] The Caliph's general protection for Jews had its limits, and had failed this time around; as the anger of the Muslim mob had to be vented away from the Caliph's Muslim elite administrators. A horrible massacre of Jews occurred in Granada.

---

[286] "Emirate of Granada - Wikipedia." https://en.wikipedia.org/wiki/Emirate_of_Granada. Accessed 9 Feb. 2018.
[287] "The Edict of Expulsion of the Jews - 1492 Spain." http://www.sephardicstudies.org/decree.html. Accessed 9 Feb. 2018.
[288] "The Caliph's Favorite." https://oi.uchicago.edu/sites/oi.uchicago.edu/files/uploads/shared/docs/the_caliph's_favorite.pdf. Accessed 9 Feb. 2018.
[289] "1066 Granada massacre - Wikipedia." https://en.wikipedia.org/wiki/1066_Granada_massacre. Accessed 9 Feb. 2018.
[290] ibid
[291] Martin Gilbert 'In Ishmael's house' 2010 page 51
[292] Bernard Lewis 'The Jews of Islam' 1987
[293] Ibid 44-45

The most prominent figure in Jewish philosophy within the Spanish Islam era is Rabbi Moshe ben Maimon[294] (Maimonides 1135-1204). Maimonides' family fled the Almohad Muslim dynasty of Spain into Morocco; as during the decline of Muslim rule in Spain, many of the Jews and Muslims had faced terrible persecutions and forceful conversions by the Christian advancing conquerors. As a young man, Maimonides then fled to Egypt due to Muslim persecution of Jews in Morocco.

Maimonides is revered among Judaic Rabbinate. So much so that a popularized saying had been created in his honour 'From Moses to Moses, no one rose like Moses'.[295] This saying elevated his influence upon Jewish philosophical thought to the level of Biblical Moses. He is also featured in Arabic literature, under his Arabic name, 'Abu Imran Musa bin Maimun bin Ubaidullah al-Qurtubi'.[296] Maimonides is also famed for being the personal physician of Egypt's most famous Sultan 'The Great Saladin'.[297] The most revered Muslim Sultan who: fought; defeated; and expelled, the Christian Crusaders from Jerusalem and Palestine. Beside Maimonides' day-to-day duties to the Great Saladin himself, and the Sultan's family, Maimonides had been required to treat many prominent Islamic officials of Cairo. His own testimony to a friend about his stressful life makes one appreciate his numerous achievements in developing Jewish thought.

'My advice is that you should not risk it. What advantage would you have in coming here, except that you would see me for a few minutes? If you want to have a private audience with me and discuss matters of wisdom, don't even hope for one hour during the day or the night. I will write you my daily schedule: I live in Fostat, and the Sultan lives in Cairo. The distance between them is 4000 cubits [a mile and a half]. My duties to the Sultan are very heavy. I must see him every morning to check on his health. If one day he doesn't feel well, or one of the princes or the women of his harem doesn't feel well, I cannot leave Cairo that day.

It often happens that there is an officer or two who needs me, and I have to attend to healing them all day. Therefore, as a rule, I am in Cairo early each day, and even if nothing unusual happens, by the time I come back to Fostat, half the day is gone. Under no circumstances do I come earlier, and I am ravenously hungry by then. When I come home, my foyer is always full of people – Jews and non-Jews, important people and not, judges and policemen, people who love me and people who hate me, a mixture of people, all of whom have been waiting for me to come home.

I get off of my donkey, wash my hands, and go out into the hall to see them. I apologize and ask that they should be kind enough to give me a few minutes to eat. That is the only meal I take in twenty-four hours. Then I go out to heal them, write them prescriptions and instructions for treating their problems. Patients go in and out until nightfall, and sometimes – I swear to you by the Torah – it is two hours into the night before they are all gone. I talk to them and prescribe for them even while lying down on my back from exhaustion. And when night begins, I am so weak, I cannot even talk anymore. Because of all this, no Jew can come and speak with me in wisdom or have a private audience with me because I have no time, except on Shabbat. On Shabbat, the whole congregation, or at least the majority of it, comes to my house

---

[294] "Moses Maimonides | Jewish philosopher, scholar, and physician ...." https://www.britannica.com/biography/Moses-Maimonides. Accessed 9 Feb. 2018.
[295] "Tzav 5763-2003 | Rabbi Buchwald's Weekly Torah Message." 17 Mar. 2003, http://rabbibuchwald.njop.org/2003/03/17/tzav-5763-2003/. Accessed 9 Feb. 2018.
[296] ibid
[297] "Saladin - Facts & Summary - HISTORY.com." http://www.history.com/topics/saladin. Accessed 9 Feb. 2018.

after morning services, and I instruct the members of the community as to what they should do during the entire week. We learn together in a weak fashion until the afternoon. Then they all go home. Some of them come back and I teach more deeply between the afternoon and evening prayers. That is my daily schedule. And I've only told you a little of what you would see if you would come.'[298]

Apart from the 'Mishneh Torah' on Jewish laws, which is his most acclaimed literary work to have been contributed to Judaic thought, Maimonides is the author of numerous well thought-out books that comment on Judaism. Maimonides is also the author of 10 medical treatises about: asthma; health regimen; toxicology; medicines, and other medical issues.

Although some of Maimonides principles on theological philosophy will never appeal to a modern secular person --- such as his 13 principles of faith --- some of his philosophies actually make complete sense, as they are formed by pairing Jewish theology with Aristotelian logic.

Maimonides claimed that any person could become a prophet --- that being so had not been exclusive to Jews; and that it is in fact the purpose of the human race. He clearly pointed to the fact that humanity's efforts to better itself involves acquiring prophetic abilities of prediction. The prediction of weather patterns and cataclysmic events --- such as tsunamis and volcanic eruptions --- in order to prevent loss of life is an example of said human desire to predict the future in a prophetic manner.

An interesting personal belief/prophecy of Maimonides had been his belief in the Biblical prophecy of the resurrection of Zion to its former state; the state of Israel. A belief that had been realized about 744 years after his death.

Another one of his philosophical assertions had been that 'evil is simply the absence of good', since God had only created good and had no role in the creation of evil --- something mainly created by humans. Maimonides suggested that learning to ignore one's bodily urges is the true way to prevent the creation of evil. This is a colossal statement as it is tangible, and has been showcased in the sense that the root cause for much suffering in the world is due to: greed; jealousy; and gluttony, that manifests in people's hearts and leads to corruption and the commitment of evil deeds.

Maimonides had often quoted, and referred to, the teachings of the Greek philosopher Aristotle; as well as the teachings of Muslim philosophers Al-Farabi and Avicenna. Some of the criticism of Maimonides' philosophy, by modern philosophers, is warranted.[299] It should however be fair to assess people's ideas in relation to the contemporary philosophers and surrounding circumstances at the time; so as to appreciate their greatness, as well as the excellent practicality of their theories.

Maimonides' view about the achievements of Jewish people in business and intellect was that the surrounding non-Jewish environment grossly underestimated the hard work and personal sacrifice made by Jews in order to attain their desired accomplishments. This statement had been practically manifested in his own life --- as was described in the above quoted letter to his friend, which demonstrates his own extreme hard work.

Humility and modesty is also highlighted throughout his works, which include medical advice about moderation with food intake and leading a balanced life. These virtues are difficult to master, as we understand all too well with regards to the temptations of the modern world and the current obesity epidemic we are all experiencing.

---

[298] http://www.jewishhistory.org/maimonides-letter-to-a-friend/ (accessed May 2016)
[299] http://plato.stanford.edu/entries/maimonides/ (accessed May 2016)

In his book 'Guide for the perplexed',[300] which is based on Talmud teachings, Maimonides demonstrates unusual insights when describing the world at the moment of creation as being no bigger than a grain of mustard that had been infinitely stretched --- an idea that had been laughable at the time, but was eventually proven true in theories of modern-era physics led by scientists such as Albert Einstein.

His published guide to philanthropy among the community is also commendable, and may be a worthwhile read for people who engage in philanthropy. Based on all his: work; insights; predictions; and lifestyle concepts, Maimonides should be considered as an all-time intellectual great --- not only by Jewish people, but by humanity in general.

Many modern ethnic-Jews, such as Mark Zuckerberg, subconsciously follow Maimonides' ways of balance and modesty --- their riches, and power, do not seem to blind them. They wear the same gray shirt every-day; and their material possessions are moderate (in comparison to their vast wealth). They look more toward improving humanity in its struggle through the great challenge of life.

Another intellectual great to have left a mark on Judaic history had existed during the Spanish Golden Age. Said intellectual is none other than Rabbi Moses ben Nachman (1194-1270), "Nachmanides".[301] A: philosopher; physician; Talmudic scholar, and Kabbalist --- this time on the Christian side of Spain.

Apart from his own interpretations of the Torah being used daily by modern Jewish Talmudic scholars, he is of fame regarding the 'Disputation of Barcelona' [302](July 20-24 1263) which had been imposed on him by the Christian King James I of Aragon upon the request and advise of Pablo Christiani; a Dominican Friar of the Church who had originally been a Jew, but had converted to Christianity. Christiani had been one of those ethnically-Jewish anti-Semites who pop up every now and again in history --- usually with some megalomaniac tendencies.

Christiani had convinced the Spanish King that he could debate the highest Jewish Rabbinical authority and prove, based on Jewish literature of the Torah and Talmud, that Jesus was the Messiah who had already arrived; in effect proving, without any doubt, that Christianity was the true faith to follow --- not Judaism.

Although both sides had complete freedom of speech, it was obviously an onerous task on Nachmanides to avoid offending the Spanish Christians. The results of this debate are contested between Christians and Jews to this day.[303]

Nachmanides had nevertheless been punished by the King, and exiled for 2 years. He departed to Palestine which had, at the time, been under the rule of the Mamluk Sultanate. His forced exile to Palestine fell upon him at his advanced age of 70. He passed away in Palestine six years later.

About two hundred years before the Nachmanides' debate, Spanish Christians had been re-conquering Spain from Muslims. During this time, the Spanish Kings had actively saught the co-operation of Jews; and so, tolerated them. King Alfonso VII had even entrusted Judah

---

[300] "THE GUIDE FOR THE PERPLEXED BY MOSES MAIMONIDES." http://www.hermetics.org/pdf/sacred/The_Guide_for_the_Perplexed.pdf. Accessed 9 Feb. 2018.
[301] "Nachmanides - Wikipedia." https://en.wikipedia.org/wiki/Nachmanides. Accessed 9 Feb. 2018.
[302] "Disputation of Barcelona - Wikipedia." https://en.wikipedia.org/wiki/Disputation_of_Barcelona. Accessed 9 Feb. 2018.
[303] http://www.jewishvirtuallibrary.org/jsource/judaica/ejud_0002_0003_0_02023.html (accessed May 2016)

ben Joseph ibn Ezra with the role of a court chamberlain.[304] Rich Jews from Muslim territories had been enticed to move over to Christian dominated areas, and help fight against Muslims. Muslims had lost territories under increasing pressure from their Christian neighbors.

After King Alfonso's death, and the Catholic church's resumption of crusades, Jews and Muslims had experienced massacres, conversions, and expulsions. The church had formed a supervising body to make sure the converted were faithful only to catholicism. This body, notoriously known as the 'Spanish Inquisition',[305] had been responsible for torturing and murdering innocent victims.

By the year 1492, under the rule of King Ferdinand and Queen Isabella, Spain had expelled all Jews from their Kingdom. By the year 1502, all remaining Muslims had also been expelled. All along these terrible periods, until days before the expulsion, Jewish people had been active participants of the Spanish economy.

According to Jewish sources, Rabbi Don Isaac Abarbanel[306] (who had been the leader of the Jewish community at the time) attempted to convince King Ferdinand to cancel the edict of expulsion by offering him a substantial amount of money --- an offer that had been turned down.

The expulsion from Spain had dispersed Spanish Jewry across Europe, the Middle-East, and North Africa. The bulk of the Jewish population had fled to North Africa (mainly Morocco, which had been close by). Substantial numbers had fared by sea to modern-day Turkey/Greece --- areas which had been under the Ottoman Empire at the time. Others had continued further up the European continent, landing in countries like Poland and Lithuania; mingling within growing Ashkenazi-Jewish communities in Eastern-Europe.

There are many surnames within Ashkenazi-Jewish populations --- such as: Hasdan; Amoils; Shaprut, and Peretz --- that are a testimony to their Spanish Jewry origins. The current Israeli prime minister --- Mr. Benjamin Netanyahu --- also claims that his family (who come from Poland) had some Spanish Jewish roots. His father, Professor Benzion Netanyahu, had dedicated most of his research to investigating what the state of affairs for Spanish Jewry during the time of the inquisition had been.

The Jewish Kingdom of Khazaria

There is very little and confusing information about this Kingdom in historical records.[307]
What is known, however, is that between the 9th and 11th century --- in and around today's modern Ukraine --- the rulers of a Kingdom mainly composed of Turkic people, may have adopted the Jewish religion for reasons of convenience; to create a neutral area between Christian and Muslim territories . . . thus promoting trade. They seem to have held some balance of power in the region between the rising Islamic Caliphate, and the Byzantines --- that is, until their eventual collapse into a Christian-Orthodox alliance of the Rus and Byzantines. This relatively poorly recorded and miniscule part of Judaic history has been used

---

[304] "Judah ben Joseph ibn Ezra - Revolvy."
http://www.revolvy.com/main/index.php?s=Judah%20ben%20Joseph%20ibn%20Ezra. Accessed 9 Feb. 2018.
[305] "Spanish Inquisition - New World Encyclopedia." 15 Oct. 2015,
http://www.newworldencyclopedia.org/entry/Spanish_Inquisition. Accessed 9 Feb. 2018.
[306] "Rabbi Don Isaac Abarbanel - Jewish Virtual Library." http://www.jewishvirtuallibrary.org/rabbi-don-isaac-abarbanel. Accessed 9 Feb. 2018.
[307] https://www.jewishvirtuallibrary.org/jsource/Judaism/khazars.html (accessed April 2016)

by anti-Semitic Islamists in their attempts to discredit the Jewish peoples' origins and historical claim to Israel.[308]

In this chapter, it has been demonstrated that the Jewish people --- who had become a persecuted minority locked within the power struggle between Christianity and Islam --- had still been true to their beliefs. They had worked hard to expand their philosophical ideas based on the Torah and Talmud; and whenever conditions had been favourable, they had managed to rise to wealth and prominence --- contributing to their environment as a result.

By producing some of the all-time best commentaries and organization of the Talmud, Rabbi Maimonides has shown all the hard intellectual work and effort that Jewish people have exhibited, over the centuries.

It has also been shown that Jewish people had a tremendous belief that one day there would be a resurrection of Zion in its own ancestral land; and that Jews would once again become masters of their own destiny --- not subject to the whims of Muslim or Christian rulers. A belief that eventually became a reality in 1948, with the independence of the state of Israel.

---

[308] "The Khazar Myth and the New Anti-Semitism | The Jewish Press ...." 9 May. 2007, http://www.jewishpress.com/indepth/front-page/the-khazar-myth-and-the-new-anti-semitism/2007/05/09/. Accessed 26 Feb. 2018.

Chapter 8

In Christian Europe of the Middle-Ages

Summary: This chapter will follow the historical facts about the formation of Ashkenazi-Judaism in Europe (mainly in lands which are part of modern France and Germany). In these lands, Jews' creative spirit had enabled them to develop the Yiddish language; a language which is based on the German language, mixed with some Hebrew words. In this chapter, it will become apparent why material wealth had become such an important issue for the Jewish people; and why some Jews had an advantage over the general population in creating material wealth. The poor and destitute had driven the expansion of Judaism into Eastern-Europe as a place of refuge and economic opportunity.

The establishment of Jews in inner continental Europe

We have already established that in the first centuries of the common era, substantial numbers of Jews had been citizens of the Roman-Empire; while some large Jewish populations had lived in Spain and France.

Sometime during the end of the 6th century CE, the Visigothic royal family --- who had ruled these lands --- converted to Christianity. Once this happened, the fate of Jews in Spain had changed dramatically.

It had begun with edict no. 613, issued by King Sisebut in the early part of the 7th century ---- ordering the expulsion of Jews who would not convert to Christianity.[309] It is estimated that many Jews had fled to the neighbouring territories of Gaul (nowadays France) and North-Africa; while many others had converted, but remained Jewish in secret. The anti-Jewish policies of Christian Visigothic Spain had remained for nearly a 100 years until the Islamic conquest of the Iberian-Peninsula in 711 CE.

When King Charlemagne[310] (768 CE --- 814 CE) rose to power and unified the collapsing Western Roman-Empire with German territories; Italian-Jews were able to migrate from Northern-Italy into German territories, safely. Jews had lived relatively peaceful lives under King Charlemagne; who became Emperor of French, German, and Italian territories.[311]

King Charlemagne's reign is considered to be successful and prosperous for its time. King Charlemagne had managed to block the Arab invasions into Europe from Northern-Spain, and the Mediterranean Sea (the daring invasion of the Abbasid Caliphate off Italy's Southern shores).[312] He made sweeping education and administration reforms of his Frankish-Empire.

---

[309] ""The Perfidy of the Jews": Visigothic Law and the Catholic Public Sphere." https://www.pdx.edu/honors/sites/www.pdx.edu.honors/files/11.%20Phillips%20Essay.pdf. Accessed 10 Feb. 2018.
[310] "Charlemagne - Facts & Summary - HISTORY.com." http://www.history.com/topics/charlemagne. Accessed 10 Feb. 2018.
[311] "CHARLEMAGNE - Jewish Encyclopedia." http://www.jewishencyclopedia.com/articles/4250-charlemagne. Accessed 10 Feb. 2018.
[312] "How The Battle Of Tours Prevented a Muslim Invasion of Europe ...." 11 Oct. 2016, https://owlcation.com/humanities/Muslim-Invasions-The-Battle-Of-Tours. Accessed 10 Feb. 2018.

It is historically recorded that King Charlemagne had used Jews as diplomats. He had sent said Jewish diplomats to his enemy --- the Islamic Caliph Harun al Rashid in Baghdad.[313] Jews had been allowed to move freely in the Frankish-Empire and employ their business activities (which had mainly been trading, as most other manufacturing and artisan trades were traditionally exclusive to Christian populations who had still been very hostile towards Jews).

A major development for Jews' at that time had been the Church's prohibition of usury by Christians. This prohibition had led to Jewish control of this despised, yet needed, financial service. Jews, who had been religiously hated, were sought after for this essential money lending financial service.[314]

Over the next two centuries, the Jewish population had grown considerably, and large communities were formed in German cities such as: Mainz; Worms; Speyer; Regensburg, and Cologne. Other smaller communities were formed in many other small towns. This had been the start of, what is today known as, the European Ashkenazi-Jewish community.[315]

The Mayence: Torah; Talmud; and Halacha centre, had been established in Mainz. Rabbi Gershom ben Judah[316] also Known as 'Our Rabbi Gershom light of the exile', is considered to be the most influential Rabbi from that era. Apart from his religious contributions to Jewish studies, he is mostly remembered for his family-law rulings against polygeny; as well as the requirement for the mutual consent of both parties in a marriage when filing for a divorce --- rulings which had a considerable effect on Judaic communities in the diaspora.

Nowadays, it is considered by some genetic studies that during this period in history there had been a substantial amount of German converts to Judaism[317] (most probably women that had been attracted to the Judaic way of family life and/or the financial edge that some male Jewish traders could provide).

Today, within many Jewish communities, there are many fair-skinned Ashkenazi-Jews with bright-coloured eyes. Ashkenazi women suffer from illnesses which are prevalent amongst Northern-European women; illnesses such as breast cancer and skin cancer.[318] These phenotype characteristics strengthen the argument that there had been genetic additions to the original Jewish community in Northern-Europe. For over more than a thousand years, there must have been a substantial back and forth flow of genes between the Jewish and German population (whether it had been willingly or forcefully). A fact that is not discussed much. There are also quite a few Germans who phenotypically resemble Middle-Eastern individuals.

---

[313] "Harun and Charlemagne - The Baldwin Project." http://www.mainlesson.com/display.php?author=audisio&book=harun&story=charlemagne. Accessed 10 Feb. 2018.
[314] "Jews and Finance | My Jewish Learning." https://www.myjewishlearning.com/article/usury-and-moneylending-in-judaism/. Accessed 10 Feb. 2018.
[315] "Who Are Ashkenazi Jews? | My Jewish Learning." https://www.myjewishlearning.com/article/who-are-ashkenazi-jews/. Accessed 10 Feb. 2018.
[316] "GERSHOM BEN JUDAH - JewishEncyclopedia.com." http://www.jewishencyclopedia.com/articles/6615-gershom-ben-judah. Accessed 10 Feb. 2018.
[317] "DNA research sheds light on ancestry of Ashkenazi Jews - ScienceDaily." 8 Oct. 2013, https://www.sciencedaily.com/releases/2013/10/131008112539.htm. Accessed 10 Feb. 2018.
[318] "Ashkenazi Jews and Breast Cancer: The Consequences of Linking ...." https://www.ncbi.nlm.nih.gov/pmc/articles/PMC1751808/. Accessed 10 Feb. 2018.

The community life of Jews in Christian-Europe

In order to further understand the development of Judaic character in Europe, it is of import to compare and contrast the Jewish community's way of life, with the lifestyle of the general population at the time.

The Judaic laws of Shabbat, as well as life around the synagogue, had compelled Jews to live in closely-knit communities amongst the general population. Jewish homes were built around the synagogue, so as to allow easy access by foot on Shabbat; as well as during the dawn and dusk prayers. The convenience of the synagogue was further enhanced when Jews had been confined to certain areas called ghettos (by order of the Christian rulers).[319]

These living conditions had ensured that the Jewish population would only mingle with the general population during business hours throughout the day, and generally on strict business terms only. This type of limited interaction with the general population would always distinguish the Jewish population from their neighbours, and had restricted assimilation. Further than that, the Judaic dress code[320] had been very different to the general population's; as men always had to wear the head cover, wear a tzitzit, and grow beards --- while women always wore headscarves. They had also spoken in Yiddish while amongst themselves[321] --- unique language being the product of the German language mixed with Hebrew.

Aren't these practices similar to the immigrant Islamic communities in modern-day Europe? For millennia, Jews had appeared different; and behaved differently, than the general population. Always to be perceived and regarded as strangers and foreigners in their place of birth. Hardly to be assimilated under normal circumstances.

Then there had been the differences between the daily lifestyle of the Jewish population compared to that of the general population. Jewish men would wake up early in the morning for prayers --- a religious duty that dictates early morning rise. Prayers had always been conducted within a group setting (usually led by the Rabbi). This would stimulate the body and mind in the early hours of the day, and awaken the individual so as to prepare them for the day of work ahead. Then, the men would return home to have breakfast with their families; and later, go to work (or study). What were the occupations of Jewish men? We know that they had normally traded goods. If a person did not work, he was expected to study Torah and Talmud in-and-around the synagogue; and strive to become a Rabbi. Therefore, an individual would either be a merchant of a kind; or, a Torah and Talmud scholar --- never to be idle, or wander around looking for mischief.

What are the skills needed for these occupations? To be a good merchant, or financier, one needs multiple skills --- excellent and energetic verbal communication, combined with convincing skills to: describe; market; sell; and buy products. Energetic behaviour and stamina, in order to source merchandise at a good price from others. A good organiser, whom can ensure the delivery of goods to places where they are accessible to customers at a good price. Good numerical skills to calculate costs and selling price, in order to make decent profit. Good assessment of risks, so as to prevent the loss of money. A good sense of the customer;

---

[319] "Ghettos - United States Holocaust Memorial Museum." https://www.ushmm.org/wlc/en/article.php?ModuleId=10005059. Accessed 10 Feb. 2018.
[320] "Jewish Dress Code Based on Torah Value of Modesty | United with ...." 15 Mar. 2015, https://unitedwithisrael.org/jewish-dress-code-based-on-torah-value-of-modesty/. Accessed 10 Feb. 2018.
[321] "Origins of Yiddish - Santa Fe Institute." https://www.santafe.edu/~johnson/articles.yiddish.html. Accessed 10 Feb. 2018.

his physical and psychological needs, and ways of servicing those needs profitably. If scrutinized carefully, it can be realized that the work done by a merchant is largely work that stimulates the mind. The physical aspect of this work can easily be achieved by hiring labour at a low cost.

What about being a good scholar and a spiritual man? There is no doubt that the skills needed here are also mind-based. A sharp memory and a quick processing ability of visual and verbal communication. Development of good logic to interpret illogical scenarios, so that they make sense. Good imagination and convincing skills are also needed, as well as psychological skills. A wide understanding of life and philosophical views, with good argumentative skills to impart confidence on the students and the community, is also a necessity.

Once the day of work had been over, a man was expected to attend the evening prayers; then go to his family for supper, and attend to his wife and children. Men and Women were expected to marry at an early age, and create as many children as they could --- a compulsory religious deed. The entirety of Jewish life had revolved around: the family; the community; learning, and trading. Hanging around, with no occupation; drinking in public places with friends and strangers, or looking for mischief, was never the Jewish way.

Having fun was always around religious festivals and plenty of community events such as Bar-Mitzvahs, weddings, and Brises (a deed and duty of male circumcision which symbolises being a Jew --- according to the religious belief of Abraham's covenant with God). There, men could have some fun with other community members, and drink some alcohol (in moderation).

This type of life had prevented mischief. It was very rare to find a Jew who had committed crimes of: murder; robbery; theft; rape, or any other negligent act, due to a drunken state of mind or financial desperation. Once again, American author Mark Twain's observations on the Jews in Austria comes in handy when attempting to understand the lifestyle of previous European-Jews. Twain continues with the following description:

'The Jew is not a disturber of the peace of any country. Even his enemies will concede that. He is not a loafer, he is not a sot, he is not noisy, he is not a brawler nor a rioter, he is not quarrelsome. In the statistics of crime his presence is conspicuously rare - in all countries. With murder and other crimes of violence he has but little to do: he is a stranger to the hangman. In the police court's daily long roll of "assaults" and "drunk and disorderlies" his name seldom appears. That the Jewish home is a home in the truest sense is a fact which no one will dispute. The family is knitted together by the strongest affections; its members show each other every due respect; and reverence for the elders is an inviolate law of the house. The Jew is not a burden on the charities of the state nor of the city; these could cease from their functions without affecting him.

When he is well enough, he works; when he is incapacitated, his own people take care of him. And not in a poor and stingy way, but with a fine and large benevolence. His race is entitled to be called the most benevolent of all the races of men. A Jewish beggar is not impossible, perhaps; such a thing may exist, but there are few men that can say they have seen that spectacle. The Jew has been staged in many uncomplimentary forms, but, so far as I know, no dramatist has done him the injustice to stage him as a beggar. Whenever a Jew has real need to beg, his people save him from the necessity of doing it. The charitable institutions of the Jews are supported by Jewish money, and amply. The Jews make no noise about it; it is done quietly; they do not nag and pester and harass us for contributions; they give us peace, and set us an example - an example which we have not found ourselves able to follow; for by nature we are not free givers, and have to be patiently and persistently hunted down in the interest of the unfortunate. These facts are all on the credit side of the proposition that the Jew is a good and orderly citizen. Summed up, they certify that he is quiet, peaceable, industrious, unaddicted to high crimes and brutal dispositions; that his family life is commendable; that he is not a burden upon public charities; that he is not a beggar; that in benevolence he is above the reach of competition. These are the very quintessentials of good citizenship. If you can add that he is as honest as the average of his neighbors - But I think that question is affirmatively answered by the fact that he is a successful businessman.'

Mark Twain's accounts are somewhat different in character than accounts of the Judaic nations during the Judaic-Roman wars of the 1st century CE. What had happened to the warring Jewish nation of antiquity? The nation that had always quarreled with their Greek and Roman oppressors --- the religious fanatics who had been warring between themselves in an uncompromising fashion during the Jewish-Roman wars in the Middle-East. Had the Jewish character changed in Europe? Can this change in character be ascertained?

It is not illogical to speculate that the changes this nation had experienced during their time in the diaspora had a lot to do with this shift in character. As a persecuted minority, any physical resistance against an overwhelming force would not only be futile; but might even turn out to be catastrophic. The generations that grew up in those communities were taught to minimise antagonism, and become non-provocative --- they had been taught to become extremely self-controlled, and keep any form of anger and resistance within themselves. Individuals that could not restrain themselves would have perished in an unforgiving anti-Semitic environment, and their genes would have been eliminated from the general genetic pool of the community. The long-term psychological effects of this suppressed, aggressive psyche could be debated by psychologists or psychiatrists. What is definitely known is that in contrast to the high IQ that Jews possess (which is disproportionate to that of the general population's IQ); Jews also suffer from phobias, anxieties, and mental illnesses on a much larger scale than the general population. Occurence of depression amongst Jews is nearly 2 fold larger than that of the general population.[322]

If one observes the behaviour of religious Jews, one may find that the quarrel and warring traits of this nation had taken on a different form. The learning and debating of the Torah and Talmud in the Yeshivas can often be aggressive and outspoken. The discussions are heated, and the speed of speech and thinking is astounding. It is as though there will be an eruption of physical violence that never materializes. This is not absolute, however; as, at times, techniques change to various forms of persuasion that will include appeasement and 'soft talk' --- a pledge to reason with the other party. Anything that will persuade the other party to recognise the truth of the opinion presented to them by the ensuing party.

The: cocktail of limitless love of the Torah and Talmud; the deep belief in the correctness of the Jewish way; the self-restraint and passive-aggressive resistance; the quick and sharp mind, to confront life situations --- all these, and probably many other similar traits, have become the weapon of the Jew. Mind-based survival strategies that had allowed them to survive as a community, and surpass their hostile environment. Beyond the physical, the Jew had become a war machine of business, finance, and intellect --- leaving very little chance for his surrounding non-Jewish environment to compete.

The pattern of this economic dominance had always culminated in an eventual apparent victory that --- during times of general hardship --- had led the general population to blame the better-off Judaic community for sinister and conspiratory conduct. The conspiracy theories

---

[322] "Higher Rate of Depression Found Among Jewish Men : Psychology: In ...." 23 May. 1995, http://articles.latimes.com/1995-05-23/news/mn-5096_1_jewish-men. Accessed 26 Feb. 2018.

and allegations were of all kind in manner, and will be discussed in chapter 14, which is about anti-Semitism.

Jewish life in Europe in the Middle-Ages became a pattern of relatively quiet periods, whereby the Judaic community would progress and prosper . . . followed by violent periods that brought death, destruction, and expulsion. The 'wandering Jew' criss-crossed Europe, back and forth --- always building new communities in order to replace the previously destroyed ones.

To survive this kind of 'lifestyle', and minimise destruction and expulsion, Jewish communities and individuals were in desperate need of money. Money, at times, would buy the feudal ruler's protection from the mob (in whichever the territory or country they had lived in). Money would also serve them while in refuge to another territory or country.

Being a poor Jewish family would spell death in the future. Wealth had been a highly-needed status --- this had probably turned into an obsession within some of the members of the community (since material wealth meant the difference between life and death). The Christian crusades period during the early part of the second millennia clearly proved this. Jews were put to a real test of life and death. Jewish communities had been extorted by being forced to contribute money to crusaders --- the ones who could not pay had received severe punishment; and, at times, were even put to death.

The Christian crusades and their impact on European-Jews

One of the most destructive periods in the history of the Judaic diaspora is the time of the Christian crusades to capture Jerusalem from the Islamic occupation.[323] The crusades had been sanctioned by Pope Urban II[324] --- his declared goal was to restore ownership of Christian holy sites in Palestine.

The crusades had taken place between the years 1096 --- 1291. The call by the Pope to free Christian holy sites in Jerusalem --- coupled with religious promises of indulgence from all personal sins --- had fueled the imagination of the masses of Christian believers who became crusaders and 'willing martyrs'. There had been much hype and stories about the 'second coming of Jesus' once the holy places had been freed from the desecrating Muslims.

This proved to be a real problem for Jewish communities, as the situation was used by greedy leaders of the crusaders to turn the mob against Jews. They had done this by promoting various religious arguments, such as: the need to first purify Christian lands from the Jewish non-believers who had crucified Christ; the argument that Jews had to have been converted first in order for the crusades to succeed; or, that Jews had been required to contribute financial resources towards crusade efforts.

---

[323] "The First Victims of the First Crusade - The New York Times." 13 Feb. 2015, https://www.nytimes.com/2015/02/15/opinion/sunday/the-first-victims-of-the-first-crusade.html. Accessed 10 Feb. 2018.

[324] "Pope Urban II orders first Crusade - Nov 27, 1095 - HISTORY.com." http://www.history.com/this-day-in-history/pope-urban-ii-orders-first-crusade. Accessed 10 Feb. 2018.

King Henry IV of Germany[325] had issued orders to protect Judaic communities. These orders had not been adhered to under the crusade frenzy. Crusade leaders such as: Peter the Hermit; Count Emicho; and Godfrey of Bouillon, either: massacred; forcefully baptized; or extorted Judaic communities, in events that are historically recorded as the 'Rhineland massacres'.[326]

Jews heading to Eastern-Europe

Following bad times in French and German lands, many Jews had fled to the relatively safe areas of the poor Eastern-European territories of Ukraine and Poland. Under the tolerant rule of Boleslaw III[327], Poland saw a large influx of Jews during the 12th and 13th centuries.

The pattern of the Jewish phenomenon had repeated itself again in Poland. From 966 CE to 1572, Jews were becoming the backbone of the Polish economy. Despite sporadic pogroms and short 'dark periods'; this era is considered to be another 'Jewish Golden Age" for Jews and their Polish hosts.[328] It is historically documented that Jews had been employed by Polish nobility in their mints (as well as in their financial and administrative affairs --- which were designed to control the large Polish peasant society).

Following the Spanish expulsion of Jews in 1492 --- as well as an increase in social and economic pressure on German-Judaic communities --- Poland, which had merged with Lithuania, had become a magnet for the immigration of European Jewry . By the year 1500, it had become the center of world Jewry.

Since the Polish nobility had been known to be protective of the Judaic communities (due to the instrumental role Jews had played in the enrichment of the ruling Polish elite) the massive population of poor Polish peasantry --- led by the Catholic Church --- had became increasingly angry and hostile towards Jews.

The most prosperous and peaceful period for Jews in Poland had been during the 14th century under King Casimir III --- he had exempt Jews from the death penalty.[329] The 15th century under King Sigismund I (followed by his son Sigismund II) had also been a good time for Jews in Poland. During the 14th century, the well-being of Jews had been a kind of 'mixed bag'

---

[325] "Henry IV | Holy Roman emperor | Britannica.com." https://www.britannica.com/biography/Henry-IV-Holy-Roman-emperor. Accessed 10 Feb. 2018.
[326] "Rhineland massacres - Wikipedia." https://en.wikipedia.org/wiki/Rhineland_massacres. Accessed 10 Feb. 2018.
[327] "Bolesław III | prince of Poland | Britannica.com." https://www.britannica.com/biography/Boleslaw-III. Accessed 10 Feb. 2018.
[328] "History of the Jews in Poland - Wikipedia." https://en.wikipedia.org/wiki/History_of_the_Jews_in_Poland. Accessed 10 Feb. 2018.
[329] "Casimir III of Poland - New World Encyclopedia." http://www.newworldencyclopedia.org/entry/Casimir_III_of_Poland. Accessed 10 Feb. 2018.

situation. Accusations for being the cause of the black plague --- as well as some blood-libels --- had been deployed by priests of the Catholic Church.[330]

Throughout those periods, the Judaic population of Poland had swelled; and, according to some accounts, it had even reached 10% of the Polish population.

The economic success of these Judaic populations under the rule of the Polish nobility (compared to the rest of the peasant Polish population) was again troublesome.

Once the Cossacks[331] had rebelled against the feudal Polish nobility; Jews had been raided, pillaged, and massacred. The Cossacks had regarded them as collaborators with Polish nobility, and part of the oppressive feudal system.

The 'Bogdan Khmelnitsky rebellion'[332] is considered, by many Jewish sources, as the most horrific time for Jews in Poland. Scores of Jewish villages and communities perished; until Polish nobility had managed to quell this rebellion and stop the massacres.

The Cossack rebellions which had followed in the East eventually separated large Eastern territories from Poland. These territories had become part of the emerging Tsarist Russian Empire. The Jewish population had still maintained its importance in Poland for hundreds of years --- that is, until its demise by the invading German army during the second World War (following Hitler and his Nazi regime's plan to exterminate the Jews of Europe).[333]

Apart from historical facts regarding Jewish life in the Middle-Ages, this chapter has explained the duress Jews had been under from living within the Christian environment of Poland. It has highlighted the constant monetary need Jews had (due to their life depending on it). This chapter has also demonstrated how Jewish people would always find ways to employ the mind, be creative, and do business. This improved themselves, as well as the economic situation of the countries that gave them some freedom from persecution. This chapter has also, once again, depicted the cycle of prosperity for Jews (which eventually leads to envy from their environment, resulting in the destruction of their communities --- forcing them to seek refuge elsewhere, and start the economic and community building cycle all over again). The role that the lifestyle of the community had played in building the Jewish character is worthwhile to assess. This will be attempted in the following chapter.

---

[330] "The Catholic Church and the Blood Libel Myth:." http://www.covenant.idc.ac.il/en/vol1/issue2/introvigne.html. Accessed 10 Feb. 2018.
[331] "Cossack uprisings - Wikipedia." https://en.wikipedia.org/wiki/Cossack_uprisings. Accessed 10 Feb. 2018.
[332] "Bohdan Khmelnytsky | Cossack leader | Britannica.com." https://www.britannica.com/biography/Bohdan-Khmelnytsky. Accessed 10 Feb. 2018.
[333] "The Holocaust in Poland - Wikipedia." https://en.wikipedia.org/wiki/The_Holocaust_in_Poland. Accessed 10 Feb. 2018.

Chapter 9

The community way of life, and Jewish character building.

Summary: This chapter will describe the Jewish community's way of life in Europe. Some of the individual characters which had been moulded by this diasporic community lifestyle will be described. The chapter will further enhance one's understanding about Jewish people's resolve to excel in their respective fields of occupation.

The day-to-day life of Jews within their minor communities had been paramount to the development of certain Jewish characteristics (as well as to the development of their intellectual and entrepreneurial spirit). These characteristics have been proven to be effective later on in history, when Jews had been allowed to engage in the study and practice of professions such as: medicine; law; accounting, and the humanities.

The lifestyle of the Jewish community must have changed much over the years, however, the basics of family life --- which had been entrenched within the Torah and Talmud --- had to have remained the same. Many of the family-life customs, and rules of the Torah and Talmud, had been developed over a long period of time --- and some still make sense today.

The Jewish home

Apart from compulsory Jewish symbols (such as the mezuzah, which is supposed to decorate the entrance of the house and protect the house with a written prayer), the traditional Jewish home was to be filled with books. The: Torah; Talmud; other books written by famous Rabbis; prayer books, and utensils for keeping Shabbat (such as the candlesticks and kiddush cups) would all be in a Jewish home.[334] Religious dressing such as Kippot, Tefillin, and Tallit would also be present in a Jewish home (as well as other ornaments which are used within specific festivals such as Hanukkah candelabras).

Within modern Jewish homes, many modern intellectual books will be found (as well as some sophisticated musical instruments --- typically the piano, violin, or clarinet). This love for books may indicate a deep-rooted love for knowledge. Although in antiquity, books had mainly been of religious substance; they had still encompassed ideas about many social and life issues. The Talmud is known for dealing with numerous moral and legal issues. The composition of books in general has changed over the years to include: science and technology; encyclopedias, and even art and culture.

Even though I had been raised in a completely secular home, my personal childhood experience had been of a home library full of books. From the age of five years, my father used to buy me books as birthday presents (mainly books about science and technology, or technical books --- but I also received books about Jewish history and Biblical stories). My home library also had books on psychology and philosophy, as well as 22 thick volumes of the Hebrew encyclopedia. The quest and encouragement for knowledge was always there. I would think that *this* is perhaps the main contributing factor in the building of character within Jewish people --- the drive to learn, and be knowledgeable.

---

[334] "Jewish Home and Community | My Jewish Learning." https://www.myjewishlearning.com/article/jewish-home-community/. Accessed 10 Feb. 2018.

To read books quickly (and properly understand them) requires visual and mental fitness that has been developed over years. There is no doubt that speed reading trains the brain to process and accumulate knowledge in an extremely efficient way. This, overtime, develops a person's capability of imagination. I would claim that the more knowledge a person obtains about various fields in life, the larger their scope for an enhanced imagination becomes. The more developed imagination an individual possess; the more possibilities they will find for solutions to various problems during their lifetime.

Therefore, the home that is empty of knowledge will likely produce people who are empty of knowledge. Same as how a house filled with knowledge will probably produce people filled with knowledge --- simple logic. Activities at home influence a person for their entire life. It is nothing but a natural behaviour to be expected. Nowadays, there is a lot of knowledge accessible on the internet. This may help children who are curious and inclined to learn. However, Judaism had another major center of influence on the members of its community . . . the synagogue (which every respected Jewish community would have built --- usually within the center of the community, so as to allow easy access).

The synagogue

Every Jewish community had a synagogue,[335] and a study place within it named 'Beit Midrash'. Many would also contain a mikvah, for women to partake in ritual baths. The synagogue had been extensively used for prayers, festivals, and gatherings of the community. The community would be led by a Rabbi and his associates; in conjunction with prominent business people.

For generations, religious leaders had been considered as the intellectuals of the community; while business leaders were revered as providers and protectors. At times, Rabbis had also excelled in business, and fulfilled the role of the financial protector of the community. One of the famous stories that demonstrates this is the story of Rabbi Abarbanel; who, according to some historical documentation, had offered money to the Spanish monarchy in exchange for the cancelation of the edict of the expulsion of Jews from Spain in 1492 CE. This offer had eventually been declined following bishop Torquemada's furious words to the Spanish King, King Fernando --- "Are you going to sell your Christian principles for money!? Like Jesus was sold!?". Since Rabbi Abarbanel's offer had been turned down, Jews had to sail off to surrounding countries (such as Portugal and Holland).

Every Jewish community had a body called 'Chevra Kadisha'[336]. This body was responsible for helping Jews who were in need --- people who fell to poverty or sickness, or became needy due to some unfortunate circumstance. Chevra Kadisha is also responsible for burying a Jew with traditional Jewish customs and ceremony. This compulsory body guarantees that Jewish people engage in 'Tzedakah' (Charity) within their communities.[337] Tzedakah is, in essence, the compulsory Jewish deed of helping the poor and other troubled individuals --- one of the pillars of Jewish faith.

Over the centuries, Jewish communities have been very organized. The community had been the center of life; while business had to be conducted with the Christian or Arab neighbours.

---

[335] "BBC - Religions - Judaism: The Synagogue." 13 Aug. 2009, http://www.bbc.co.uk/religion/religions/judaism/worship/synagogue_1.shtml. Accessed 10 Feb. 2018.
[336] "Chevrah Kadisha - Home." http://www.jhbchev.co.za/. Accessed 10 Feb. 2018.
[337] "Tzedakah - Wikipedia." https://en.wikipedia.org/wiki/Tzedakah. Accessed 10 Feb. 2018.

Jewish communities had been small, and were isolated from the general population's environment. This meant that the market for their products and services had existed in their surrounding external environment. But, when a day of work had ended; Jewish men came back to their communities and dealt with community issues.

The community as the center of life

As described earlier, ethnic-Jews in Europe had lived in relatively secluded communities within the larger Christian populations. Since they had been under considerable pressure and stress from their hostile surrounding external environment, there was much need for internal help from members within the community. Solidarity and co-operation between members had to be developed.[338] The smaller communities had many familial relationships between the members. This then also made familial solidarity a factor in the relationship between the community members. Marriages had been arranged based on familial strength or apparent intellectual/economical strength; which meant that it had not been uncommon for a Rabbi's child, to marry a businessman's child (and vice-versa).

The financial success of a member of the community created a lifeline for others in the community. Some religious deeds were geared towards helping a fellow Jew in need --- to save another's life if possible. The success of one member had been the success of *all* members.

This solidarity and co-operation is not, however, present in every single Jewish community. In Jewish communities (like in any other human community) there are feelings of jealousy, coveting, and hate. But perhaps the balance between positive and negative behaviour had been better within Jewish communities (due to the outside pressure on the community from the gentile population).

Over the centuries in Feudal-Europe; It has been documented that Jews had survived expulsion and harm, by paying substantial sums of ransom money to greedy monarchs and nobility. Therefore --- money always had to be made (and lots of it), as it would be the factor that determined life or death for the community.

This meant that within the community, many cohesive forces had been at work. Jews would employ other Jews in the community (which, in many instances, would also be family members). A culture of teamwork and mutual support between the community members was developed. A sense of mutual destiny regarding life and death had been built over many generations.

All this indicates to what is commonly viewed by non-Jews today as the biased support of Jews towards each other in business --- whereas actually, this is simply a culmination of thousands of years of mutual: lives; family connections; and the development of a mutual understanding between the members of small cohesive communities. Even though many Ashkenazi-Jews had originated from different parts of Europe --- where their native spoken languages had differed --- they all held a kind of similar 'hidden behaviour language' (accompanied by the Yiddish language; which had been widely used, up until a couple of generations ago).

---

[338] "Jewish Solidarity: Living in a post-persecution era - Diaspora ...." 19 Aug. 2017, http://www.jpost.com/Jerusalem-Report/Solidarity-The-morning-after-persecution-500776. Accessed 10 Feb. 2018.

I myself have experienced such solidarity and co-operation amongst Jewish students in university. They assist each other in understanding study material, assigning tasks for individuals, and using the ability of stronger members to enhance weaker members' understanding. Eventually, they all do well as a group.

The Jewish entrepreneurial spirit

Shakespeare's play, 'The Merchant of Venice', about Shylock (a Jewish merchant) is quite damning; and in line with anti-Semitic indoctrination. The blatant anti-Semitic portrayal never considered the harsh realities of Jewish life in Christian-Europe, and the need to become an entrepreneur and accumulate wealth. This life pressure on Jews to become entrepreneurs had also been pertinent within the Islamic world. By analysing the Islamic writings of the Persian ibn Khordadbeh,[339] one can learn about Jewish entrepreneurship. He writes about a class of Jewish merchants named Radhanite;[340] who had been trading between the Islamic and Christian world. They had been fluent in: Arabic; Persian; Roman; Slav; Frank (German) and Spanish, and their trade routes had spanned from Spain to China. The Radhanite had been operating up until the 11th century (due to the collapse of the Abbasid Islamic Caliphate by the Mongol and Turkic invasions, as well as the eventual collapse of the Jewish Kingdom of Khazaria --- rendering the trade routes extremely dangerous and non-operational).

The great success that Jews had achieved in various trades (especially in the then new profession of banking) has been shown repeatedly in previous chapters. It should be noted that trade has always been the preferred practice for Jews. When done correctly, it can yield great profits. This is also true regarding some of the first American-Jewish merchants heading to the West-coast of America (such was the Goldwater family; of which, stories regarding their trade activities are recorded).[341]

The storyteller

The other character that supplements the merchant and entrepreneur is the storyteller. Perhaps this character is a precursor to many Jewish people in the entertainment and media industries of today --- including Hollywood itself.

Over the centuries, Jews had been exposed to a vast abundance of stories. From Biblical stories, to Talmudic stories; legends from various eras in their history, to real life situations --- stories that have been passed down the generations, in families and communities.

Many times, a specific person with the ability to tell stories had been assigned by the community; and named 'the Maggid'[342] ('teller' in Hebrew). Some of these people had eventually adopted this name as a surname (when Jews in Europe were forced to assign to themselves surnames).

---

[339] "Book of Roads and Kingdoms (ibn Khordadbeh) - Wikipedia." https://en.wikipedia.org/wiki/Book_of_Roads_and_Kingdoms_(ibn_Khordadbeh). Accessed 10 Feb. 2018.
[340] "The Radhanite Merchants | Brian Gottesman - Academia.edu." http://www.academia.edu/4810020/The_Radhanite_Merchants. Accessed 10 Feb. 2018.
[341] http://www.acjna.org/acjna/articles_detail.aspx?id=426 (accessed April 2016)
[342] "Maggid - Wikipedia." https://en.wikipedia.org/wiki/Maggid. Accessed 10 Feb. 2018.

Every year, Jewish children had been encouraged to listen and tell stories during holiday celebrations; and create a moral for each of the stories they told. The active and successful lives of fellow ethnic-Jews over the years have added enriching stories about all walks of life (including stories about business and academia).

Following those practices, Jews have a rich source of stories to draw from. You will find many who are excellent in telling convincing stories. This storytelling characteristic is an essential component in sales and marketing professions --- which is the core of many businesses. It is also the core of success in the movie industry for instance. It has already been mentioned that hollywood was literally founded by Jews; and many current script writers, producers, and actors are of ethnic-Jewish origin. Much of the content in hollywood is written by ethnic-Jews. The following short-story may again demonstrate, and magnify, what Judaism's biggest concern of all time had been.

The story begins with a rich businessman, who approaches his Rabbi and tells him of a new fortune that he has made. He tells the Rabbi that, with his new found fortune, he wishes to build a fancy house; with a modern and decorated carriage --- but his wife told him not to do so, as he might become the terrible envy of other Jews. He then asks the Rabbi for his opinion. The Rabbi then asks him: "Is there any Jewish Talmudic book that you know well?" The man answers in the negative. The Rabbi then asks him, "Is there any Talmudic chapter that you are well conversed in?" The man, again, answers in the negative. The Rabbi then asks him, "Is there any Talmudic issue within a chapter that you know well and could debate and argue properly?" The man, once more, answers in the negative. The Rabbi then nods his head and tells the businessman . . . "I can not see any reason why other Jews may envy you."

Within true Judaism; *nothing* is more revered than knowledge. Knowledge of the scriptures, and especially the Talmud, is what has been considered supreme. Over thousands of years, Jews have: learned; argued; and debated, the Talmud.

Steadfast, debative and argumentative Nation

In recent years, many business books had been written in order to unveil the underlying foundations for the success of business people. Attempting to discover certain distinguishable character traits of these successful personalities, is a common technique that has been used. This technique can also be used to discover some Jewish characteristics that have been developing over the millennia --- both for the community, and for the individuals within the community.

After learning the history of the Jewish nation --- and gleaning into its culture --- it may be easier to analyse what traits have been built; and how, over time, said traits have served Jews around the world.

We already know that this nation had been a warring one in antiquity. A stubborn-headed nation that believed, unwaveringly, in the correctness of its way of life; and truly believed itself to be 'the chosen nation' of God. As with any acquired trait of stubbornness, following this type of uncompromising belief can be a mixed blessing.

When the Jews had been a substantial minority during the time of the Roman-Empire, this fervent trait unleashed destruction upon them; as many times, these religiously inspired Jewish fanatics had underestimated the sheer size and strength of the Roman-Empire, and blindly believed that their 'God' would deliver them from the Romans.

This fatal mistake had culminated in the large diaspora revolt --- which brought death and destruction to *many* Jews within the Roman-Empire. The Romans' resolution to crush this religion had ended with the destruction of the second Temple; and other attempts to erase all memory of Judaism's existence: the renaming of Judea to 'Palestine' (and Judea's capital city, Jerusalem, to Aelia capitolina); the decree that Jews could not set foot in these places; and the massacre and enslavement of all Jews on the Island of Cyprus, and the province of Cyrene (nowadays Libya).

During the ensuing diaspora life --- when Jews had been subdued and could not even attempt to resist --- this trait of steadfastness to the Jewish faith had served them in the form of mental exercise (while debating the correctness of their religious beliefs --- within themselves, and with other religious denominations). Said debate had also brought groundbreaking ideas to the fore --- concepts relating to the nature of life and Godly powers (resulting in the creation of the Kabbalah, and various mystical theories --- a sort-of pseudo-science).

To this day, Jews are known and famed for their love of argument --- their famous chutzpah[343] (audacity) and debating powers. Children are allowed to ask questions, and challenge their elders. Arguments and counter-arguments are many times accompanied with passionate vocality. The mental challenge is ongoing. Even the most hard-headed and non-conceding person is wisened somewhat.

This character of pride also promotes an uncompromising drive to learn and achieve; and prove mental superiority over other fellow Jews in the community (later on, even over foreigners outside the community).

A brainy nation in the European Middle-Ages

Much has already been discussed about the effects that constant Judaic studies have on the brain. One's environment and physical conditions must also have an effect on brain function and development.

While Europe had experienced an intellectual decline during the Middle-Ages --- due to religious Christian intolerance for intellectual activity which had not been confined to religious standards[344] --- Jews had suffered the most terrible anti-Semitic conduct. However, the Middle-Ages reveal a further development of Judaism as a brain centralized nation.

The confinement in Ghettos within European cities, as well as the ban of Jews from most professions, had resulted in lack of normal physical activities. This led to the invention of the 'Cheder'[345]. A relatively small room whereby children as young as 4 years of age studied Torah under the guidance of a learned adult individual.

The effects of this practice can only be speculated. The children were required to memorize entire sentences and chapters of the Torah --- as well as said sentences' their numerical references. They had to recite these sentences in front of their teacher, and to their

---

[343] "What Is Chutzpah? - And is it good or bad? - Chabad.org." http://www.chabad.org/library/article_cdo/aid/1586271/jewish/Chutzpah.htm. Accessed 10 Feb. 2018.
[344] "The Middle Ages." http://webspace.ship.edu/cgboer/middleages.html. Accessed 10 Feb. 2018.
[345] "Heder - The YIVO Encyclopedia of Jews in Eastern Europe." http://www.yivoencyclopedia.org/article.aspx/Heder. Accessed 10 Feb. 2018.

classmates.[346] A practice that undoubtedly enhances: memory; and verbal and numerical skills. It also enhances group work, as the individual had received help and feedback from the teacher and other children.

The studies would have developed the children's imagination, and mentally transport them into the far and distant lands of the Middle-East (which are riddled with different: human characters; their lives and circumstances; their physical and emotional struggles, and their solutions in overcoming the challenges and obstacles they had faced). The confinement aspect would have compelled the children to escape the 'Cheder' through their imagination.

The studies would have further developed the child's understanding of human nature, and tint their life with philosophical arguments revolving around God, God's laws, and the Jewish purpose of life (which is to follow God's laws). So --- from a young and tender age, children's brains had been developed and conditioned . . . enhancing: memory; imagination, and verbal and numerical skills.

Since the Church had prohibited usury lending, only Jews had been able to lend money to their neighbouring Christians. This had become a Jewish profession, that supplemented the traditional trading activity of Jews. This practice must have also enhanced memory and computational skills.

In the morning, the gates of the Ghettos would open to let Jews enter into town and conduct their commercial activities. Then, before nightfall, Jews had been required to return to the Ghetto until the next morning.

The Ghettos became very crowded spaces; forcing the population to maintain hygienic conditions. Although, hygiene customs had already been embedded within the Jewish religious way of life --- such as the deed (Mitzvah) of washing hands before meals, and of keeping clean during menstruation (as well as the deed of thoroughly cleaning dwellings before Passover and New year, and the deed of being clean and pure before the holy day of Shabbat enters).

None of these customs of cleanliness are recorded in any of the other populations of Western-Europe. Some, like the French, had been notorious for leading a dirty lifestyle. It is documented that during the Black Plague of Europe, Jews were the least affected of all populations[347] --- something which bred many anti-Semitic blood-libels blaming Jews for poisoning Christian populations.[348] Those libels had ignited numerous pogroms and hardships for Jewish communities. Nevertheless, Jewish communities had fared much better than their Christian neighbours against the Black Plague epidemic in Europe.

What I have learnt from my personal encounter with Jewish characters in the diaspora

The following short stories may shed some light on Jews in the diaspora --- how they think, and what they do, can demonstrate their way of life (and the Jewish philosophy that is subconsciously entrenched within them).

---

[346] "Education and Learning | Key Documents of German-Jewish History." http://jewish-history-online.net/topic/education-and-learning. Accessed 10 Feb. 2018.
[347] "Black Death Jewish persecutions - Wikipedia." https://en.wikipedia.org/wiki/Black_Death_Jewish_persecutions. Accessed 11 Feb. 2018.
[348] "the black death and the burning of jews - Oxford Academic." https://academic.oup.com/past/article-pdf/196/1/3/4310993/gtm005.pdf. Accessed 11 Feb. 2018.

There is no doubt that, over the centuries, commerce had been the backbone of financial success for Jews. The following personal short-story may highlight the significance of commerce within the Jewish mind.

Sometime in 1993 (as a young chemical engineer looking for ways to promote myself economically) I heard of a certain Jewish man in his late sixties, Mr. Sam Immelman --- the owner of a large chemical and food company named Royco. I had approached him for a meeting in his offices in Midrand. (a new-and-fancy area just North of Johannesburg).

After arriving to his fancy offices, I was told by his secretary to wait for him; as he would be arriving in the next 15-20 minutes. As I was sitting --- waiting at the second floor, close to the secretary --- she pointed outside to an approaching Jaguar sports car, and informed me that M. Immelman had arrived.

Mr. Immelman entered, greeted me and his secretary, and went into his office. Shortly afterward, I had been instructed to enter his office. Mr. Immelman, seated in his magnificent chair, lit a cigar and began chatting with me. After a short introduction, he asked me what business ideas I had in mind.

I told him that I was thinking of manufacturing a certain needed chemical compound. Mr. Immelman immediately grinned and told me: "Look here, you come from Israel and you have been remodeled" (meaning corrupted). I asked him: "what do you mean by that?" Then, he asked: "where did your grandfather come from, and what had he done for a living?"

I thought for a minute and then answered --- "my grandfather came from Greece, and my father told me that he had been an antique dealer". "Aha", Mr. Immelman answered --- "my ancestors were wood merchants in Eastern-Europe. Traders --- that is who we are. Jewish occupation for generations. Not manufacturers, We buy and sell . . . buy, and sell. This is the Jewish way, we buy and sell products and promote deals. That is what we are good at. Manufacturing is done by others. That is what *they* are good at." He then bragged a bit about his sales force of about 35 salesmen who service the mining industry (as well as about a multi-million dollar food merchandise deal that he and his son, Vivian, were concluding with the American conglomerate, Del Monte).

As he had excused me from his office, he said to me: "Just always remember . . . buy and sell, buy and sell." I can't say that I orthodoxly remembered and applied his advice, but it made me realise something . . . we *all* need to sell something in this world in order to survive. What is more important from this experience, is that traditional Jewish business expertise had been in 'buying and selling' and deal-making --- trade, which requires skills such as marketing and logistics.

The fame of Jewish merchants and business people over the millennia has, at times, been recorded in the most sinister way. As mentioned earlier, Shakespeare's 'Merchant of Venice' portrays the darkest side of the Jewish merchant; and might only be an expression of Shakespeare's own upbringing within his own anti-Semitic English society.

The reality is --- merchants had advanced the world in many untold ways; bringing ideas and technology from far places (at times, in ways that had been extremely perilous to travelers in general).

My own encounter with entrepreneurial Jews in the diaspora

My search for help to finance the manufacturing of my product had landed me on yet another Jewish businessman --- Mr. Wolfowitz. He had owned a company by the name of Chemico.

This time, I was lucky enough to be invited to his home in Hyde park --- a very upmarket suburb in Johannesburg. The house had been surrounded by armed guards with shotguns (since house breaking in this residential affluent area must have been a lucrative activity for criminals).

I had entered the house, and Mr. Wolfowitz' wife attended to me --- guiding me to a lounge full of a collection of old clocks hanging on the walls around. She told me that Mr. Wolfowitz was on his way, asked the maid to serve me some tea, and told me that her husband has just received some innovation prize in Russia. As we heard the bell, she requested that I greet Mr. Wolfowitz. He had arrived, driven by his chauffeur. He seemed to be struggling with his weight --- occupying most of the backseat of his luxury Mercedes car. The Wolfowitz couple seemed very focused on their relationship, as there were no signs that they had any children.

Mr. Wolfowitz had listened to my product idea, and told me that it was too complicated and niche. His advice was to look for something that could be sold to masses of people. As I asked him for his secret to business success, his answer had been: "one always needs to be entrepreneurial". He boasted that, "he did not start one company at a time, but 10 companies at the same time . . . more or less. This way, when the companies reach maturity, the value may be 10 times more than someone who starts 1 company at a time." I could not completely comprehend this strategy, but it seemed to have worked very well for Mr. Wolfowitz.

My encounters with professional scientific Jews

As a pushback to anti-Semitism, Jews' will to prove anti-Semites as being wrong and inferior has been overwhelming. I have listened to stories of Jewish families from Russia, about their experiences during the communist era. In this particular case, the father had been a Professor; with over a 100 patents to his name. The mother had been a school principal. The children were often mocked for being Jewish, and for being short and small. These children were forced to study and achieve, in order to prove that they were smarter than all their contemporaries. This had been a huge effort to silence and humiliate the anti-Semitic non-Jews. So much so that today, the son is a nuclear physicist professor; and the daughter is an accomplished engineer, with a PhD in mechanical engineering.

This is by no means an odd story among Jews in the diaspora. In the era shortly after the enlightenment age (whereby Jewish communities had been emancipated from the ghettos) Germany and Austria were experiencing a massive population explosion of Jewish intellectuals --- a tidal wave, that eventually led to the creation of famous world ethnic-Jewish scientists such as Sigmund Freud and Albert Einstein.

Conclusion

This chapter has further examined how the Jewish way of life had, over time, influenced and built the Jewish character (which is, first and foremost, a family and community oriented type of individual). It is a knowledge-based character --- with a built-in intellectual and entrepreneurial spirit (one which is: persistent; highly communicative; and above all, imaginative). These traits --- which had been nurtured over the years within the Jewish individual and community --- are conducive for intellect and business. The Jewish lifestyle is a family-orientated one --- with very little alcohol consumption, and zero use of any abusive substances. It is a clean type of life, which revolves around: learning; work; family, and the community. It is a life of daily routine --- waking up early, so as to face the day's challenges; and a life of teamwork in studies or business.

Modern living today has removed some of these values within Jewish people. Assimilated ethnic-Jews may have lost some of these values even further. I would think that retaining and restoring some of these values (in a balanced way within a secular lifestyle) is a challenge for secular people today.

Chapter 10

The age of enlightenment, and the emancipation of Jews

Summary: This chapter will explain the emancipation of Jews in Europe, and the intellectual and business opportunities this emancipation process had provided for them. It will also describe how --- following this emancipation process --- the explosive number of Jewish intellectuals that had been generated, left a profound impact on the world at large.

The French revolution,[349] and Napoleon's conquests[350] of Europe, had no doubt been the event to relieve Jews from the oppressive and tyrannical stranglehold of medieval Christian anti-Semitism. The revolution, and Napoleon's conquests, had spread the ideals of equality amongst human beings. These events had also promoted the separation of the Church from the state (as well as the secularization of Europe).[351]

Napoleon's instruction on developing the legal body of laws known as the Napoleonic Code,[352] had the promise of equality for any human being before the law --- no matter his or her religious or ethnic background. For the first time in many centuries, Jews had enjoyed the same legal freedoms that the general Christian population had enjoyed. The right to own property became a major improvement to the status of Jews' welfare.

However, this change had not been a smooth one; as anti-Semitism had remained entrenched in Europe for centuries. After the emancipation --- in countries such as Germany --- there had been periods of pogroms (as well as many attempts to manipulate the law in order to restrict Jews again).[353]

The newly acquired freedoms had enabled Jews to: secularize; burst out of their traditional confined spaces, and engage in full-force with the social and economic life of the European countries. But, this new-found freedom had also damaged the communal structure; as secularism, and assimilation, had been magnified. Traditional Jewish religious belief systems --- as well as the concept of a Jewish communal hierarchy --- were questioned, and destabilized. Converting for convenience; assimilated, and mainly secularised, Jews rose to prominence.[354] Jews had then been permitted to: enroll in academic studies; learn professions; become members of these professions societies, and engage in work with the public as professionals. Many had enrolled to study in the medical and physical sciences (as well as in the humanities).[355]

---

[349] "French Revolution - Facts & Summary - HISTORY.com." http://www.history.com/topics/french-revolution. Accessed 11 Feb. 2018.
[350] "Napoleonic Wars (1799-1815)." http://www.historyofwar.org/articles/wars_napoleonic.html. Accessed 11 Feb. 2018.
[351] "BBC NEWS | Europe | The deep roots of French secularism." 1 Sep. 2004, http://news.bbc.co.uk/2/hi/europe/3325285.stm. Accessed 11 Feb. 2018.
[352] "Napoleonic Code | Definition, Facts, & Significance | Britannica.com." 19 Jan. 2018, https://www.britannica.com/topic/Napoleonic-Code. Accessed 11 Feb. 2018.
[353] "The Jews in the Age of Emancipation | Sotheby's." 3 Apr. 2013, http://www.sothebys.com/en/news-video/blogs/specials/a-treasured-legacy-history-of-the-jewish-people/2013/04/jews-age-emancipation.html. Accessed 11 Feb. 2018.
[354] "Jewish emancipation - Wikipedia." https://en.wikipedia.org/wiki/Jewish_emancipation. Accessed 11 Feb. 2018.
[355] ibid

This freedom --- coupled with the ferocious ability for intellectual pursuits and creative powers --- had enabled secularised Jews (or first-generation secularised converts) to reach new heights in academia, business, and many other professions. Even within art, culture, and music. Hundreds had risen to exceptional prominence in their fields.[356] Some individual stories are inspiring and noteworthy.

Mayer Amschel Rothschild[357] had been born in the Jewish ghetto of Frankfurt. Through hard work and clever business transactions, he managed to turn his family into the wealthiest family in human history --- deploying his sons to establish Banks in Europe's central cities of: London; Frankfurt; Paris; Vienna; and Naples. He is considered to be 'the founding father of international finance'.

The Rothschilds are considered to be the first family of Jews who managed to immune themselves from mob violence or the confiscation of their wealth by greedy monarchs (behaviour that had been conducted against Jews in previous generations). Financial instruments such as: stocks; bonds; and debt --- as well as keeping absolute secrecy and tight control in family hands --- had provided this immunity.

Other Jewish families (such as the Seligman's and Bischoffsheim, who had also become banking dynasties) emulated the Rothschilds' success. These banking firms became the finance powerhouses of Europe --- soon thereafter expanding into the United states of America.[358]

Even though not all Rothschilds had been affiliated with Zionism, large tracts of land were bought from the Ottoman-Empire in 1882, by Edmond James de Rothschild[359] (in order to initiate the process of the first Zionist settlements of Zichron Ya'akov and Binyamina, areas within what is now the State of Israel).

In the shipping industry, German-Jew Albert Ballin[360] had invented the business concept of cruise shipping. He had done very well until the first World War (when his ships had been seized by Great Britain and the U.S.A. as war reparations from Germany). Ballin had also been one of the first world business leaders to have engaged in philanthropic activities.

Some of the most well-known Nobel prize winners had been Jews --- Albert Einstein[361] and Max Born.[362] Among the most influential Jews were: Karl Marx,[363] who is considered to be the

---

[356] https://www.geni.com/projects/Notable-German-Jews/17009 (accessed 08/04/2016)
[357] "Mayer Amschel Rothschild (1744-1812) | Rothschild Family." https://family.rothschildarchive.org/people/21-mayer-amschel-rothschild-1744-1812. Accessed 11 Feb. 2018.
[358] "Birdman Bryant: The Role of Jewish Finance in 19th Century America." http://www.thebirdman.org/Index/Others/Others-Doc-Jews/+Doc-Jews-Power&Influence&Dominance/TheRoleOfJewishFinanceIn19thCentturyAmerica.html. Accessed 11 Feb. 2018.
[359] "Baron Edmond James de Rothschild (1845–1934)." https://knesset.gov.il/lexicon/eng/rotchild_ad_eng.htm. Accessed 11 Feb. 2018.
[360] "Ballin, Albert | International Encyclopedia of the First World War (WW1)." 25 Nov. 2015, https://encyclopedia.1914-1918-online.net/article/ballin_albert. Accessed 11 Feb. 2018.
[361] "Albert Einstein - Biographical." https://www.nobelprize.org/nobel_prizes/physics/laureates/1921/einstein-bio.html. Accessed 11 Feb. 2018.
[362] "Max Born - Biographical." https://www.nobelprize.org/nobel_prizes/physics/laureates/1954/born-bio.html. Accessed 11 Feb. 2018.
[363] "BBC - History - Historic Figures: Karl Marx (1818 - 1883)." http://www.bbc.co.uk/history/historic_figures/marx_karl.shtml. Accessed 11 Feb. 2018.

father of Socialism; and Sigmund Freud,[364] who is considered to be the father of Psychoanalysis. Felix Mendelssohn[365] and Gustav Mahler[366] in the classical music fields --- both were of Jewish origins. Jews had even dominated in intellectual sports (Wilhelm Steinitz had been the first chess world-champion, [367] while Emanuel Lasker[368] --- a renowned Mathematician --- had been the second).

In England, for the first time in history, there had been a prime minister of Sephardic-Jewish origin (who was also proud of being so within the English political circles) --- Benjamin Disraeli[369] was a young politician and writer, whose parents had converted to the Anglican Church for reasons of convenience. Disraeli is credited for: some Acts Of Parliament which had substantially improved workers' standing against employers; important diplomatic achievements for England in Europe against Russia; and some brilliant world diplomatic and commercial maneuvering, which had secured England's ownership of the suez canal --- benefiting English commerce for decades. One of his famous quotes is: 'The secret of success in life is for a man to be ready for his opportunity when it comes'.[370]

The list of Jews who had risen to prominence in their fields in Europe is extremely long, and cannot be dealt with in detail. What *is* unique, and important to notice, is that the influence of these Jews on their countries --- and the world --- had been highly disproportionate to their numbers within the general population. In most European countries, Jews had consisted between 0.5% to 1% of the population; while their numbers as successful: entrepreneurs; scientists; and professionals, would come to 30, 40, 50 . . . and at times up to 80%, in a specific field. For example, 85% of the German Stock Exchange had been composed of ethnic-Jewish individuals.

This domination had been in-spite of anti-Semitism, and it is most probable that --- due to their Jewish origins --- many Jews had been denied recognition in many public fields. Once Jewish domination had been established in a specific field, there had been little chance for non-Jews to enter the field (especially in the fields of commerce and finance).

As has been shown throughout this book, once given freedom from prosecution; Jews always seemed to float to the top of society within two or three generations (that is, until the next calamity befell on them). The extensive historical analysis conducted in previous chapters points to a long-and-hard process of building a national Jewish character of survival whilst within extremely inhospitable environments.

This process had required resilience and steadfastness --- traits which had promoted learning and the pursuit of knowledge. Said pursuit of knowledge and skills involves an almost obsessive-compulsive type of personality; people who are willing to sacrifice long hours, and hard work, to achieve their goals.

---

[364] "Sigmund Freud - Psychiatrist, Scholar - Biography." 4 Dec. 2017, https://www.biography.com/people/sigmund-freud-9302400. Accessed 11 Feb. 2018.
[365] "Felix Mendelssohn | Biography, Music, & Facts | Britannica.com." 9 Jan. 2018, https://www.britannica.com/biography/Felix-Mendelssohn. Accessed 8 Mar. 2018.
[366] "Gustav Mahler - Wikipedia." https://en.wikipedia.org/wiki/Gustav_Mahler. Accessed 8 Mar. 2018.
[367] "Wilhelm Steinitz - Chess Corner." http://www.chesscorner.com/worldchamps/steinitz/steinitz.htm. Accessed 11 Feb. 2018.
[368] "Chess World Champions - Emanuel Lasker - Chess Corner." http://www.chesscorner.com/worldchamps/lasker/lasker.htm. Accessed 11 Feb. 2018.
[369] "History of Benjamin Disraeli, the Earl of Beaconsfield - GOV.UK." https://www.gov.uk/government/history/past-prime-ministers/benjamin-disraeli-the-earl-of-beaconsfield. Accessed 11 Feb. 2018.
[370] "Benjamin Disraeli Quotes - BrainyQuote." https://www.brainyquote.com/authors/benjamin_disraeli. Accessed 11 Feb. 2018.

Thinking that changed the world

The age of enlightenment and the Industrialisation of Europe are considered to be the impetus that had profoundly changed the world. Taking the world from: Feudal systems controlled by monarchs and Churches in the Middle-Ages; to the egalitarian systems we know today (which are controlled by secular governments, and the law).

In Western-Europe, some democratic systems began to emerge; whilst monarchies, and the Church, waned. In England, the monarchy had gradually lost its status; and became a representative role --- while church had an even greater decline. In Eastern-Europe, monarchy and religion had eventually lost their statuses all together (due to the emerging communist system).

It is a common mistake to confuse Russia's communist system with Karl Marx's theories about socialism, and his communist manifesto.[371] The reality is that Russia's communist system is just a derivation of the socialist system that Karl Marx had envisioned. A derivation that had promoted the total ownership of the economy belonging to the working class. It had been devised by Lenin, and his comrades, in Russia.[372] Marx's ideas are considered to be original, and novel, by many historians. It is the interest of this book to determine how these ideas had been influenced by Jewish thought.

Marx had been a converted ethnic-Jew in childhood. His views about Jews and Judaism are scant; as he probably tried to renounce his own Jewish origins (so as to prevent his theories from being associated, or confused, with Jewish philosophy --- ensuring no anti-Semitic criticism would be received).

Marx, however, did not exhibit any anti-Jewish thoughts while pressed by Engels to convey his opinion on 'the Jewish question'[373]. Being an atheist, his answer had been that religion is unimportant; and that once the Socialist system would entrench itself, religion would fade naturally. Karl Marx will be revisited in the next chapter (regarding Jews fighting for human freedoms and rights).

This chapter empirically reaffirms that over many generations, Jews had developed sharp brain skills; and, when the opportunity arose in Europe, many Jews had shined in intellectual and business pursuits. These fields had required powerful skills of creativity --- creativity developed from abilities of heightened imagination. This chapter had also reviewed how Jewish people had worked together in a tightly-knit fashion; helping each other, in order to promote their success in various countries. They *had* to work together --- due to a generally hostile environment.

It has been shown --- in Chapter 8 --- that in the Middle-Ages, money would have saved the life of a Jew. With strong anti-Semitism manifesting within Europe, Jews had been exposed to terrible pogroms. Many times, they sought protection from the mob and Church. The Monarch, or Feudal authority, would only provide this protection for money. At times, they would take

---

[371] "Did Karl Marx really create Communism? | eNotes." https://www.enotes.com/homework-help/karl-marx-communism-347635. Accessed 11 Feb. 2018.
[372] "What is the difference between Communism and Socialism ...." 5 Jan. 2018, https://www.investopedia.com/ask/answers/100214/what-difference-between-communism-and-socialism.asp. Accessed 11 Feb. 2018.
[373] "On The Jewish Question by Karl Marx - Marxists Internet Archive." https://www.marxists.org/archive/marx/works/1844/jewish-question/. Accessed 11 Feb. 2018.

the money; and not even provide protection. In such cases, Jews had to flee to other territories. Such efforts again required money. For the Jew, money had become as basic a need in life as water or oxygen --- a much greater essential than for any other member of society. Lacking money would have guaranteed impending death once pogroms had resumed. Even though money would not completely guarantee survival, it would improve a rich Jew's chance of buying his/her freedom and security. The poor Jew had been doomed to extermination, or drifting to his non-Jewish environment before calamity strikes again; while the wealthier and more intelligent Jew would escape and survive (a type of natural selection).

This process --- consistent for over more than a 1000 years in European and Arab countries --- had resulted in wealthy Jewish populations normally possessing a greater capacity for intelligence, and a greater capability to survive, than their surrounding populations.

The debate about whether or not this relentless drive to succeed is genetic has yet to be resolved; however, the genetic debate is really not of much significance (since if there had been any genetic predisposition, it had probably occurred through a process of natural selection; whereby successful individuals survive the harsh environment, and can find female mates to carry their genes). Females in this environment had also been programmed to seek out the best-educated and wealthiest individuals; so as to increase their offspring's chances of survival.

Chapter 11

Within the legal profession --- fighting for human rights

Summary: This chapter will explain why ethnic-Jews are so prominent in the field of law. It will also explain the historical background for the relentless drive that Jewish people had for establishing human rights.

The legal profession

In his 1994 autobiography, Nelson Mandela wrote the following about South-Africa's Jewish lawyers who had fought Apartheid, and had given him his first Legal job.

'It was a Jewish firm, and in my experience, I have found Jews to be more broadminded than most whites on issues of race and politics; perhaps because they themselves have historically been victims of prejudice.'

'The fact that Lazar Sidelsky, one of the firm's partners, would take on a young African as an articled clerk — something almost unheard-of in those days — was evidence of that liberalism.'[374] --- (Mandela's 1994 autobiography, 'Long Walk to Freedom.')

Jewish people had played an instrumental role in the negotiation of South-Africa's Constitution, and its Legal development. Mandela's trust in Chief Justice Arthur Chaskalson[375] --- and other ethnic-Jewish lawyers such as: Ackerman; Goldstone; Sachs, and acting Judge Kentridge --- speaks for itself. Thirty-five percent of the first South-African constitutional court had been comprised of ethnic-Jews[376] (*way out of their proportion of around 0.1% of the population*). The head of this court at the time of its formation, Chief Justice Chaskalson, is considered by South-African lawyers as the main pillar in the development of South-Africa's Constitutional law.

This example of the excellence of Jews within the legal profession is not unprecedented. Today's Jurisprudence (Philosophy of law) studies, in most universities around the world, are dominated by the legal writings of scholars/professors such as: Ronald Dworkin[377](American), Herbert Hart [378](British) and Joseph Raz[379](Israeli/British) --- all ethnic-Jews. These philosophy of law studies encompass many fundamental aspects of Law (which include: natural law; positive law, and law and morality).

---

[374] "Amazon.com: Long Walk to Freedom: The Autobiography of Nelson ...."
https://www.amazon.com/Long-Walk-Freedom-Autobiography-Mandela/dp/0316548189. Accessed 12 Feb. 2018.
[375] "Arthur Chaskalson - Wikipedia." https://en.wikipedia.org/wiki/Arthur_Chaskalson. Accessed 12 Feb. 2018.
[376] "Historical Background of the Constitutional Court | South African ...." 24 Mar. 2016, http://www.sahistory.org.za/article/historical-background-constitutional-court. Accessed 12 Feb. 2018.
[377] "Ronald Dworkin obituary | Law | The Guardian." 14 Feb. 2013, https://www.theguardian.com/law/2013/feb/14/ronald-dworkin. Accessed 12 Feb. 2018.
[378] "H.L.A. Hart | English philosopher, teacher, and author | Britannica.com."
https://www.britannica.com/biography/H-L-A-Hart. Accessed 12 Feb. 2018.
[379] "Joseph Raz | Oxford Law Faculty." https://www.law.ox.ac.uk/people/joseph-raz. Accessed 12 Feb. 2018.

Fighting for human rights

Nearly 70 years ago (1948), René Cassin[380] (also ethnic-Jew) --- an esteemed French Legal professor --- had been commissioned by the United Nations to finalize the Universal Declaration of Human Rights. Professor Cassin (who had also been a member and president of the European Court of Human Rights, and was instrumental in its development) received the Nobel Peace Prize for his life-long efforts.[381] The European court of Human rights in Strasbourg had been built on Rua ('street' in French) René Cassin. In his later years, seeing the need to secure Jewish lives, he became an active Zionist[382] (this had been in conflict with European-Islamic leaders who had rejected Zionism).

Three of the nine Judges in the current sitting of the United States Supreme Court are of Jewish origins. Justice Ruth Bader Ginsburg[383], Justice Stephen Breyer[384] and Justice Elena Kagan.[385] Chief Justice Roberts'[386] mother's name (Rosemary Podrasky) is suspiciously also of Jewish origins. This is a minimum of 33% ethnic-Jewish representation.

Far more telling about the talent of Jews in Law, is the history of American Law within the last century. Justice Louis Brandeis[387] (Supreme court 1916-1939) graduated from Harvard law school with the highest marks ever; and was honoured as a valedictory. Over his lifetime, He was renowned for groundbreaking work on individual rights to: privacy; protection laws against monopolies, and big corporations. The redefining of the life-insurance industry --- and the famous 'Brandeis brief' regarding labour laws and the protection of women's health --- is also thanks to Brandeis. Justice Louis Brandeis came to be known in America as 'the people's attorney';[388] and it is of a shame that today, his legacy of fighting 'mass consumerism' --- which is employed ruthlessly by big corporations in America and the world --- has been abandoned. Brandeis University, the famous American university in Massachusetts, is named after him.

Justice Benjamin Cardozo[389] (Supreme Court 1932-1938) --- an American Jew of sephardic origin who had graduated from Columbia law school in New York --- had been highly regarded at the time of his original contract and tort law rulings, during his work in the New York court of appeals. Justice Cardozo passed away in 1938.

---

[380] "René Cassin." http://www.renecassin.org/. Accessed 12 Feb. 2018.
[381] "René Cassin - Biographical." https://www.nobelprize.org/nobel_prizes/peace/laureates/1968/cassin-bio.html. Accessed 12 Feb. 2018.
[382] "René Cassin, Human Rights, and Jewish ... - Brandeis University." http://www.brandeis.edu/tauber/events/CassinMoyn.pdf. Accessed 12 Feb. 2018.
[383] "Ruth Bader Ginsburg - Supreme Court Justice - Biography." 22 Jan. 2018, https://www.biography.com/people/ruth-bader-ginsburg-9312041. Accessed 12 Feb. 2018.
[384] "Stephen Breyer - Supreme Court Justice - Biography." 15 Jul. 2015, https://www.biography.com/people/stephen-breyer-40553. Accessed 12 Feb. 2018.
[385] "Elena Kagan - Educator, Supreme Court Justice, Lawyer - Biography." 6 May. 2016, https://www.biography.com/people/elena-kagan-560228. Accessed 12 Feb. 2018.
[386] "Chief Justice John Roberts - Wikipedia." https://en.wikipedia.org/wiki/John_Roberts. Accessed 12 Feb. 2018.
[387] "Louis Brandeis - Supreme Court Justice - Biography." 1 Apr. 2014, https://www.biography.com/people/louis-brandeis-39048. Accessed 12 Feb. 2018.
[388] "Louis Brandeis Biography - life, family, parents, history, school ...." http://www.notablebiographies.com/Br-Ca/Brandeis-Louis.html. Accessed 12 Feb. 2018.
[389] "Benjamin Cardozo - Supreme Court Justice, Judge, Journalist, Lawyer ...." 1 Apr. 2014, https://www.biography.com/people/benjamin-cardozo-40728. Accessed 12 Feb. 2018.

Justice Felix Frankfurter[390] (Supreme court 1939-1962) had been a descendant of a family who had produced many well known Rabbi's in Europe. He has been regarded as 'the best graduate from Harvard law school since Louis Brandeis'. He had helped in the founding of The American Civil Liberties Union,[391] and was known for his fight for socialists and religious minorities. He is a controversial Justice due to his ways of 'Judicial restraint', and avoidance of making 'unpopular decisions'.

There are a few others on the list, such as Justice Arthur Goldberg and Justice Abe Fortas (as well as the current Justices, including Justice Breyer who is consistent in his support for abortion rights).

One of the interesting facts for the purpose of this book is the work-ethic that some of these individuals testify to. Justice Louis Brandeis many times described the law as his mistress. Justice Cardozo described himself as a 'plodding mediocre' but industrious; and Justice Frankfurter is credited with writing hundreds of opinions for the court.

This work-ethic originates somewhere . . . the order: 'You should delve into it day and night'[392] from the Bible can be a possible source of this work-ethic. Dare we say that Talmudic yeshivas' work-ethic may have been the ancestral precursor for these individuals work-ethics?

There are many more famous current --- and noteworthy past --- American-Jewish professors of law. They can easily be searched on the internet. Harvard Professor of law Alan Dershowitz[393], known for: his fight for civil liberties; unusual success in criminal trials defending celebrities; and a staunch advocate of Israel, is a real media favourite.

One of the most important freedom fighters in America (although not as famous and flamboyant) is Joseph Rau Jr.[394] --- again a Harvard law school graduate, that finished first in his class. He is credited for his involvement in, and lobbying of, congress for the passage of the most important Human Rights Acts --- The Civil Rights Act (1964 and 1968), and The Voting Rights Act (1965). He had marched with Martin Luther King Jr. ; and had been a member of the National Association for the Advancement of Colored People, for many years. Dare we say that he did more for African-Americans than many people? He had been hated for being such a liberal, as well as for being an ethnic-Jew. Only after his death, during the Clinton Presidency, had he properly been recognised and awarded the 'Presidential Medal of Freedom' --- the highest civilian honour in America.

There had been many other Jews --- not from the Legal profession --- who were instrumental in the fight for civil liberties for African-Americans. Some like Andrew Goodman and Michael Schwerner --- who had both been murdered in the Mississippi swamps by the Ku Klux Klan --- had paid with their *lives* for their activism.[395]

---

[390] "Felix Frankfurter - Supreme Court Justice, Educator, Scholar - Biography." 3 Mar. 2016, https://www.biography.com/people/felix-frankfurter-9301106. Accessed 12 Feb. 2018.
[391] "American Civil Liberties Union." https://www.aclu.org/. Accessed 12 Feb. 2018.
[392] "Mishna 15(a): The Song of the Soul • Torah.org." 5 Dec. 2016, https://torah.org/learning/pirkei-avos-chapter1-15a/. Accessed 12 Feb. 2018.
[393] "Alan M. Dershowitz | Harvard Law School." http://hls.harvard.edu/faculty/directory/10210/Dershowitz. Accessed 12 Feb. 2018.
[394] "Who Was the Unsung Hero of the 1964 Civil Rights Act? - The Root." 30 Jun. 2014, https://www.theroot.com/who-was-the-unsung-hero-of-the-1964-civil-rights-act-1790876217. Accessed 12 Feb. 2018.
[395] "Murders of Chaney, Goodman, and Schwerner - Wikipedia." https://en.wikipedia.org/wiki/Murders_of_Chaney,_Goodman,_and_Schwerner. Accessed 12 Feb. 2018.

Even famous American Rabbis (such as the leading Jewish philosopher Rabbi Abraham Joshua Heschel)[396] were instrumental in the African-American struggle for freedom. Martin Luther King Jr. , who had been close friends with Rabbi Heschel, was puzzled by the high tendency of African-American anti-Semitism.

'How could there be anti-Semitism among Negroes when our Jewish friends have demonstrated their commitment to the principle of tolerance and brotherhood not only in the form of sizable contributions, but in many other tangible ways, and often at great personal sacrifice. Can we ever express our appreciation to the rabbis who chose to give moral witness with us in St. Augustine during our recent protest against segregation in that unhappy city? Need I remind anyone of the awful beating suffered by Rabbi Arthur Lelyveld of Cleveland when he joined the civil rights workers there in Hattiesburg, Mississippi? And who can ever forget the sacrifice of two Jewish lives, Andrew Goodman and Michael Schwerner, in the swamps of Mississippi? It would be impossible to record the contribution that the Jewish people have made toward the Negro's struggle for freedom—it has been so great'.[397]

(Essential writings of Martin Luther King Jr. --- 1965)

The abolition of slavery

Nearly a 100 years earlier, the struggle for the abolition of slavery in America had been championed by American president Abraham Lincoln.[398] Lincoln's warm relations with the minority Jewish population can be determined from his personal letters, as well as from the deep grief felt by the Jewish community following his assassination.[399]

There are conspiracy theories as to Lincoln's Jewish ancestry in England (given all the Biblical names of his relatives --- but especially the use of the Jewish name 'Mordecai', which had not been used by Christians).[400]

There is no real merit in those conspiracy theories; as Lincoln had been secular, with American evangelical tendencies. He had, however, placed high value on the Hebrew Old Testament and ancient Jewish thought.

Lincoln had once summed up his faith: 'When I do good I feel good, and when I do bad I feel bad, and that's my religion'[401]. Perhaps it is no accident that the sentiment is remarkably close to what Rabbi Hillel had urged in his teachings: 'To forbear doing unto others what would displease us'.[402]

---

[396] "Abraham Joshua Heschel: A Prophet's Prophet | My Jewish Learning." https://www.myjewishlearning.com/article/abraham-joshua-heschel-a-prophets-prophet/. Accessed 12 Feb. 2018.
[397] "As allies of Martin Luther King, Jews must fight for the civil rights of ...." 9 Jan. 2017, https://www.jta.org/2017/01/09/news-opinion/opinion/as-allies-of-martin-luther-king-jews-must-fight-for-the-civil-rights-of-muslims. Accessed 12 Feb. 2018.
[398] "Abraham Lincoln Biography - Biography." 24 Jan. 2018, https://www.biography.com/people/abraham-lincoln-9382540. Accessed 12 Feb. 2018.
[399] https://www.jewishvirtuallibrary.org/jsource/loc/abe1.html (accessed April 2016)
[400] "Mordecai Lincoln - Wikipedia." https://en.wikipedia.org/wiki/Mordecai_Lincoln. Accessed 12 Feb. 2018.
[401] "When I do good, I feel good. When I do bad, I feel bad. That's my." https://www.brainyquote.com/quotes/abraham_lincoln_106095. Accessed 12 Feb. 2018.
[402] "Do Unto Others: Living Reciprocity | Yedid Nefesh." 29 Apr. 2011, https://ynefesh.com/2011/04/29/do-unto-others-living-reciprocity/. Accessed 12 Feb. 2018.

As evidenced by Lincoln's saying, the trend of Jewish freedom fighters in general --- as well as legal freedom fighters in particular --- had begun long before Lincoln's time. Rabbi Hillel had shown Jews and Christians the way.

President Lincoln, as a child to Christian Puritans and later in life an educated lawyer, must have known far more about the Old Testament (as well as about Judaism's laws on slavery). There had been many issues about slavery in the ancient world --- but unlike the: Persians; Greeks; Romans; and Arabs, the Judaic religion had many prohibitions against owning and treating slaves badly. The most central Biblical law was that a slave should be released on the 7th year, after 6 years of work.[403]

Equality for women

Fighting for women's liberties can also be found within Rabbinical teachings. Rabbi Gershom had already mentioned with regards to women's rights within Judaism. His ruling on the abandonment of polygamy in Judaism (nearly a 1000 years ago) must have been a real improvement for Jewish women at the time.

Rabbi Maimonides ruled that a woman who finds her husband repugnant is entitled to a divorce, as she should not be a captive and subjected to intercourse with someone she hates.[404] Rabbi Perez ben Elijah, and other Rabbis, had considered domestic violence as a 'heathen' gentile practice that is not Judaic; and is ground for divorce.[405]

The Jewish religion, like any other religion, is still far from modern concepts of equality for women --- however, it should be considered in light of the historical timeline. The spirit of these rulings must have contributed to famous Jewish freedom fighters, and modern fighters for human rights .

One of the most remarkable fights for freedom in world history had been the proletariats' fight against the oppression of capitalists. This fight had been ignited by the philosophical writings of Karl Marx.

Considered to be one of the most influential people in world history, Karl Marx --- an ethnic-Jew who had been converted into christianity during childhood --- had constructed a philosophy for equality called Marxism (after his own name).

This fight for equality grew, and had encompassed many issues such as: equality for women; racial equality, and equality for all religions and beliefs. Marxism had developed all over the world, in all kind of ways. From the Soviet communist regime of the USSR; to China's current central government planning. It had been instrumental in shaping third-world/developing countries like South-America, Africa, and the Arab world. It has been relied upon in the battle against colonialism and imperialism. It is still with us today, looming as an alternative to American capitalism. The fight is still in its midst, and ongoing.[406]

---

[403] http://www.jewishencyclopedia.com/articles/13799-slaves-and-slavery (accessed April 2016)
[404] "Ishut - Chapter Fourteen - Chabad.org."
http://www.chabad.org/library/article_cdo/aid/952888/jewish/Ishut-Chapter-Fourteen.htm. Accessed 12 Feb. 2018.
[405] "Women in Judaism - Wikipedia." https://en.wikipedia.org/wiki/Women_in_Judaism. Accessed 12 Feb. 2018.
[406] "Marx Continues to Influence 125 Years After His Death | Germany ...." 14 Mar. 2008,
http://www.dw.com/en/marx-continues-to-influence-125-years-after-his-death/a-3190306. Accessed 12 Feb. 2018.

In any human rights fight --- and societal issue --- in America today, ethnic-Jews are prominent; and many times, take the lead. This freedom has reached absurd levels whereby some would fight for the extensive rights of their enemy --- the same enemy that yearns for their demise.

From: Zionism rights to Palestinian rights; Trade Union and workers rights; rights to bear arms, and lobbies against arms --- you will find ethnic-Jews either: finalizing the Law on those rights; or, within movements that fight for those rights. It had intrigued me to discover that the president of the National Rifle Association of America, between 2005 to 2007, had been an ethnic-Jewish woman by the name of Sandra Froman.[407] Another weird and puzzling conflict is the well-known capitalist George Soros, acting as a left-wing activist.[408]

Beyond the fact that Judaic people had to fight for their own rights and freedoms in Europe and America (and had therefore been sympathetic to the African-American cause and other fights for the rights of minorities); the fight for freedom had been ingrained within the Jewish Biblical and Rabbinical culture. Over the years, said Jewish culture of progressivism had allowed people to question and challenge authority and world order. This, in turn, had created individuals that found a cause, and fought for it.

Freedom of thought --- and the expression of it --- is what created Karl Marx and Albert Einstein. The freedom of the mind to wander beyond the physical boundaries of human existence --- whether that means contemplating social imagination, or outer-space physics. The liberty to express this freedom of thought is what had created America's materialistic success as we know it today.

This freedom is not as simple and trivial as it sounds. Today, many societies struggle to provide such freedom to their populations. China still heavily controls individual expression and thought processes.[409] Many Islamic countries struggle between the rigidity of their religion; and the freedom to express contrary views. In some of these countries, a person will literally lose their head for thinking otherwise.[410]

This chapter had begun with Mr. Nelson Mandela's statements about Jewish liberalism. The Judaic people had never been properly credited for their monumental fight against Apartheid in South-Africa.

Just observing the famous Rivonia trials[411] will reveal the overwhelming involvement of Judaic people. Six people out of the 13 arrested had been ethnic-Jews. They included: Arthur Goldreich (who had owned the Rivonia farm); Denis Goldberg; Lionel Bernstein; Bob Hepple; Harold Wolpe, and James Kantor. Joe Slovo[412] from the communist party --- who had also been the leader of the ANC military wing --- had been incredibly instrumental in the fight against Apartheid. He had lost his wife, Ruth, who had been assassinated by the Apartheid regime's secret service.

---

[407] "Froman, Sandy (Board Member) - NRA On the Record." http://nraontherecord.org/sandy-froman/. Accessed 12 Feb. 2018.

[408] "George Soros." https://www.georgesoros.com/. Accessed 12 Feb. 2018.

[409] "Freedom of Expression in China: A Privilege, Not a Right ...." https://www.cecc.gov/freedom-of-expression-in-china-a-privilege-not-a-right. Accessed 12 Feb. 2018.

[410] "'Muslims do not believe in the concept of freedom of expression' - The ...." 9 Jan. 2015, https://www.washingtonpost.com/news/volokh-conspiracy/wp/2015/01/09/muslims-do-not-believe-in-the-concept-of-freedom-of-expression/. Accessed 12 Feb. 2018.

[411] "Rivonia Trial 1963 -1964 | South African History Online." 13 Apr. 2017, http://www.sahistory.org.za/article/rivonia-trial-1963-1964. Accessed 12 Feb. 2018.

[412] "Joe Slovo | South African lawyer and activist | Britannica.com." https://www.britannica.com/biography/Joe-Slovo. Accessed 12 Feb. 2018.

It is very easy to just throw anti-Semitism as a blanket answer for this lack of proper recognition of Judaic people in the fight for the liberation of African people in America and South-Africa --- however, the reasons are more complex, and are (again) related to the illogicality of a situation. From the one side, the oppressed see Jewish freedom fighters as soldiers to their cause; but on the other side, they see extremely successful Jewish people becoming notable capitalists, and obscenely wealthy. The way they see it, the Jew has no regard for their struggle and will, without any hesitation, take economic advantage of their poverty. Their perception is that Jews are part of their economic oppression. Whether their perception is true or not is irrelevant --- the emotions of blame, hate, and jealousy are natural human reactions.

The fact that the Jewish brethren of the capitalists arrive to help the oppressed in their fight against political oppression may even become puzzling to them. It does not make sense to them. Their emotions become mixed, and other sinister thoughts come to mind (such as conspiracy theories).

This dichotomy is also a major part of modern anti-Semitism, as Jewish culture has never been truly understood. Any deeds on the part of a Jewish person have always been interpreted as another Jewish ploy for profitability.

Apart from the observations of Mark Twain regarding the fact that Jews had never been a burden on their surrounding gentile society (in terms of poor and incapacitated individuals); the best proof that Jewish people genuinely care about the weak in society lies in their religious philosophy itself.

The three pillars of Judaism will reveal that further than the study of Torah and the divine work that is required to be part of Jewish life; the other, indispensable, element is 'Gemilut Hasadim' (an expanded form of the ancient Jewish pillar of Tzedakah). It can be translated as 'good deeds', but the meaning goes far deeper than this rudimentary translation. The harsh religious verdict was that a person is simply not a *Jew* if they do not engage in 'Gemilut Hasadim'.

'Gemilut Hasadim' is not just charity --- it involves a Jew's active physical help, for people who are in need of physical help. It involves giving help anonymously, so that the person who receives said help will not feel ashamed when they encounter the giver (and vice-versa). It involves rehabilitation of: the sick; the incapacitated; the orphaned, and other members of the community who have run into misfortune. It even involves the dignified burial of the dead.

The concept of 'Gemilut Hasadim' had been developed over many years in Jewish communities; and had created a socialistic type of Jewish community (within the capitalistic nature of the community toward the outside gentile world).

Following gentile society's oppression of Jews in the Middle-Ages; Jews had been forced to deal with movable property in general, and money loans in particular. A money loan to a fellow Jew in need would not bear interest. This was another kind of social arrangement --- that a Jew will not take advantage of another Jew's misfortune (since they had all been subject to the cruelty of their surroundings). It is considered a good deed to help fellow Jews in their time of difficulty. Perhaps Marx's observations about all those intricate social arrangements of sharing within the Jewish community had lead him to his socialist ideas.

What is important --- for the purpose of this book --- is to realise that there are many pans to Judaism; and beyond Jews who became successful in business, there had been many others with ideals about creating just societies. These people had been willing freedom fighters for other oppressed groups (such as African-Americans, as well as indigenous Africans in Apartheid South-Africa).

The phenomenal success of Jews in the Legal profession and academics, highlights the fact that this cannot simply be a co-incidence. Generations of Talmudic study includes complicated legal issues; and debates and arguments about social justice, and just causes. This filters down in family cultures over generations. This can especially be true if members of the family become Lawyers.

Law in general, and Contract Law specifically, is vital for business. A fault in a contract or a beneficial clause can determine a business' fate. Ethnic-Jews have proven their skill in business contracts. Every individual who aspires to create a decent business should have a good understanding of Contract and Business Law.

Law is also very important in the fields of human rights and Social Justice. Lawyers who are engaged in such fields will have an added advantage if they come from a tradition of good morality, and care about fellow human beings.

Over the millenia, Talmudic studies have dealt with all aspects of life --- including Social Justice. Between person to person, between husband and wife, and between the public and private.

I am of a conviction that Karl Marx's observations, or even absorption of Jewish values from his converted parents, had lead him to his philosophical writings. These writings have had the most profound impact on the world since the beginning of the previous century, starting with the Russian Communist revolution.

Chapter 12

From Russia to the promised land of America and the troubled state of Israel

Summary: This chapter will describe the the physical immigration of Jewish people from Eastern Europe to the new worlds of America, England, Israel(Palestine), South America, Australia and South Africa. It will also explain the Zionist movement, the struggle for a Jewish state and the eventual establishment of the State of Israel in 1948.

In 1881 CE, the Russian Czar Alexander II was assassinated by Polish revolutionaries who were descendants of polish nobility that lost their power to Russia's Cossacks.[413] Since, in the eyes of the Russians, the historical connection between Polish nobility and Jews had still been strong; Jews were blamed for the assassination of the Russian Czar, and pogroms as well as anti-Jewish laws were implemented in Russia.[414] These events initiated a big immigration move into the U.S.A., and a much smaller stream of immigration to Palestine (which had then been part of the Turkish Ottoman empire at the time).

Most Russian Jews travelled to England; and from there to the USA. On the way to America, some Jews remained in England while others preferred immigrating to other newly established countries such as South Africa, Argentina and Australia --- creating new Jewish communities in what was considered to be the 'new world'.

Marx's theory of equality --- which began to take shape in the turmoil of Eastern-Europe --- further exacerbated this trend of Jewish immigration. In Russia, the revolutionary Ilya Vladimirovich Lenin championed a variation of Marx's theory --- naming it... Communism.[415] Defeating the Russian army, and executing the whole of the Romanov royal family in order to eliminate any future claims to the restoration of monarchy in Russia.

At first, many Russian ethnic Jews joined Lenin's ranks in the hope that this new secular ideology of equality would finally be their salvation from the anti-Semitic tyranny of the Russian monarchy and the Christian orthodox church. Communism promised equality to all secular citizens.[416] This seemed, to many ethnic Jews, a logical proposition.

Again, as many times before in history, ethnic Jews had abandoned their religion, as they had perceived religion in general to be the discriminating and dividing force that prevented equality between populations. Secularization had already become a trend in Europe, and was rapidly infiltrating Russia among all ethnic groups.

Unlike Marx's beliefs about a natural peaceful social revolution of the working class, Lenin believed in a forceful and quick takeover of power in Russia. Russian monarchy and royalty represented the evil father; religion represented the mother of all evils, and its effect on the population had been compared to that of opium --- keeping the people subdued to the monarchy and church. Lenin defined this in his following speech:

---

[413] "Czar Alexander II assassinated - Mar 13, 1881 - HISTORY.com." http://www.history.com/this-day-in-history/czar-alexander-ii-assassinated. Accessed 28 Jan. 2018.
[414] "The Reign of Alexander III: From Pogroms to Counter-Reforms.." 9 Mar. 2009, http://www.uni-heidelberg.de/fakultaeten/philosophie/zegk/sog/loewe_artikel_the_reign.html. Accessed 28 Jan. 2018.
[415] "communism | Definition, Facts, & History | Britannica.com." https://www.britannica.com/topic/communism. Accessed 28 Jan. 2018.
[416] "Communism - The YIVO Encyclopedia of Jews in Eastern Europe." http://www.yivoencyclopedia.org/article.aspx/Communism. Accessed 12 Feb. 2018.

'Religion is one of the forms of spiritual oppression which everywhere weighs down heavily upon the masses of the people, over-burdened by their perpetual work for others, by want and isolation. Impotence of the exploited classes in their struggle against the exploiters just as inevitably gives rise to the belief in a better life after death as impotence of the savage in his battle with nature gives rise to belief in gods, devils, miracles, and the like… Religion is opium for the people'[417] --- (extract from Lenin's speech)

Lenin's 'Russian revolution' was assisted by ethnic Jews who turned their back on Judaism, became secular, and assumed Russian names. From Leon Trotsky (Lev Davidovich Bronstein)[418] who became Lenin's deputy; to many other individuals who filled the ranks of the bolsheviks (meaning the majority in Russian).

While Lenin's father's ethnicity is illusive, his mother (Maria Alexandrova Blank) was definitely of some ethnic Jewish background.[419] However, contrary to conspiracy theory advocates, Lenin's Bolshevik party 'old guard' had been primarily comprised of ethnic russians; however, his closest comrades had been mostly ethnic Jews whom had changed their ethnic affiliation in favour of secular communism.

The first politburo (cabinet) had been comprised of Lenin, and six of his closest comrades. Four members were of ethnic Jewish background. They Included, Leon Trotzki[420] (Lev Bronstein), Grigory Zinoviev[421] (Hirsch Apfelbaum), Lev Kamenev[422] (Lev Rosenfeld), Grigory Sokolnikov[423] (Hirsh Yankelevich). Only Stalin and Bubnov were of Georgian and Russian ethnic background. We can only speculate as to why this was so. Energetic individuals, organizing efficiency and new innovative ideas were needed during and after the revolution. Lenin seemed to be attracted to his ethnic Jewish confidants who probably possessed these qualities. People with vision that, in effect, renounced their ethnic and religious background to work hard towards an egalitarian secular society.

The rise of Stalin (who was not an ethnic Jew) after Lenin's death, and his purging of the communist party of his opponents who were mainly ethnic Jews (mostly by their execution and assassination) only proves the conspiracy theory that Jews always control power, to be no more than a myth.

Ethnic-Jews that became disappointed during the communist revolution --- as their property had been confiscated and they had been forced to do labour work for little compensation --- searched for a new destination to root up. The new communistic experiment did not prove itself economically, and Russia and its occupied territories went through much hardship; including loss of production, and generally low economic output.[424]

---

[417] https://www.marxists.org/archive/lenin/works/1905/dec/03.htm (accessed April 2016)
[418] "BBC - History - Historic Figures: Leon Trotsky (1879 - 1940)." http://www.bbc.co.uk/history/historic_figures/trotsky_leon.shtml. Accessed 28 Jan. 2018.
[419] "Maria Alexandrovna Ulyanov (Blank) (1835 - 1916) - Genealogy - Geni." 18 Feb. 2017, http://www.geni.com/people/Maria-Alexandrovna-Ulyanov/6000000010018910359. Accessed 28 Jan. 2018.
[420] "Leon Trotsky - Activist - Biography." 27 Apr. 2017, https://www.biography.com/people/leon-trotsky-9510793. Accessed 12 Feb. 2018.
[421] "Grigory Yevseyevich Zinovyev | Russian revolutionary | Britannica.com." https://www.britannica.com/biography/Grigory-Yevseyevich-Zinovyev. Accessed 12 Feb. 2018.
[422] "Lev Kamenev | Soviet government official | Britannica.com." https://www.britannica.com/biography/Lev-Kamenev. Accessed 12 Feb. 2018.
[423] "Grigorij Sokolnikow – Wikipedia, wolna encyklopedia." https://pl.wikipedia.org/wiki/Grigorij_Sokolnikow. Accessed 12 Feb. 2018.
[424] "The Soviet Economy in the 1920s and 1930s - University of Warwick." https://warwick.ac.uk/fac/soc/economics/staff/mharrison/public/1978_cc_postprint.pdf. Accessed 12 Feb. 2018.

During the pogroms and anti Jewish laws that preceded the communist revolution many Jews were desperate to leave Russia. The United states of America sounded like, and appeared to be, the new 'promised land'. America had been established on a constitution that had promised not to infringe on their: ethnicity; religion; and, entrepreneurial spirit. Many German Jews who had already migrated there were doing reasonably well.

The old world of Europe had been highly anti-Semitic, densely populated, and highly competitive. Other european continental Jews, and non-Jews alike, were also trying to immigrate to America. Droves of Eastern-European Jews tried to find their way into the United States of America. Some had to compromise and immigrate to other destinations such as South American countries, and South Africa.

At first, most Jewish newcomers to America had found themselves inhabiting the poor neighborhoods of New York city --- mainly in the lower east side of Manhattan.[425] From there they spread around the country; mainly to Los Angeles and San Francisco. Their position today as a major economic and political force in American life is a testimony of the great potential of ethnic Jews to propel economies to great heights.

The Zionist movement and the birth of Israel

Due to: the state of Russia and Europe with regards to Jews; realising the rise in anti-Semitism in Europe and especially Germany, as well as Austria (whereby ethnic Jews became extremely wealthy and vastly hated); and also observing the flight of Jews from pogroms organised by the Russian government, a new Jewish movement named the Zionist movement was founded by a Jewish journalist named Theodor Binyamin Ze'ev Herzl.[426]

Theodor Herzl was an Austro-Hungarian Jew, who considered himself an atheist, and had tried to assimilate into the German culture. He was a successful journalist who initially believed that all Jews should be assimilated into their country of birth.

Witnessing the fact that even well-off assimilated Jews in Germany were never fully accepted as German, he began to realise that Jews were in need of their own homeland. In his diary, while visiting in France during the Dreyfus trial, he wrote:

'In Paris, as I have said, I achieved a freer attitude toward anti-Semitism . . . above all, I had recognized the emptiness and futility of trying to 'combat' anti-Semitism'.[427] --- (Theodor Herzl's Diary - June 1895)

Soon afterward, Herzl published his philosophical book about the creation of a Jewish state --- in the German language "Der Judenstaat" (The Jewish state).[428] His vision had been that anti-Semitism could not be combated, but rather avoided, by separating Jews from Europeans.

Herzl's predictions about the Jewish state and its birth labours were quite accurate. However, true to his Judeo-German culture, Herzl imagined the new Jewish state to be modelled upon European German culture with German as the official language of the state. This however did not materialize, as the Hebrew language was revived by Jews who had

---

[425] "Brooklyn Jews – The Peopling of New York - Macaulay Honors College." https://macaulay.cuny.edu/eportfolios/napoli13/brooklyn-jews/. Accessed 12 Feb. 2018.
[426] "Theodor Herzl | Austrian Zionist leader | Britannica.com." https://www.britannica.com/biography/Theodor-Herzl. Accessed 28 Jan. 2018.
[427] "Learning with the National Library of Israel | Herzl, Zola, and Dreyfus." http://www.nli-education-uk.org/herzl-zola-dreyfus. Accessed 12 Feb. 2018.
[428] http://www.zionism-israel.com/js/Jewish_State.html (accessed April 2016)

already settled in the country.[429] Hebrew eventually become Israel's official language, coupled with Arabic as a second official language. This had to be done, as Arab palestinians had an enormous growth rate via immigration from surrounding Arab countries, and a high natural birth rate with good access to medical facilities operated mainly by Jewish doctors within British mandate Palestine. Resulting in many Palestinian villages surrounding the fast growing Jewish urban developments within British mandate Palestine.

On the way to America

As most Jews headed to America via England, some decided to settle in England, or venture into other destinations around the world.

England

Some decided to stay in England, where Jews were allowed to re-settle after Oliver Cromwell's reform in the year 1650.[430] By the year 1656, 400 Jews of Sephardic origin were recorded in England (mainly merchants who conducted big business with: the Levant; Brazil; West Indies; The Netherlands, and Spain). Since then, the English Jewish population has swelled to the current approximate of 300,000 people.

The resettlement of Jews in England is credited to Menasheh ben Yosef ben Israel[431] (1604-1657). A portuguese Rabbi and kabbalist, who had also been the founder of the first Hebrew printing company in Amsterdam. Ben Israel convinced Cromwell of the need to allow Jews to resettle in England. For commercial reasons as well as based on Cromwell's reforms and just ideas regarding those reforms.

In 1798 CE, the Rothschilds of Germany had opened their branch in England.[432] Providing large finance to the British government. Finance to assist in the war against Napoleon's expansion, suez canal purchase and finance for Cecil Rhodes'[433] economic expansion in Africa.

The Rothschilds, and other Jewish persons, rose to prominence in England in the 18th century. Sir Moses Haim Montefiore[434] (1784-1885), an Italian Jewish immigrant to England, received a knighthood from Queen Victoria in 1837 for his business innovations that benefited the British Empire. He is well revered in Jewish communities around the world for his engagement in philanthropy for persecuted Jews. Engaging in these philanthropic activities

---

[429] "The Revival of the Hebrew Language | Behold Israel." http://beholdisrael.org/news-israel/articles/revival-hebrew-language. Accessed 13 Feb. 2018.
[430] "Oliver Cromwell - Cromwell and the Jews." http://www.olivercromwell.org/jews.htm. Accessed 13 Feb. 2018.
[431] "MANASSEH BEN ISRAEL - JewishEncyclopedia.com." http://www.jewishencyclopedia.com/articles/10345-manasseh-ben-israel. Accessed 13 Feb. 2018.
[432] "Rothschild banking family of England - Wikipedia." https://en.wikipedia.org/wiki/Rothschild_banking_family_of_England. Accessed 13 Feb. 2018.
[433] "Why is Cecil Rhodes such a controversial figure? - BBC News." 1 Apr. 2015, http://www.bbc.co.uk/news/magazine-32131829. Accessed 13 Feb. 2018.
[434] "Sir Moses Montefiore's life and times – Montefiore Endowment." https://www.montefioreendowment.org.uk/sirmoses/about/. Accessed 13 Feb. 2018.

until his death at the age of 100 years. In 1841 Isaac Lyon Goldsmid[435] was made a baronet. In 1855 Sir David Salomons[436] was elected as the first Jewish Mayor of London. In 1868 Benjamin Disraeli became the first ethnic Jew who became prime minister. Ethnic-Jews in England have contributed to British: economy; science; and technology, and had participated in British war efforts.

Another famous contribution was that of Dr Chaim Azriel Weizmann's[437] acetone production bacterial fermentation patent, which had been of much importance to Britain's production of explosives during the first world war. Dr Weizmann became a well respected persona within the British political establishment. This helped him secure the "Lord Balfour declaration"[438] for a homeland for the Jews in Palestine. The British control of Palestine followed their world war I victory over the Turkish Ottoman Empire in the Middle-East. Dr. Weizmann, who became head of the Zionist movement, eventually became the first president of Israel.

After Dr. Weizmann's death in 1952, American/German Professor Albert Einstein, who was assisting Zionist projects and donated all of his intellectual property to the Hebrew university of Jerusalem, declined an offer for this post.[439]

South-Africa

Some other Jews from this Eastern-European Jewish immigration ventured into South-Africa (which had become a british colony).

At its height in the 1980's, the South-African Jewish community amounted to approximately 120 000 individuals. In recent years, due to mass immigration of especially the younger generation, the community is estimated at half of this figure. Mainly the mature and elderly population remain.

The first big wave of Jewish immigration to South Africa came from Lithuania at the late part of the 19th century and early 20th century. A smaller number of German Jewish refugees arrived between 1933 to 1939.[440]

The impact that Jewish people had on South Africa was substantial. Most big businesses in Johannesburg had been started, and developed, by them. The city, at times, had been called 'Jewburg'.[441]

---

[435] "Sir Isaac Lyon Goldsmid, 1st Baronet | British political activist ...." https://www.britannica.com/biography/Sir-Isaac-Lyon-Goldsmid-1st-Baronet. Accessed 13 Feb. 2018.
[436] "David Salomons - Wikipedia." https://en.wikipedia.org/wiki/David_Salomons. Accessed 13 Feb. 2018.
[437] "Chaim Weizmann | Israeli president and scientist | Britannica.com." 28 Dec. 2017, https://www.britannica.com/biography/Chaim-Weizmann. Accessed 13 Feb. 2018.
[438] "Balfour Declaration letter written - Nov 02, 1917 - HISTORY.com." http://www.history.com/this-day-in-history/the-balfour-declaration. Accessed 13 Feb. 2018.
[439] "Albert Einstein's complete archives to be posted online | Science | The ...." 19 Mar. 2012, https://www.theguardian.com/science/2012/mar/19/albert-einstein-archives-theory-of-relativity. Accessed 13 Feb. 2018.
[440] "Community in South Africa :: World Jewish Congress." http://www.worldjewishcongress.org/en/about/communities/ZA. Accessed 13 Feb. 2018.
[441] "Jewburg - Oxford Reference." http://www.oxfordreference.com/view/10.1093/acref/9780199829941.001.0001/acref-9780199829941-e-25536. Accessed 13 Feb. 2018.

Perhaps this success had been due to the circumstances of South Africa at the time. A country that possessed: vast amounts of natural resources; a large population of uneducated African people; Dutch Afrikaners who were concentrated mainly in agriculture; and British individuals, whom had mainly been involved in mining, engineering, and infrastructure. Jews literally built: the textile industry; the retail and property development industry, and a myriad of: health; financial; and insurance, conglomerates. Massive companies such as Investec[442], Liberty life[443] and Discovery health[444] are known to have been established, and still run, by ethnic-Jewish people.

Perhaps the most well-known ethnic Jew in South-Africa was Harry oppenheimer[445] who built and controlled the Anglo American corporation which, at some stage, had been the biggest gold mining company in the world. Mining world giant Glencore CEO Ivan Glasenberg[446] is also an ethnic-Jew who originated from South-Africa, but today resides in Switzerland. There had been little assimilation in this community. This is probably due to the conservative nature and racial character of South-Africa's various populations over the years.

Australia

Around 15000 German-Jews escaping Hitler's Nazi regime found their way to Australia --- a country which already had a similar number of Jews of English origin, who had become prominent Australian figures. The most famous of said Jews of English origin is General sir John Monash,[447] who successfully led the Australian troops in the Gallipoli battles in Europe during World War I on the side of the allied forces. Sir Monash had been memorialized by naming the Australian Monash university on his name, as well as by printing his image on the highest denomination of the Australian currency --- the $100 Australian dollar bill.[448]

After the second World War, Australia had received some holocaust survivors; and in recent years, quite a few South-African Jews have immigrated to Australia. Although Australian-Jews are about 0.5% of Australia's population, they are heavily involved in the Australian economy; and some hold huge business enterprises. Among many successful big businesses i will mention, the huge packaging company Visy Industries --- which has nearly 10 000 employees --- was established by a holocaust survivor named Richard Pratt.[449] The company is now controlled by his son Anthony Pratt, who is considered to be the richest man in Australia.[450]

---

[442] "Investec | Specialist Bank and Asset Manager." https://www.investec.com/en_gb.html. Accessed 13 Feb. 2018.
[443] "Liberty | A leading financial services group." http://www.liberty.co.za/. Accessed 13 Feb. 2018.
[444] "Discovery." https://discovery.co.za/. Accessed 13 Feb. 2018.
[445] "Obituary: Harry Oppenheimer, diamond baron | News | The Guardian." 20 Aug. 2000, https://www.theguardian.com/news/2000/aug/21/guardianobituaries.davidpallister. Accessed 13 Feb. 2018.
[446] "Our Board of directors | Glencore." http://www.glencore.com/who-we-are/board-of-directors/. Accessed 13 Feb. 2018.
[447] "Biography - Sir John Monash - Australian Dictionary of Biography." http://adb.anu.edu.au/biography/monash-sir-john-7618. Accessed 13 Feb. 2018.
[448] "RBA Banknotes: $100 Banknote - Reserve Bank of Australia Banknotes." https://banknotes.rba.gov.au/australias-banknotes/banknotes-in-circulation/hundred-dollar/. Accessed 13 Feb. 2018.
[449] "Richard Pratt (Australian businessman) - Wikipedia." https://en.wikipedia.org/wiki/Richard_Pratt_(Australian_businessman). Accessed 13 Feb. 2018.
[450] "Anthony Pratt (businessman) - Wikipedia." https://en.wikipedia.org/wiki/Anthony_Pratt_(businessman). Accessed 13 Feb. 2018.

Another is the property empire Westfield, which owns shopping centers around the world, and was built and owned by another holocaust survivor named Frank Lowy.[451]

South and central America

The Jews who landed in South and central America are concentrated mainly in Argentina and Brazil. Brazil already had Jews that came over from Morocco and the Middle-East. Today, the community there is estimated at around 100 000 people. It consists of 25% Sephardic-Jews, and 75% Ashkenazi Jews. The most famous for his business success is the banker Joseph Safra, whose family had come over from Syria. Mr. Safra is considered to be the second richest person in Brazil, and one of the richest bankers in the world.

In Argentina, the Jewish population is estimated at around 200 000 individuals, and its composition is about 80% Ashkenazi and 20% Sephardic. The Jews in Argentina do not seem to be among the top business people in the country. Most of them are of middle-to-upper-class economic status. Quite a few have immigrated to Israel due to inherent anti-Semitism in Argentina (largely in part of Catholicism).

Canada

Most of the Jews in Canada are Ashkenazi-Jews who had arrived from Eastern-Europe during the early part of the previous century, and after World War II. At that time, a tiny Sephardic-Jewish community of a couple hundred individuals had already been established in Canada. Since then, there has been growing immigration of Sephardic-Jews from France and Morocco into French-speaking Quebec, and mainly to the city of Montreal. Today, the total population of Canadian-Jews --- which include a substantial number of Israelis --- is estimated at around 400 000.

Canadian-Jews are also prominent in the Canadian economy. Some of the top businessmen are of Jewish origin. Some Canadian Jewish billionaires are: internet and media investor, Jeffrey skoll[452]; Israeli-Canadian real estate tycoon, David Azrieli[453] ; and Big-Pharma businessmen, Daryl Katz[454] and Bernard Sherman.[455]

The United States of America

Jewish immigration to the United States of America had already been described in chapter 1. Apart from the earlier immigration of Sephardic-Jewish people, the majority had come from Germany and Eastern-Europe. German-Jews who had escaped the anti-Jewish laws and restrictions --- and the occasional pogroms against them in Germany in the late 19th century --- had created the basis for the Jewish people's 'American Dream'.

The economic success of those German-Jewish immigrants had become a beacon of hope for the masses of dispossessed Eastern-European Jews in the early part of the 20th century.

---

[451] "Frank Lowy - Wikipedia." https://en.wikipedia.org/wiki/Frank_Lowy. Accessed 13 Feb. 2018.
[452] "Jeffrey Skoll - Forbes." https://www.forbes.com/profile/jeffrey-skoll/. Accessed 13 Feb. 2018.
[453] "David Azrieli & family - Forbes." https://www.forbes.com/profile/david-azrieli/. Accessed 13 Feb. 2018.
[454] "Daryl Katz - Forbes." https://www.forbes.com/profile/daryl-katz/. Accessed 13 Feb. 2018.
[455] "Bernard (Barry) Sherman - Forbes." https://www.forbes.com/profile/bernard-barry-sherman/. Accessed 13 Feb. 2018.

To them, America seemed to be the new Biblical 'promise land'; with limitless possibilities, and an end to thousands of years of persecution.

Most newcomers from Eastern-Europe had filled New York's poor neighbourhoods. Many went into the clothing industry business; as quite a few Jewish women, and men, had been skilled in this profession in Eastern-Europe.

From New York, Jews had expanded all over America; creating businesses everywhere. There is no doubt that their intellectual capacity, and entrepreneurial spirit, has driven America to economic heights never before seen on this earth. The list of Jewish intellectual and business personalities is too long to describe in this book. Some have been mentioned in chapter One, as well as in other parts of this book. Apart from America, the most interesting development of Jewish life had been in its Biblical ancestral land of Israel.

Israel

As European-Jews had searched for refuge in America, and new European individuals had settled in countries such as Australia, South-Africa, and Canada --- by the year 1924, America had begun to close the gate on indiscriminate Jewish immigration. Many of the Jews in Europe began to sense the growing anti-Semitism in the continent (especially in Germany, which had been immersed in anger from their humiliating defeat in World War I; and their miserable, hyper-inflated economy thereafter --- for which many middle-to-lower-class Germans blamed the Jews).[456]

The newly-formed Zionist movement had been in a deep search for a safe haven for European-Jews --- a haven which could also become a home to persecuted Jews from around the world in the future.

Although some Jews had already settled in Ottoman-Palestine, it had not looked like a viable option to many of the Zionist movement leaders. The country had a reputation of being uninhabitable --- desertous in large areas in the South, and malaria stricken in the North. It had also lacked natural resources.[457]

Instead of Palestine, other countries had been considered. Uganda had been proposed by the British[458] (and even Madagascar,[459] later on by the Nazi's). Unlike Palestine, these countries had been bountiful in natural resources; and seemed to be better suited for sustaining millions of people.

As mentioned above, Ottoman-Palestine had mainly been a desert. Large tracts of land had been infested with malaria. Even the Arab bedouins never dared to live there. The Zionist movement had considered the efforts of Ukrainian-Jews to settle in these areas of Palestine,

---

[456] "Antisemitism in History: World War I." https://www.ushmm.org/wlc/en/article.php?ModuleId=10007166. Accessed 13 Feb. 2018.
[457] "Habitation of Palestine - Arabs Speak Frankly." https://www.arabsspeakfrankly.co.uk/pdfs/5-habitation-of-palestine.pdf. Accessed 13 Feb. 2018.
[458] "The Uganda Proposal (1903) - Jewish Virtual Library." http://www.jewishvirtuallibrary.org/the-uganda-proposal-1903. Accessed 15 Feb. 2018.
[459] "The Madagascar Plan - Jewish Virtual Library." http://www.jewishvirtuallibrary.org/the-madagascar-plan-2. Accessed 15 Feb. 2018.

as being unrealistic and nostalgic --- a mere dream of some die-hard ideological movements. The dire state of the Ottoman-Palestinian territory in 1867 was recorded by Mark Twain, in his 'innocents abroad' travel journal.[460]

'. . . A desolate country whose soil is rich enough, but is given over wholly to weeds . . . a silent mournful expanse . . . a desolation . . . we never saw a human being on the whole route . . . hardly a tree or shrub anywhere. Even the olive tree and the cactus, those fast friends of a worthless soil, had almost deserted the country.'[461]

Jerusalem's population was quoted at 14,000 people and comprised of Arabs, Jews, Greeks and Armenians . . . 'Jerusalem is mournful and dreary, and lifeless . I would not desire to live here'.[462]

Nevertheless, only 13 years after Twain's visit to Ottoman-Palestine, ideologically Zionist inspired Jews from the Russian-Empire --- in the areas which are now under modern-day Ukraine --- began to arrive in Ottoman-Palestine. They had begun settling into those desolated and malaria-stricken areas in the Galilee, and around lake Tiberias; draining and clearing the land from the malaria mosquitos[463] --- many dying in the process.

In 1909, still under the Ottoman-Empire's rule, some 66 Jewish families began building the city of Tel-Aviv. It had been built upon the sand dunes just North of the city of Jaffa (which had a majority Arab population). From historical records, it is apparent that the founders had aimed to establish a European-style city, which would be clean and modern --- with: a proper sewage system; electricity; roads, and other modern amenities. Unlike its neighbouring city, Jaffa.

In 1917, during the first World War, the inhabitants of Tel-Aviv were briefly expelled by Ottoman authorities. Following the defeat of the Ottomans by the British army, said inhabitants had returned to their homes immediately.

At first, under the British rule and following the historically renowned Balfour declaration, Jews had enjoyed the freedom to build and create settlements and industry all over British-Palestine. However, many of the areas had been uninhabitable and malaria-stricken --- as many as half of the first zionist settlers died from malaria complications.

An American-Jewish zionist named Dr. Israel Jacob Kligler[464] had changed this situation. The brilliant Dr. Kligler had devised a plan to rid the area of the dreaded malaria. This plan had included a novel education system of preventing the breeding of mosquitoes --- a plan which had eventually succeeded in eradicating malaria from British-Palestine.[465] His methods to combat malaria are still used around the world today.

Following the eradication of malaria, many zionist settlements began to spring up --- further attracting Jewish zionist settlers (as well as a high influx of Arabs from the nowadays neighbouring countries of: Iraq; Syria; Jordan, and Egypt --- individuals who had sought after a better life than the one they had in the surrounding Arab territories).

---

[460] https://archive.org/stream/innocentsabroad02twai#page/240/mode/2up (accessed May 2016)
[461] Ibid 242-347
[462] Ibid 328-329
[463] "The key to successful malaria eradication in Palestine/Israel 90 years ...." 1 Jun. 2012, https://malariaworld.org/blog/key-successful-malaria-eradication-palestineisrael-90-years-ago. Accessed 13 Feb. 2018.
[464] "Israel Jacob Kligler - Wikipedia." https://en.wikipedia.org/wiki/Israel_Jacob_Kligler. Accessed 13 Feb. 2018.
[465] "Elimination of Malaria in Palestine 90 years ago ... that Dr Kligler did.." https://www.eradication-of-malaria.com/elimination-and-after.pdf. Accessed 13 Feb. 2018.

In 1924, the construction of the City of Herzliya[466] had begun; and in 1928 --- following the discovery of underground water --- the construction of the City of Netanya[467] had begun. New small settlements (known as kibbutzim) began popping up all over British mandate Palestine.

The major development of British-Palestine had enhanced further Jewish manpower from Eastern-Europe (as well as Jewish investments and 'knowhow' from rich Western-European Jews). Arabs from the surrounding areas of the newly-created countries of Syria and Lebanon --- carved out of territories of the French mandate --- had also arrived in British Mandate Palestine; looking for work opportunities. Others from British mandate Transjordan, and the Arab Republic of Egypt (who had already gained independence from Britain in 1922) had arrived in British Mandate Palestine --- some had come from as far as the Kingdom of Iraq (who had gained independence in 1932). Many of the Arab surnames indicate their place of origin: Al-Masri (the Egyptian); Al-Huri (the person from Ur in Iraq); Al-Halabi (the person from Haleb in Syria), and Al-Cahiri (the person from Cairo) are some of those surnames.

The high rate of Arab and Jewish population growth in British-Palestine --- as well as the will by both populations to gain independence from Britain --- had created friction and growing animosity between the two populations.

The first protesting incident is recorded as the 1920 Nebi Musa Arab riots[468] in Jerusalem; where 5 Jews, and 4 Arabs, had died. By 1929, a major eruption of Arab violence against Jews --- known as the 1929 Hebron massacres[469] --- had commenced; beginning in Jerusalem, then spreading into Hebron and Safed. The end result had been the death of 133 Jews, and 110 Arabs.

The story of the Hebron massacre is especially revealing. Following initial tensions with Arabs, the mainly religious Jews who inhabited Hebron rejected an offer from the secular 'Haganah' Jewish military organization to send armed men to protect them. Their argument had been that they had trust in their long historical positive relationship with the local Arab leaders (Jews had continuously lived in Hebron for thousands of years, and many Arabs there can even trace their family origins to Jews who had converted to Islam, over hundreds of years). This fatal mistake resulted in 69 Jews massacred, and the fleeing of survivors. That had been the *end* of the long historical Jewish settlement in Hebron (that had lasted for thousands of years[470] --- only to be revived some 38 years after that massacre, following the 1967 war between Israel and its surrounding Arab neighbours).[471]

The British managed to quell the massacres and riots of 1929; however, by 1936, a massive uprising by the Arabs had erupted --- demanding an end to the British mandate, as well as an end to Jewish immigration from Europe.[472] This uprising had been implemented by terrorist attacks on British soldiers, and Jews, around the country. It had lasted 3 years; by which

---

[466] "Herzliya - Wikipedia." https://en.wikipedia.org/wiki/Herzliya. Accessed 15 Feb. 2018.
[467] "History." http://www.netanya.muni.il/Eng/?CategoryID=1617. Accessed 15 Feb. 2018.
[468] "1920 Nebi Musa riots - Wikipedia." https://en.wikipedia.org/wiki/1920_Nebi_Musa_riots. Accessed 15 Feb. 2018.
[469] "1929 Hebron massacre - Wikipedia." https://en.wikipedia.org/wiki/1929_Hebron_massacre. Accessed 15 Feb. 2018.
[470] "1929: Hebron massacre begins, with a big push from the mufti - Haaretz." 23 Aug. 2016, https://www.haaretz.com/jewish/1929-hebron-massacre-begins-1.5427655. Accessed 15 Feb. 2018.
[471] "History & Overview of Hebron - Jewish Virtual Library." http://www.jewishvirtuallibrary.org/history-and-overview-of-hebron. Accessed 15 Feb. 2018.
[472] "1936–1939 Arab revolt in Palestine - Wikipedia." https://en.wikipedia.org/wiki/1936%E2%80%931939_Arab_revolt_in_Palestine. Accessed 15 Feb. 2018.

thousands of Arabs had been killed, or hanged, by the British. Hundreds of Jews were murdered, raped, and pillaged by Arabs. 262 British soldiers and citizens had also been killed.

The impact that this violent Arab uprising had on the Jewish settlement of Palestine had been the opposite of what the Arabs had hoped for. A further 50 000 Jews had arrived into the country during that period; while a replacement for the Jaffa seaport had been constructed in Tel-Aviv.[473] The new Tel-Aviv seaport had effectively eliminated the reliance on the Jaffa seaport, and the Arab workforce there.

However, the British realized that their involvement in the Arab-Jewish conflict had damaged their relations in the Arab world in general; and had put their oil companies interests at risk. Due to the looming confrontation with Germany in Europe, the English had concluded that they would rather limit Jewish aspirations than risk further confrontation with the Arabs. The British prime minister Neville Chamberlain's famous quote had been: 'If we must offend one side, let us offend the Jews rather than the Arabs'[474] . . . and so the British did (the new found oil in Arab Gulf countries and Saudi Arabia had been too tempting to surrender).

This change of policy had been translated to restrictions on Jewish immigration, and a host of raids on Jewish settlements to confiscate arms, and catch/execute leaders who had blatantly resisted the British mandate.[475]

Although during World War II the situation in British-Palestine had been relatively calm --- and co-operation between the Jews and the British had begun to take form --- Jewish resistance had intensified; as nearly a million Jewish holocaust survivors became refugees in Europe. Many traumatized Jews began adopting the idea that only an independent, Jewish state could provide protection from a repeat of the horrors they had experienced under the Nazis in Europe.

Following a bitter attrition war of terrorism by the Jewish resistance movements --- against the 100 000 British troops stationed in Palestine, as well as against British economic interests --- rendering Palestine ungovernable; the British had realized that they could no longer stand between Arabs and Jews in Palestine, as neither party had desired British presence there. Britain had also been faced with growing pressures from the world community regarding the immigration restrictions on European-Jewish holocaust survivors, who were now desperate to get into Israel.

By late 1946, Winston Churchill had called to leave Palestine, and hand it over to the United Nations.[476] This had also been in line with the earlier handing of independence to the Arab territories of: Syria; Lebanon; and TransJordan (during 1946) that had been carved from the French and British mandates.

By 1947, the British had hastily organised their departure from Palestine. The United Nations was to determine the future of Palestine. The Jewish population had been looking for a partition of Palestine into a Jewish state, and an Arab state --- while the Arabs, backed by the newly-formed Arab league of States, had been adamant in rejecting any solution (save a One-State solution, ruled by the Arab majority in Palestine).

---

[473] "Tel Aviv Port - Wikipedia." https://en.wikipedia.org/wiki/Tel_Aviv_Port. Accessed 15 Feb. 2018.
[474] "Britain's role in bringing in illegal Arabs and keeping out Jews, trying ...."
http://www.eretzyisroel.org/~jkatz/return.html. Accessed 15 Feb. 2018.
[475] "The British Army in Palestine, 1945-48 | National Army Museum."
https://www.nam.ac.uk/explore/conflict-Palestine. Accessed 15 Feb. 2018.
[476] "Churchill and the Jews - Churchill, Zionism, & the Holocaust."
https://www.winstonchurchill.org/publications/finest-hour/finest-hour-170/churchill-and-the-jews/.
Accessed 15 Feb. 2018.

On 28th of November 1947 --- after a vote by the United Nations that had partitioned Palestine and recognized the Jewish part as the State of Israel[477] --- violence and full-scale civil war broke out between the Arabs and Jews.

Although the Palestinian-Arab population had been greater in numbers, they were no match for the highly-sophisticated and well-organized Jews of European descent. Around 700 000 Arabs had fled from Palestine, into the the surrounding Arab countries. Around 100 000 had been concentrated on the borders of Egypt (in what is known today as the Gaza strip), while most had landed in refugee camps in Jordan, Syria, and Lebanon. Violence, killings, and restrictions had been implemented against Jews in Arab countries --- while the Arab armies had waited to intervene, and wage war against the Jews in Palestine.[478]

On the 14th of May, 1948 --- the last day of the British mandate --- the Jewish people had declared the State of Israel. The following day, the combined armies of: Egypt; Jordan; Syria; and Iraq, began to invade Palestine, and the newly formed State of Israel. A bitter war between the newly-formed State of Israel, and its surrounding Arab countries, had begun --- war that had lasted for nearly a year. It came to an end with an armistice agreement on March 1949.[479]

The outcome of this war had been that Israel managed to keep most of the Jewish territories allotted to them by the United Nations partition resolution (as well as 50% of the land allotted to the Arabs). The Egyptian, Syrian, and Iraqi armies had been defeated. Only the Jordanian army had partly succeeded by capturing most of the West Bank; which had included the Jewish territories of Gush-Etzion, and East-Jerusalem (with all its holy places --- including the Jewish quarter. Overall, the league of Arab States had been physically and a strategically defeated.

Threatened by mass-scale retribution by Arab governments --- and having already experienced violent crimes by the hands of neighbouring Muslim-Arabs --- nearly one million Arab-Jews, within the Arab world, had fled the countries of their birth. With the help of Israeli and American Jewish organisations, Jews had evacuated countries where Judaic people had been living for thousands of years --- even long before Arabs had occupied them. It is estimated that around 850 000 Arab-Jews had eventually found refuge in Israel, while another 150 000 found their way to other Western countries (mainly: the United States; France; England; and Canada).

While many of the Jews that came from North-Africa and Yemen had not been wealthy; a large amount of Jews that came from Iraq and Egypt were considered to have been highly educated and wealthy --- holding high statuses in their countries of origin. In order to leave, their governments had given the Jews an ultimatum: they had to abandon their property, and renounce their citizenship --- leaving with naught but one individual suitcase (which could not even contain any valuables; only clothing, and personal items).

This forgotten piece of history is still crying out for justice. The Palestinian-Arab refugees have been recognized by the United Nations and various other agencies; and have been helped for generations . . . while the Arab-Jewish refugees had never never assisted whatsoever by any of said entities.

---

[477] "C h a p t e r - the United Nations." http://www.un.org/Depts/dpi/palestine/ch2.pdf. Accessed 15 Feb. 2018.
[478] "Jewish exodus from Arab and Muslim countries - Wikipedia." https://en.wikipedia.org/wiki/Jewish_exodus_from_Arab_and_Muslim_countries. Accessed 15 Feb. 2018.
[479] "The Arab-Israeli War of 1948 - Office of the Historian - Department of ...." https://history.state.gov/milestones/1945-1952/arab-israeli-war. Accessed 15 Feb. 2018.

The Israeli government (mainly of Jewish-European descent) had also been inconsiderate to these people. They had welcomed all Jews in order to 'beef up' the Jewish population in Israel; but at the same time, dumped most of these 'Arab-Jews' in the outlying border areas of Israel. Over the years, these Jews have been systematically discriminated against; and relatively neglected for generations by the succeeding Israeli governments.[480]

Due to my surname that is associated with Sephardic-Jewish ancestry, I have personally experienced the inherent discrimination and prejudice of Israeli Ashkenazi-Jews --- who come from Europe --- towards Israeli Sephardic-Jews (who had originated mainly in Arab countries). Nevertheless, I will not be elaborating on this type of discrimination, as I had still recieved a good education in Israel, and have done relatively well in my life abroad.

This discrimination, however, had eventually assisted me in my understanding of anti-Semitism and racism as a fact of life. The realization that there is even discrimination between Jews *themselves* simply based on their perceived geographical origin, has cemented many of my ideas about anti-Semitism itself. My life experience in South-Africa has also contributed to my understanding about racism and ethnic discrimination between African nations (and within the country's own tribes). All those experiences in my life have made me realize that racism and anti-Semitism are related in many ways --- there are many reasons why they cannot be eradicated (this will be discussed in more detail in Chapter 14 on anti-Semitism, and in my next book about human life).

Since 1948, the State of Israel has experienced about 6 major wars with its surrounding Arab neighbours, as well as tens of thousands of terrorist attacks; with thousands of casualties. A few immigration waves of self-proclaimed Jews from around the world had also been recurrent since 1948 (the largest being of about 1 000 000 people from the former Soviet Union).[481]

Today, Israel has a population of nearly nine million people --- all of diverse religious affiliations that range from completely secular atheists, to ultra-religious Jews who dress uniformly with black-coloured clothing. There are about one-and-a-half million Arabs that hold Israeli citizenship, but claim to be Palestinian-Arabs. There are also another combined four million Arabs in the West Bank and Gaza strip, who claim to be Palestinians. A total of 13 million people on an area of about 27,000km squared --- One of the most densely populated areas in the world. A place that, only 130 years ago, had been one of the least populated areas in the world . . . completely barren and desolate.

Through all this strife and tension between all those populations, Israel has become a successful country in computer high-tech (as well as in other high-tech industries). This small country had an export revenue from high-tech of nearly $23 billion in 2017; and a GDP of nearly $400 billion (with a GDP per capita of around $44,000 --- surpassing some long-established European countries such as: the U.K.; France; Italy, and Belgium.[482]

These economic indicators are significant, as most of the country is: desertous, with almost no natural resources; has high military-defense and security costs; and, has a third of its population consisting of Ultra-religious Jews and Palestinian-Arabs who receive state aid (yet contribute very little to the economy). Nevertheless, the other half of the population seem to

---

[480] "Racism in Israel - Wikipedia." https://en.wikipedia.org/wiki/Racism_in_Israel. Accessed 15 Feb. 2018.
[481] "1990s Post-Soviet aliyah - Wikipedia." https://en.wikipedia.org/wiki/1990s_Post-Soviet_aliyah. Accessed 15 Feb. 2018.
[482] "Israel - A Successful Powerhouse in the Collapsing Middle East - Mida." 15 Jan. 2018, http://en.mida.org.il/2018/01/15/israel-successful-powerhouse-collapsing-middle-east/. Accessed 15 Feb. 2018.

advance the country towards new heights within the high-tech computer and cyber technology fields. As the world becomes more and more technological, the ethnic-Jewish mind and entrepreneurial spirit may yet-again prove itself to be a formidable force to be reckoned with.

The way forward

Apart from the historical value of the above paragraphs, it has been established that today; the majority of ethnic-Jewish people live in the USA and Israel. In chapter One, the achievements of American ethnic-Jews in the vast American land of opportunity had been described. This chapter has mainly described the much smaller ethnic-Jewish groups who had landed in Israel, and had to endure extremely inhospitable physical conditions (such as the desert, malaria, and very hostile neighbours). Yet, through determination and innovation, they had prevailed and prospered.

The nearly 70 year old state of Israel is still expanding economically; with one of the highest foreign reserves per capita, in the world. This trend of economic expansion may become even stronger as Israel engages with the innovation and exportation of computer and cyber technologies --- industries which are considered to be most lucrative.

However, the political and demographic future stability of Israel is still very unpredictable . . . but the same applies for the entire Middle-East, as it is mired with conflicts between the various ethnic-Arab populations.

Chapter 13

The Inherent conflict between religions, and the new-world religions

Summary: This chapter will try to explain why there are religious conflicts around the world. It will also argue that many of the modern social and financial systems around the world are akin to religions. The insights about religious, and ideological, conflicts may partially explain anti-Semitism --- which is, in its core, an ideological conflict.

'Religion is opiate to the masses' --- Karl Marx

This chapter is about trying to understand religion in-depth. Why were religions formed, and why is there a deep-rooted historical conflict between religions? Such understanding may further explore, and explain, anti-Semitism and racism. It will also be very useful for understanding the current problems that the world is facing (mostly with regard to the gruesome fights in the Middle-East and Yemen between the Sunni-Muslims, and the Shia-Muslims). The historical: Jewish; Muslim; and Christian conflicts, as well as the conflicts between modern countries' social and economic systems, will also be explored in this chapter --- social and economic systems which may be considered akin to religions.

This chapter is based on a research essay that I had done as part of my final year LLB studies at the Witwatersrand university in Johannesburg, South-Africa. However, I have realized that writing according to stringent academic requirements turns a document into a monotonous and boring piece of writing; rendering it an unfulfilling read.

I have therefore written and explained the essence of this research essay, and have added material for a religion that is not covered in the essay --- the new 'capitalistic religion'. This capitalistic religion is incredibly interesting, as it has managed to capture the masses in the Western world under a slogan of secular liberalism and freedom. This kind of religion is efficiently promoted on a daily basis by the electronic media. The capitalistic elite use the media as a tool to produce fiction and manipulate the minds of individuals . . . very similar to the historical indoctrinative role the Church had played during the Middle Ages in Europe. This stranglehold on the information that the public receives promotes their action in a way that enhances capitalism and consumerism further --- enriching the political and business leaders of this modern 'religion'.

Like any religion throughout the course of history, once the religion controls the mind of the people, it can control their actions in order to benefit the religious leaders of the system. Today, this process of exploitation is carried out better than ever. Most of the world's population are glued to screens that constantly preach what the capitalist owners of society want to convey; prompting action that benefits the capitalist owners. This process is almost full-proof, and truly acts --- as Karl Marx defined it --- as an opiate to the masses. The addiction is stronger than ever --- yet there is some hope . . . the internet. The internet can be used by people who would like to provide alternative options.

The internet has proven that the traditional media of T.V. programs and newspaper writings can be challenged now. This had been proven in the recent American presidential elections. The media totally blasted, and heavily disapproved of, Mr. Donald Trump. Yet, when push came to shove; he had been elected as president of the U.S. (due to a mostly internet-based campaign using twitter). Another example of the internet defying the media is the cryptocurrency phenomenon, which is largely driven by the internet as opposed to traditional financial media.

The deep-rooted conflict of religions

The following is an abstract from my research essay. It briefly explains what the essay was about. Although it had been research aimed at explaining the existence of deep-rooted conflict between traditional religions in general --- and conflicts within the modern secular Legal system (another kind of system which is akin to religion) --- it may also enlighten the reader as to why traditional religions, such as Christianity, had a high content of anti-Semitic write-up. It may also explain why Islamic scriptures have a high content of anti-Christian *as well as* anti-Semitic, write-up.

It might come as a surprise to many of the readers that religion is very hard to define. The oxford dictionary definition can demonstrate the complexities regarding the definition of religion.[483] Even the oxford dictionary definition still lacks many aspects which are connected to religion (such as ethnicity, morality, and social order).

A major aspect of a newly-founded religion is about domination of the new, over the old. A new religion is basically offering a new product, while at the same time discrediting the old product. This is a kind of survival mechanism (even though the new product may be quite similar to the old one). It is the way of nature in general; as the old must be forgotten, in order for the new to flourish. However, the old always fights back. Nothing wants to lose its power, die off, and be forgotten. Everyone, and every system, wants to be relevant. My research abstract, which pits the Western world's rule of law against religious countries' Legal systems, may explain some of those points further:

'Religious wars and terrorism around the world have developed between Theocratic states and their affiliated factions such as ISIL who claim divine religious laws as their legal and moral foundations and Secular states which are governed by a human rights based legal system. This points to a deep inherent conflict between Theocratic States and Secular States. This paper strives to explore and explain the roots of the conflict through a historical journey and analysis of the religious and secular belief systems. It is also claimed that historical movements and regimes such as Marxism, Communism, Fascism and Nazism, as well as Apartheid, were also historical belief systems akin to religion that faltered thus helping to shape the current secular human rights belief system.

The paper then explores the relatively recent and novel beliefs of human rights such as: the right to life; freedom; security, and women's and children's rights, as opposed to older religious legal systems which emphasize duties that might result in capital punishment if breached. Ancient religious crimes such as adultery, apostasy, and heresy --- which are no longer considered crimes in the secular state --- are still followed by capital punishment in Theocratic states; violating the secular most sacred right to life. All this results in a seemingly unbridgeable legal and moral gap between those systems of belief.

The paper also describes the suspicion that religious states and entities have towards the secular states, viewing them as: ungodly; immoral; indulgence and greed oriented societies,

---

[483] "religion | Definition of religion in English by Oxford Dictionaries."
https://en.oxforddictionaries.com/definition/religion. Accessed 17 Feb. 2018.

that should be subjected to a Holy war. Following the historical and current analysis which proves the deep inherent conflict, some thoughts about ways of resolving the conflict are discussed. Finally, education is identified as the tool that provides a ray of hope for the resolution of this inherent conflict'.

Working on this essay gave me the realisation that firstly, throughout history, people had been concerned with their ethnic survival --- religion had simply been a powerful means of this ethnic survival. That is why Sunni-Muslims --- who are mostly associated with Arabs --- are at odds with Shia Muslims (who are mostly associated with Persians). The hate between them is historical and deep-rooted. Religious differences had been created to distinguish between those ethnic groups. Some minor ethnic-Arab groups, like the Syrian Alawites, have adopted their own modified Shia religious stream as a resistance tool against their larger oppressive Arab groups.

Secondly, the survival motive is also rooted deep within the ethnic groups themselves; right into the influential families within those ethnic groups. In the Jewish religion, it had been the Levi's and Cohen's who were treated as a kind of religious royalty; with a direct lineage to the prophet Moses,[484] receiving privileges and benefits. While in Islam, it had been the Abbasids who claimed a lineage to Muhammad's family --- even naming their first Caliph as Muhammad. In Christianity the spread of the religion in the Roman-Empire had at first been strongly linked to the political maneuvering and survival of Emperor Constantine the Great.[485] He had built a ring of new loyal Christian supporters around him, and successfully shielded his reign from the traditional power-hungry conspiring pagan-Roman elites.

Thirdly, it has been shown through historical documentation that religions evolve and create new branches. Like Christianity, which had generated a whole array of denominations in Europe and America: Orthodox; Catholic; Lutheran; Calvinist; Protestant; Evangelists; Newborn, and many more smaller denominations over the years.[486] A process which is still ongoing in modern times. Judaism as well had sects such as: Orthodox; Karaites; Hasidic; other Haredi factions; Conservatives, and Reform.[487] This is also true to any religion (at some stage of its life cycle).

In the research essay, I have shown that the new movements in the beginning of the last century (namely Communism, Fascism, and Nazism) were akin to religion. They all had ideological ideas and symbols that had been followed in a kind of a religious manner. They were also determined to ruin all other religious systems (a practice that had been especially evident in communist Russia, when communism nearly wiped out the Russian Church).[488] It was also apparent in Hitler's Nazi regime, which completely weakened the German Christian Churches, and was recorded with intent to demolish Christianity at 'the right time' in the

---

[484] "The Tribes Today - Kohens, Levis & Yisraels - Jewish Virtual Library." http://www.jewishvirtuallibrary.org/the-tribes-today-kohens-levis-and-yisraels. Accessed 17 Feb. 2018.
[485] "Controversial Constantine | Christian History." http://www.christianitytoday.com/history/issues/issue-27/controversial-constantine.html. Accessed 17 Feb. 2018.
[486] "List of Christian Denominations & Their Beliefs | churchrelevance.com." 22 Jun. 2012, https://churchrelevance.com/qa-list-of-all-christian-denominations-and-their-beliefs/. Accessed 17 Feb. 2018.
[487] "Judaism 101: Movements of Judaism." http://www.jewfaq.org/movement.htm. Accessed 17 Feb. 2018.
[488] "Russian Christianity and the Revolution: What Happened? | Christian ...." http://www.christianitytoday.com/history/issues/issue-18/russian-christianity-and-revolution-what-happened.html. Accessed 17 Feb. 2018.

future.[489] Those secular communist and Nazi systems --- which are akin to religions --- had eventually collapsed due to their own brutality and clashes between themselves (as well as due to better designed systems such as America's capitalist system). Now, we are witnessing perhaps the strongest religion so far --- the religion of capitalism.

Although I am a minor beneficiary of this religion, I am not in love with it; as I believe it harbours a lot of harmful elements. In recent years --- after the 2008 financial crash --- this system has been developed into an even more greedy system than the one before 2008.

I would like to write my views on this religion, and will be happy if my learned readers can enlighten me regarding said religion. It seems to me that today, it has the Western world in a tight grip; with no signs to indicate that this religion will fade anytime soon. This religion is of interest for this book, because many of the leaders of this religion are ethnic-Jews. Some estimates are as high as 40% of America's financial personalities are of Jewish origin.

Turning capitalism into one of America's religions

The basis was there. Many of the new settlers of America were Christian Protestants. To become rich in America was not only desirable, but it had become a great religious deed. One of the most famous personalities advocating for wealth and philanthropy had been the Scottish-American industrialist Andrew Carnegie (who is also considered to be the wealthiest man in the modern-era).[490] His published essay, 'the gospel of wealth'[491] has influenced generations of America's wealthy individuals. For a few hundred years now, America has been revering the rich, and some would even say that America has built a culture of indifference towards the poor.[492]

This reverence and respect for rich people in America in the 18th century can also be gleaned upon from Mark Twain's open letter, which has been quoted in this book a few times. As Mr. Twain speaks about the Jew, he expresses his own American culture's feelings about money.

'He long ago observed that a millionaire commands respect, a two-millionaire homage, a multi-millionaire the deepest deeps of adoration. We all know that feeling; we have seen it express itself. We have noticed that when the average man mentions the name of a multi-millionaire he does it with that mixture in his voice of awe and reverence and lust which burns in a Frenchman's eye when it falls on another man's centime.'

This American setting had been perfect for Jewish people who, throughout their history, needed to find ways of making money in order to survive in the hostile world around them. This time 'round, there had been no greedy monarchs who would take their money away. There was no mob organized by the Church to kill and rob them of their possessions. This time, there had been a democratic system; with a written constitution that had promised

---

[489] "Hitler, Himmler, and Christianity in the Early Third Reich." http://digitalcommons.iwu.edu/cgi/viewcontent.cgi?article=1200&context=constructing. Accessed 17 Feb. 2018.
[490] "Andrew Carnegie's Story - Carnegie Corporation of New York." https://www.carnegie.org/interactives/foundersstory/. Accessed 17 Feb. 2018.
[491] "The Gospel of Wealth : Publications | Carnegie Corporation of New York." https://www.carnegie.org/publications/the-gospel-of-wealth/. Accessed 17 Feb. 2018.
[492] "Poverty in America is a moral outrage. The soul of our nation is at ...." 16 Dec. 2017, https://www.theguardian.com/commentisfree/2017/dec/16/poverty-america-moral-outrage-nation. Accessed 17 Feb. 2018.

equality before the Law. Further than that, the general population --- who were mainly of British descent --- had not encountered Jews for more than 500 years since the expulsion of Jews from England in the year 1290. They did not harbour any deep animosity toward the Jews. They had also been different than their English ancestors. Their puritan base had filled them with many ancient Jewish ideals. They saw themselves as the continuation of ancient Israelites from the Torah's stories.[493] It may be that some were even mixed descendants of converted ethnic-Jews before the expulsion of Jews from England in 1290, as most of their values had emphasized the Old Testament (this had been in contrast with the majority of Christian-Europe which had only promoted the New Testament, and neglected the Old Testament). The prophet Moses --- the Biblical liberator --- in particular had occupied a special place in their heart. The Hebrews' exodus from Egypt into the promised land of Israel had been the puritans' inspiration. They had equated it to their own exodus out of England and into the new promise land of America[494] --- a divine repetition of history according to their belief.

Following the establishment of these new Christian denominations, Jews had been accepted at first; as sort of 'old distant relatives'. Quite a few of the new arrivals of Sephardi-Jews had been assimilated, and formed mixed Christian communities which had been far less hostile toward Jews than the old European-Christian populations.

This new accepting environment was most probably a magnificent surprise to the first Western-European Jews who had journeyed to America in the 19th century. The opportunity was there --- German-Jews knew how to: start businesses; trade; market; and sell, better than any ethnic group in America. There are many stories --- some about Levi Strauss, the innovator of 'Levi's' jeans and trousers. Another story is of the writings of B.E. Lloyd, about the leadership of Jews in business in California. These stories are testimony to the Jews' business success in America.[495]

The rapid success and inhostility made many ethnic-Jews integrate with the population in the West of the United States. Many became mayors of small towns, and instrumental in many endeavours (such as the bringing of railway to Los Angeles). This trend of integration and assimilation has featured all-along Jewish history (as has been shown throughout this book).

When traditional religion becomes less of a factor and loses its importance, Jews --- like anybody else --- would integrate and assimilate. The conditions in America were, and still are, conducive to this process. It is however important to note that *the assimilated* bring their own culture to the table. Some of their values stick, eventually changing the general population's values and perceptions. A new mixed and evolving culture develops --- the American business-oriented culture.

If Protestant-America had revered the entrepreneurial capitalist; it has now become all engulfed, and admiring of the Jewish 'money-making machines'. Both populations become more and more secular and money-orientated. Protestants become more Jewish-business like and secularized; while Jews become more secularized. All forming a new American culture. All reaching for the lowest common denominator between them; the one which mostly represents America today --- business and money making, secularism, and allegiance to the new capitalist system.

---

[493] "PURITANS WERE MORE JEWISH THAN PROTESTANTS." http://www.christianity-revealed.com/cr/files/puritansweremorejewishthanprotestants.html. Accessed 17 Feb. 2018.
[494] "God In America: People: The Puritans | PBS." 11 Oct. 2010, http://www.pbs.org/godinamerica/people/puritans.html. Accessed 17 Feb. 2018.
[495] http://www.acjna.org/acjna/articles_detail.aspx?id=426 (accessed April 2016)

A new system akin to religion has been established in America. A secular capitalist system which is 'highly contagious' --- for it provides some people with an unbelievable sense of power. It is also a sweet dream to the rest of the aspiring American population all over the U.S.A. (as well as a magnet to populations around the world, who become willing dreamers to its promise). This religion uses sophisticated and effective marketing systems --- such as the media --- to promote its values. Values of which investments and consumerism are featured as supreme. It runs through multiple business conglomerates which persistently preach the 'American dream' of becoming either rich or famous . . . or both.

Show business is one perfect example of the dream that the capitalist system provides. This does not only include Hollywood, but also: sports; television shows; multiple new reality T.V. shows, and even politics.

Although ethnic-Jews are still the drivers of this showbusiness dream economy (as was demonstrated in chapter 1) they are also a major power behind the endless marketing and organization of the industry of showbusiness. There have been a multitude of beneficiaries and absurds to this massive wheel of capitalistic fortunes.

Big and tall basketball players like Lebron James and Michael Jordan (who is said to be worth a billion dollars). Football, baseball, and tennis players like Serena Williams. People like: Oprah; Degeneres; the Kardashians; and Kanye West, have become billionaires/multi-millionaires. Politicians such as the Clinton family (who are supposed to be modest public servants) command hundreds of millions of dollars in those so-called 'Maverick' investments. Barack Obama becoming 'the first African-American president' campaigned for by the ethnic-Jew political strategist David axelrod.[496] Obama has become a big celebrity, even receiving a highly controversial 'token' nobel prize for peace.

Many of these people in previous generations would hardly scrape by (due to lack of opportunity and prejudice). Today, they are a kind of nobility that is marketed over and over around the world. They are gladly part of the new religious system of money and power. The rest of the population unconsciously works for them --- paying for their lavish lifestyle (all the while being continuously brainwashed that this system is brilliant). The American dream at its best . . .

This is the brilliance of the application of selling dreams and good storytelling. It makes people like Oprah command more than $2 billion; or the Clintons command hundreds of millions dollars (insane amounts of money) --- while most professional people such as: doctors; engineers; and scientists, who actually improve people's lives, will be lucky to save a mere $1 million in their lifetime. All those other celebrities will command thousands of millions of dollars. Where is this money coming from? From the rest of the population who are convinced to spend this money to support this industry --- hand-in-hand with big corporates . . . all promoting mass-consumerism that feeds this massive show-business industry.

One would think that there cannot be much room for anti-Semitism within those American nobilities --- and if there is, it is pretty-well hidden; as said nobilities, just like ethnic-Jews, are part-and-parcel of the new American Capitalist system . . . devouring the resources of the people they pretend to care about in all their reality shows.

This new American religion is not in isolation --- it has been affecting the world. It has integrated the world economy into a financial system which is under America's control. A control that is applied by the dollar being the world's reserve currency; as well as by American bonds, and other financial derivative instruments --- and above all, by debt . . . a continuous and everlasting debt cycle within America, and around the world.

---

[496] http://www.biography.com/people/david-axelrod-431900 (accessed May 2016)

Can anyone figure out where this system is leading America and the world? I would think that no one can tell at this stage where it's heading.

The religion of financial speculation

It is of no secret any longer that most of the world's financial system is run by the USA. Many of the key players in: the Federal Reserve Bank; American financial institutions; and U.S. government institutions, are ethnic --- or partially-ethnic --- Jews.

Many of those people are graduates of the best American academic institutions. Some held professor posts in those institutions, and some are Nobel prize winners in economics.

Over the last 30 years, the Federal Reserve Bank (also named The FED) has been headed by ethnic-Jews. Alan Greenspan[497] (1987-2006), Ben Bernanke,[498] (2006-2014) and Janet Yellen[499] (2014-2018). The most influential economists in America --- and around the world --- are also of ethnic-Jewish origin. To name some of the most famous ones: Milton Friedman[500]; Joseph Stiglitz[501], and Paul Krugman[502] --- all Nobel prize winners for their economic theories and models. Leaders of the biggest financial institutions: Lloyd Blankfein[503] of Goldman Sachs; Laurence Fink[504] of Blackrock solutions; Stephen Schwarzman[505] of Blackstone group; Bill Gross of Pacific investment; Carl Icahn of Icahn enterprises --- the list is long, but the pattern is the same. Jews dominate at least 40% of the sector of finance and banking in the USA. The other 60% --- who originate from other ethnic backgrounds in America such as Henry Paulson, Warren Buffett, and Bill Gates --- share the same financial philosophy in how to enrich themselves within the global economy. We can dare say that their philanthropic marketing strategy is a necessary component to their American and world image.

It would be foolish and naive to think that nations in general, and the USA in particular, are primarily concerned with the well-being of the world. Their concern is first to themselves, their organisations, and their own country. Absolutely natural human behaviour.

The American economy, and the world's interests are conflicting in many ways. Whether the conflict is in relation to the interests of American financial institutions, or the American economy as a whole.

---

[497] "Alan Greenspan | Federal Reserve History." https://www.federalreservehistory.org/people/alan_greenspan. Accessed 17 Feb. 2018.
[498] "Ben S. Bernanke | Federal Reserve History." https://www.federalreservehistory.org/people/ben_s_bernanke. Accessed 17 Feb. 2018.
[499] "Janet Yellen - Wikipedia." https://en.wikipedia.org/wiki/Janet_Yellen. Accessed 17 Feb. 2018.
[500] "Milton Friedman: The Concise Encyclopedia of Economics | Library of ...." http://www.econlib.org/library/Enc/bios/Friedman.html. Accessed 17 Feb. 2018.
[501] "Joseph Stiglitz | The Guardian." https://www.theguardian.com/profile/josephstiglitz. Accessed 17 Feb. 2018.
[502] "The Prize in Economic Sciences 2008 - Press Release." https://www.nobelprize.org/nobel_prizes/economic-sciences/laureates/2008/press.html. Accessed 17 Feb. 2018.
[503] "Lloyd Blankfein - Wikipedia." https://en.wikipedia.org/wiki/Lloyd_Blankfein. Accessed 17 Feb. 2018.
[504] "Larry Fink | BlackRock." https://www.blackrock.com/corporate/en-ch/about-us/leadership/larry-fink. Accessed 17 Feb. 2018.
[505] "Stephen Schwarzman - Blackstone." https://www.blackstone.com/the-firm/our-people/person?person=1000272. Accessed 17 Feb. 2018.

As the U.S.A. lost its manufacturing competitive advantage to the far-East --- and mainly to China --- The U.S. had been in need of other ways to generate revenue. Trading and creating global debt through financial instruments[506] seems to have been the path chosen by economic policy advisors in America. This system of debt allows the U.S. to control the world economy through the American government's bonds, as well as the American dollar (which has become the world's reserve currency since the end of World War II). The International Monetary Fund and World Bank have become powerful instruments in the hands of the U.S. in implementing control over the rest of the world.[507]

This would not have been achieved if other important nations such as: Japan; the U.K; Germany; and France, had not co-operated. Hints for this underlying co-operation can be found in professor Zbigniew Brzezinski's proposals in the 70's[508] . . . and they do co-operate, as they themselves also use the financial system of debt to their own advantage.

The problem with this debt system is that the world seems to have come to a state of 'saturation in debt'[509]. Many countries cannot really service their debt anymore, and one of the best examples is Greece. Greece has fallen further into the hands of their own culture of nepotism and extremely greedy and corrupt political leaders.[510]

There are many other problems with this system. It encourages corruption and nepotism in highly indebted countries. Governments in: South-Africa; Brazil; Argentina; and many others, found this system to be attractive and addictive.[511] They expand their government's spending by increasing personnel, as well as implementing unnecessary programs. An entire corrupt industry of tenders and services for the government develops --- a corrupt and nepotistic industry that only provides for people who are close to the government officials. Brazil is a good example.[512] Other sectors of the economy are neglected, and many just want to work for the government in order to gain benefits for hardly any work done. The results in the long run are devastating for all those countries, as they become less and less productive; but more corrupt and addicted to debt.

This system also seems to corrupt the U.S.A. as well. Since the indebted world cannot repay the American financial institutions that lend the money, the U.S. government look to the Federal Reserve Bank for replenishment. The bank obliges, as they cannot afford bankruptcy of those American financial institutions; since said bankruptcy would mean the end of countless jobs. It will also diminish America's financial power in the world. So the bank provides 'cheap money' (money lent at a low interest rate and a long and flexible return) to the American financial institutions.

---

[506] "Global debt: Why has it hit an all-time high? And how worried should ...." 5 Jan. 2018, http://www.independent.co.uk/news/business/analysis-and-features/global-debt-crisis-explained-all-time-high-world-economy-causes-solutions-definition-a8143516.html. Accessed 17 Feb. 2018.
[507] "The "Globalization" Challenge: The U.S. Role in Shaping World Trade ...." https://www.brookings.edu/articles/the-globalization-challenge-the-u-s-role-in-shaping-world-trade-and-investment/. Accessed 17 Feb. 2018.
[508] "Trilateral Diplomacy: the United States, Western Europe and Japan." https://2001-2009.state.gov/r/pa/ho/time/qfp/103525.htm. Accessed 17 Feb. 2018.
[509] "Fed tightening 'threatens disaster for debt saturated global economy ...." 15 Sep. 2015, http://www.telegraph.co.uk/finance/economics/11867177/Fed-tightening-threatens-disaster-for-debt-saturated-global-economy.html. Accessed 17 Feb. 2018.
[510] "Why can't Greece shake its corruption problem? - Tufts University." https://ase.tufts.edu/economics/documents/newsIoannidesGreece.pdf. Accessed 17 Feb. 2018.
[511] "Corruption in South Africa - Wikipedia." https://en.wikipedia.org/wiki/Corruption_in_South_Africa. Accessed 17 Feb. 2018.
[512] "BRAZZIL - News from Brazil - Corruption, bribery, and nepotism in ...." http://www.brazzil.com/cvrmar97.htm. Accessed 17 Feb. 2018.

This 'cheap money' not only increases America's deficit, but it also causes havoc on pricing around the world. The financial institutions are busy creating trades in everything (more like bets than real trade). Options on: stocks; bonds; various currencies, and many other 'financial instruments' that the general public can never comprehend.

While the American economy was boasting to have been generating around 10% of American GDP from this financial world trade in the 1980's, it has since ballooned to more than 30% in recent years --- to what is probably more of a generation of internal growing American deficits and debt, rather than real GDP. This system has created huge economic meltdowns, of which the first big test was in 2008.

Mineral resources are erratically priced, and servicing the debt for the capital that was needed to develop said resources is heavy. This further impoverishes natural resources and emerging markets in Africa and South-America.

Currently many of the developing nations --- such as the BRICS nations --- are in the midst of deep economic recessions. Nowadays, many respected economists are of the opinion that this system is unsustainable; as even in America, it mainly supports Wall Street, while 'Main street' (everyday people) don't really benefit. This may have also been the reason for the surprise election of Mr. Donald Trump as the President of the U.S.

The solutions for this remain to be seen. Some are of the theories that Karl Marx had propagated (such as the notion that the boom and bust of capitalist systems is now obviously right, and perhaps some of his socialist views such as limitations to consumption and manufacturing, may be part of the solution). The verdict is out there, and the future will tell if the capitalist religion --- as it has evolved --- had been the optimal system.

We will not be able to properly glean into this created and conspired world of capitalist finance. Most of the time, the world will feel the economic pain (as was felt in the 2008 financial crisis) in a sudden and surprising fashion. It will probably be some financial instrument that will trigger a crisis (like the American invented mortgage backed securities that were sold around the world and had eventually become worthless, creating havoc in the world). We will also never know what the real prices of commodities are, as we don't know what the real value of the dollar is (which has been shuffled, expanded, and contracted around the world according to these American financial institutions' master trading and profit plans).

The next American-invented economic instrument that will hit the world cannot be predicted. What is of certainty is that the economic lives of billions of people are controlled by New York (for the foreseeable future).

What has become of the capitalist system can be further compared to a controlling religion. Millions of people are working within it, and many more billions of people are following it religiously. People are glued to their screens and television sets, and incessantly follow share prices and currency fluctuations; as well as the values of their portfolios. Most are puzzled continuously, and will probably lose money over their lifetime.

The high 'clergy' within this religion are full of themselves as the new elite, who benefit in hundreds of billions of dollars annually. Just a few years ago, Goldman Sachs' CEO Lloyd Blankfein was caught with the unfortunate saying "we do God's work"[513] --- infuriating many people who can see beyond the woods. Mr. Blankfein might have also been servicing the Greek Gods, when the connection between Goldman Sachs and the corrupt Greek

---

[513] http://www.businessinsider.com/lloyd-blankfein-says-he-is-doing-gods-work-2009-11 (accessed May 2016)

government's debt had been exposed.[514] When business leaders try to boast about providing finance to grow companies (which in-turn create jobs), transparency would be to their benefit; since there is high public suspicion that most of the Federal Reserve Bank's 'cheap money' --- that Goldman Sachs uses --- mainly goes to quick and risky financial bets that might eventually turn sour (as they had, during the 2008 financial crisis --- with no real benefit to America, or the world economy).

The sad fact is that although the American system is flawed in many ways, there seems to be no good alternative around the world. China is a one-party state that mainly benefits its communist party members and their families, while Russia is a hidden type of dictatorship; whereby a ruler sets his reign forever, and is heavily considerate towards himself and his oligarch friends (many of whom --- without co-incidence --- are highly capable ethnic-Jews who are invested, and do business around the world. Russia's president, Vladimir Putin, may be a hidden dictator --- but he is no fool. He knows how to maximize his benefits, while still retaining friendships with many people and nations around the world. An astute politician.

Having written my take on this religion of capitalism, I would think that America's relatively new religion of capitalism is unabated; and will remain intact for the foreseeable future (since it still provides freedom for technological advancements, and awakens the entrepreneurial spirit within individuals).

As with any new economic system, one will find out that ethnic, and assimilated, Jews are dominant and active. In America (as this book has demonstrated) Jews are heavily involved within the capitalist system --- but there are many other willing participants who have nothing to do with Judaic people . It seems that as long as real productivity and creation will surpass virtual financial trade; the capitalist system will not collapse so easily. What the future holds for this American world-dominant capitalist religion, still remains to be seen.

The main lesson from this chapter is that world movements and systems are akin to religion; and as such, will do anything in their power to undermine other systems and religions that compete --- or are perceived to be competing --- with them.

That is why Communism and Fascism had been at odds. That is why Russian-Communism tried to eliminate the Russian Church. That is why Capitalist America fought Communism in America, and around the world; and it is also the reason for historical hate amongst religions. This is also a factor in the makeup and sustainability of anti-Semitism over the long run of history --- which is the topic of the next chapter.

---

[514] "Greek Debt Crisis: How Goldman Sachs Helped Greece to Mask its ...." 8 Feb. 2010, http://www.spiegel.de/international/europe/greek-debt-crisis-how-goldman-sachs-helped-greece-to-mask-its-true-debt-a-676634.html. Accessed 17 Feb. 2018.

Chapter 14

Anti-Semitism forever

Summary: This chapter will attempt to explain anti-Semitism as being a natural phenomenon which, at its core, is similar to racism. Based on this understanding, the new age anti-Semitism --- which is disguised as anti-Zionism or anti-Israelism --- will be discussed. There is no conduct that has puzzled and confused ethnic-Jews (as well as famous non-Jewish philosophers) as much as the anti-Semitic conduct.

The popularization of the term anti-Semitism is credited to the German agitator and publicist Friedrich Wilhelm Adolph Marr (1819-1904) in his publishing 'The Way to Victory of Germanism over Judaism, 1879'. [515] Marr --- who in his own personal life had been attracted to assimilated Jews and had married and divorced a few of them over his lifetime --- claimed that there had been a hidden war between the Jewish and German spirit; whereby the Jewish spirit was winning. He offered ways for Germans to combat and win this war. It is interesting to note that after a lifetime of anti-Semitic conduct, Marr published a final essay --- '*Testament of an anti-Semite*' --- whereby he denounced his conduct, and acknowledged it as being a misjudgement of the social upheaval in Germany at the time. In the essay, he openly apologizes to Jews for his mistakes.[516]

There are many bright and intelligent world-renowned philosophers who have attempted to explain/define anti-Semitism. The famous french philosopher Jean-Paul Sartre (1905-1980 CE) defined anti-Semitism as being 'a criminal passion similar to hysteria'.[517] There has been much criticism of Sartre's analysis,[518] as it had not taken historical anti-Semitism into account.

There is a good reason to suspect that in Germany, most of the philosophers that had written about anti-Semitism were anti-Semitic themselves; as they had addressed their anti-Semitic German readers, and probably deliberately excluded Jewish writings.

Jews had not only been unable to defend themselves physically, but they had also been spiritually oppressed for most of the 17th to early 20th century in Germany --- they had no voice, and could not stand up for themselves in the form of intellectual writings. By that time, the accumulation of venomous anti-Semitic indoctrination had been so high that the ground was ripe for characters like Hitler to spring up and flourish. Moreover, the build-up of ethnic-Jewish domination in: medicine; law; science; and the economy, had probably been used as tangible evidence for the Nazi's anti-Semitic claims of a full-scale war between the 'races'.

All anti-Semitic theories seem to have lacked some components. The best way to understand anti-Semitism is probably by the description and analysis of specific circumstantial anti-Semitic verbal and physical conduct. There is no doubt that anti-Semitism has been around since at least soon after the Greek occupation of the Middle-East by Alexander The Great.[519]

---

[515] "Wilhelm Marr - Academic Dictionaries and Encyclopedias." http://enacademic.com/dic.nsf/enwiki/43774. Accessed 27 Jan. 2018.
[516] "Wilhelm Marr - Wikipedia." https://en.wikipedia.org/wiki/Wilhelm_Marr. Accessed 27 Jan. 2018.
[517] "Anti-Semitism's many expressions - Opinion - Jerusalem Post." 3 Mar. 2011, http://www.jpost.com/Opinion/Editorials/Anti-Semitisms-many-expressions. Accessed 27 Jan. 2018.
[518] http://www.academia.edu/1502580/Jean-Paul_Sartres_positioning_in_Anti-Semite_and_Jew (accessed April 2016).
[519] "Antisemitism (1) - Livius." 16 Dec. 2016, http://www.livius.org/articles/concept/antisemitism/. Accessed 27 Jan. 2018.

In previous chapters, we had discussed the differences between the Jewish populations and their Greek and Roman contemporaries of the era. We spoke about the puzzling illogicality that Jewish people's success had presented before the all-powerful conquering Romans and Greeks.

The illogicality of the fact that the Greeks and Romans, as powerful warriors, eventually landed up financially indebted to ethnic-Jews. The puzzling fact that the ethnic-Jew would always, over the medium-to-long run, become the richer and smarter individual --- always there to be noticed. It must have been a humiliating state of affairs for the Greek or Roman occupier.

This always breeds jealousy, fear, and hate. These unsavoury feelings in turn lead to anger, feelings of a desire for revenge, and a general outrage of the mind. This mentality also leads to imaginary explanations and self-justification. Said feelings had led to some of the most vicious and ludicrous: theories; stories; and myths, for over more than two millennia.

One of the first known anti-Semitic writings of antiquity is the writing of Apion of Alexandria. This had been a blood-libel about the Jews fattening a Greek prisoner, so as to devour him on their holidays.[520] This libel has been recycled against Jewish people in various forms over two and a half millennia (mainly as the christian child who is killed, by Jews, in order for his blood to be used to bake Jewish shabbat challah [bread] or Passover Matzah).

'Against Apion' had been Josephus Flavius' response to this blood-libel[521]. He pointed to the fact that it had lacked any concrete details or names . . . simply bare allegations. Why, in the blood-libel story, does King Antiochus --- who supposedly found the fattened up Greek man --- not glorify him for his perseverance in any records. How could one Greek person satisfy thousands of hungry celebrating Jews that had taken an oath not to murder. Josephus states that this blood-libel is a complete, cruel and audacious, fable.

Flavius' writing, 'Against Apion', had discreted Apion as a neutral historian regarding ethnic-Jews, and had provided a multitude of arguments to prove the Hellenistic bias of Apion. It further argued in favour of the Jewish culture's superiority over Greek culture (in terms of family values and education).[522]

The physical destruction of Jewish lives and property in the city of Alexandria --- during the beginning of Emperor Caligula's reign --- had preceded Flavius' writings. At the time, the governor was a fellow by the name of Flaccus. The Greeks in the city had weaved a sophisticated anti-Semitic plot --- they had positioned a statue of the Emperor in their Temples, and stated that the Jews had not honoured the Emperor, as they had not done same (well-knowing that idolatry is strongly forbidden in the Jewish religion).

The Roman Governor Flaccus --- either knowingly or as a sign of dominance --- had forced the placement of statues in Jewish Temples of worship; causing widespread riots within Alexandria, resulting in: deaths; pillaging, and the destruction of Jewish homes by the Greeks, Egyptians, and Romans (confining Jews to only one district of the city). Flaccus was eventually arrested, demoted, and put to death by Rome for his conduct. For many years before this incident, the Jews were considered allies and trustees of the Romans against the Greeks and Egyptians; and governor Flaccus has breached this trust.

---

[520] "Apion: Intellectual and Anti-Semite - Blogs - Jerusalem Post." 10 Jan. 2016, http://www.jpost.com/Blogs/Past-Imperfect-Confronting-Jewish-History/Apion-Intellectual-and-Anti-Semite-440996. Accessed 27 Jan. 2018.
[521] http://penelope.uchicago.edu/josephus/apion-2.html (accessed April 2016)
[522] http://penelope.uchicago.edu/josephus/apion-1.html (accessed April 2016)

A noteworthy observation is that anti-Semitism is in fact a product of a kind of cultural war that, at times, erupts into extreme physical violence. This cultural war has been brewing for thousands of years; and is at the root of the cultural conflict between two, or multiple, cultures.

While many nations such as the Persians, Greeks, and Romans have been battling wars with armies and occupations (causing physical destruction); the minority of Judaic people in these areas had survived by using their uncompromising culture --- a culture that uses a God and his commandments as a front. The effective outcome of these beliefs in this God being: the rapid expansion of the family; their uncompromising education; and, the process of making them astute as to life and economic success. While others had built powerful armies to fight against each other, the Jews had built armies of 'pen pushers' --- economically astute traders and observant intellectuals. All of whom had been family, and community, oriented individuals.

Whenever there had been an explosion of the Jewish population, and an attempt by some radicalized minorities within the community to take up arms against gigantic powerful Empires, Jews had generally failed (since the odds during ancient wars of: sword; shield; and muscle, had been heavily tipped against them).

This Jewish cultural war over thousands of years cannot be underestimated, as it has eventually won many battles in the long run of history; and many of its components are still dominant in today's world.

The famous open letter of Mark Twain, which has been accompanying this book, can also attest to this cultural war eventually leading to economic and intellectual dominance. Twain begins with the Biblical story of Joseph, as an example of how a slave manages to become the all-powerful economic ruler of Egyptians. Thereafter, he describes the parallelled situation between the Christian and the Jew in Europe (thousands of years later).

'I am persuaded that in Russia, Austria, and Germany nine-tenths of the hostility to the Jew comes from the average Christian's inability to compete successfully with the average Jew in business - in either straight business or the questionable sort. In Berlin, a few years ago, I read a speech which frankly urged the expulsion of the Jews from Germany; and the agitator's reason was as frank as his proposition.

It was this: that eighty-five percent of the successful lawyers of Berlin were Jews, and that about the same percentage of the great and lucrative businesses of all sorts in Germany were in the hands of the Jewish race! Isn't it an amazing confession? It was but another way of saying that in a population of 48,000,000, of whom only 500,000 were registered as Jews, eight-five percent of the brains and honesty of the whole was lodged in the Jews.

I must insist upon the honesty --- it is an essential of successful business, taken by and large. Of course it does not rule out rascals entirely, even among Christians, but it is a good working rule, nevertheless. The speaker's figures may have been inexact, but the motive of persecution stands out as clear as day. The man claimed that in Berlin the banks, the newspapers, the theatres, the great mercantile, shipping, mining, and manufacturing interests, the big army and city contracts, the tramways, and pretty much all other properties of high value, and also the small businesses, were in the hands of the Jews.

He said the Jew was pushing the Christian to the wall all along the line; that it was all a Christian could do to scrape together a living; and that the Jew must be banished, and soon --- there was no other way of saving the Christian.'[523]

As a Christian, Mark Twain must have also harboured some subconscious anti-Semitic feelings as he states the following:

---

[523] https://legacy.fordham.edu/Halsall/mod/1898twain-jews.asp (accessed April 2016)

'In estimating worldly values, the Jew is not shallow, but deep. With precocious wisdom he found out in the morning of time that some men worship rank, some worship heroes, some worship power, some worship God, and that over these ideals they dispute and cannot unite --- but that they all worship money; so he made it the end and aim of his life to get it.

He was at it in Egypt thirty-six centuries ago; he was at it in Rome when that Christian got persecuted by mistake for him; he has been at it ever since. The cost to him has been heavy; his success has made the whole human race his enemy - but it has paid, for it has brought him envy, and that is the only thing which men will sell both soul and body to get.

He long ago observed that a millionaire commands respect, a two-millionaire homage, a multi-millionaire the deepest deeps of adoration. We all know that feeling; we have seen it express itself. We have noticed that when the average man mentions the name of a multi-millionaire he does it with that mixture in his voice of awe and reverence and lust which burns in a Frenchman's eye when it falls on another man's centime.'

Mr. Twain had been blessed with a great gift of analytical observation, however, his above statement alludes to a conscious effort by the Jew to control his environment. An effort that earns the Jew hate from his non-Jewish environment--- shifting the blame of hate onto the victim.

There is no consideration of: the Jews' cultural life of supporting large families; the constant death and dispossession threats to the breadwinner and his family; and the extreme need for money in the events of: expulsion; a need for protection; ransom payouts, and satisfaction of the pure greed of various: Kings; rulers; and common thugs, over the course of history.

In addition, the historical inaccuracies about financing the crusades, as if Jews had any choice in that matter --- it has been historically documented how Jews had been forced to finance the crusades.

Nevertheless, Mark Twain had made one of the most valiant efforts of a non-Jew to understand the Jews, their underlying history, and anti-Semitism. His accurate record of his voyage to Palestine in 1865, also serves as a good starting point in understanding the Jewish-Arab conflict.

The holocaust as the pinnacle of anti-Semitism

One of Napoleon's famous quotes (which can be used to describe the internal torture of an anti-Semite) is:

"Death is nothing; but to live defeated & inglorious is to die daily." --- **Napoleon Bonaparte**

This had probably been the feeling of many Germans in general --- as well as the sentiments of the sizable minority of German anti-Semites in particular --- as they had felt disenfranchised by their defeat in the first World War to the allies externally, and had felt as though they had been losing their cultural war to Judaic values and Jews internally.

The plotting of revenge was on its way. Based on other anti-Semitic scriptures such as the 'elders of Zion', Hitler had written his own anti-Semitic book, 'Mein Kampf'. In a blind spot of history, this mediocre person rose to power; resulting in conduct that would change modern history profoundly.

The ethnic-German, Friedrich Marr's, apology to the Jews mentions the 'Beer drinking' German anti-Semites; and the pretentious 'German cultural' romanticist --- both of whom had been too egotistical to bring and raise any children into the world. This description fits Hitler; who had initially spoken in Beer Halls, and adorned Wagner's polemic music.

The arrogant anti-Semite

Most assimilated Jews in Germany had still held a fare share of their ancestral culture. Families were smaller, but care and love for their children's well being and educational needs had been a top priority.

A simple comparison of the Nazi leader Hitler, with German-Jewish assimilated political leaders at the time; will explain the cultural differences (and hence the 'cultural warfare') between Germans and Jews better than hundreds of philosophical articles on anti-Semitism, or writings of anti-Semitic apologetics.

The son of a maid to a father and mother who, on various accounts, seemed to have been first cousins; Hitler was mediocre in his education despite his mother's efforts to provide him with one. After his mother's early death, he become almost destitute; as he did not work. He had found his calling in the army, and later on in anti-Semitic politics. He never raised a family; and symbolically married his woman Ms. Eva Brown at the age of 56 (just a few days before the end of World War II). They had allegedly committed suicide together to avoid capture by the Soviet Red Army.

Hitler never created anything but: destruction; warmongering; anti-Semitic politics; egoism, and megalomania. Even he himself admitted that his book, 'Mein Kampf', had been of such poor quality and completely illogical; and that if it were not for circumstantial calling, he would have never written it.[524]

Just before Hitler's rise to power, there had been a few well-known assimilated Jewish politicians who featured in German politics. Reviewing these individuals' skills and personal lives may highlight their intellectual and business capabilities; as well as explain their contributions to German society at the time. Hugo Preuss, a lawyer and lithographic business owner (who at the height of his political career drafted the German constitution)[525] was married and had four sons.[526] Hugo Haase,[527] credited as the first socialist lawyer in Prussia, had rendered his services to lower-class individuals who could not afford high fees. He had fought

---

[524] "Inside The Third Reich: Amazon.co.uk: Albert Speer: 9781842127353 ...." https://www.amazon.co.uk/Inside-Third-Reich-Albert-Speer/dp/1842127357. Accessed 27 Jan. 2018.
[525] "Hugo Preuss | German political theorist | Britannica.com." https://www.britannica.com/biography/Hugo-Preuss. Accessed 27 Jan. 2018.
[526] ibid
[527] "Hugo Haase | German politician | Britannica.com." https://www.britannica.com/biography/Hugo-Haase. Accessed 27 Jan. 2018.

within the German SPD party against some of the war finance plans. He was also married, and raised a child.

Kurt Eisner[528] --- who had headed the socialist revolution in Bavaria, overthrowing the monarchy --- was an educated philosopher and journalist; married, with five children. Gustav Landauer, a graduate in Philosophy, German studies, and the arts --- married with two children. These assimilated Jews are in complete contrast to Hitler's associates, who had mostly received lower educations, and had been of low moral standings.

In close scrutiny of Hitler's associates and first members of the S.S. , it is apparent that most had mediocre achievements in life. Most were rank and file soldiers in the first World War, and had behaved like thugs after World War I. When their numbers had increased substantially, some of their former members who fell out of Hitler's favour --- or other new top S.S. commanders --- had been executed in what was termed 'the Night of the Long Knives'.[529]

They had only brought misery to their Jewish victims, and to Germany's people (who had lost more than 5 million lives in the war). They had also brought death and destruction upon themselves and their families.

There are still enough culturally impaired individuals in the world that revere those invalids. Thugs can never get very far . . . they always fall into their own bad character and die-hard habits --- as history always shows. Their unfounded arrogance always betrays them.

The new age anti-Semitism

Anti-Semitism never dies . . . it only changes forms, and arrives within new packaging. Its latest form has heavily manifested in Europe; with an alliance between old European anti-Semitic guard on the one hand, and a new alliance between the leftist socialists (as well as with the new generation of ethno-Islamic immigrants to Europe and the U.K). The new declared target of this left-wing Muslim alliance is Israel. This in an attempt to hide their real anti-Semitic feelings against the ethnic-Jewish population in Europe and America.

Multiple organisations such as BDS had been formed to do physical harm to Israel and its Jewish population.[530] The Palestinian population is portrayed as the oppressed, and Israel is portrayed as an 'Apartheid state oppressor'.

All is forgotten as to why Israel was created --- the European-Jewish holocaust surviving refugees that came to find sanctuary within Israel; the nearly one million Arab-Jewish refugees

---

[528] "Kurt Eisner | German journalist and statesman | Britannica.com." https://www.britannica.com/biography/Kurt-Eisner. Accessed 27 Jan. 2018.
[529] "Night of the Long Knives - Jun 30, 1934 - HISTORY.com." http://www.history.com/this-day-in-history/night-of-the-long-knives. Accessed 27 Jan. 2018.
[530] "BDS Movement |." https://bdsmovement.net/. Accessed 27 Jan. 2018.

that ran for their lives from the murderous Islamic countries of: Iraq; Iran; Egypt; Syria; Lebanon; Morocco; Algeria; Tunisia; Libya, and Yemen . . . leaving their property, and in some cases their vast wealth, behind. These Jews were, in effect, refugees who had lost almost everything.

All is forgotten about the wars and extermination efforts perpetrated against Israel by those same Arab countries; and the Palestinian-Arab population's hate and terror attacks toward all those Jewish refugees in their new refuge homeland of Israel (since its independence in 1948).

According to the new anti-Semitic organizations, Israel is now 'responsible' for the miserable lives of nearly 2 000 000 Palestinians living in the Gaza strip --- hardcore Islamists who had been composed of a mere 100 000 people nearly seventy years ago, and have since multiplied nearly 20 fold due to their religious culture and way of life. Israel is further 'responsible' for said Palestinians' constant terrorism against Israel (implying that their thinking and culture is any different from their brethren in: Syria; Iraq; Libya; Lebanon, and other Arab countries who use terrorism on a daily basis).

Israel is also 'responsible' for the Palestinians in the West Bank, who have been running their own affairs independently for the past 20 years; receiving unprecedented world aid which has been wasted on corruption and nepotism. Israel is also 'responsible' for their suicide bombings and their hate --- ignoring the fact that their Arab brethren blow themselves up in the name of Allah, daily, in: Iraq; Syria; Libya, and every-so-often in Egypt and Lebanon.

Israel is to blame for Al-Qaeda and Isis' creation. Israel is to blame for everything bad that the Arabs do. What would all these blamers do if Israel did not exist? Who would they blame then?

As was discussed earlier in Chapter 12, Israel is far from a perfect country (with all its own internal and external problems). It is, however, still considered as the only real free country in the Middle-East; and one that provides relative: peace; security; and opportunity, to its 1.5 million Arab citizens, and around 500,000 Christians and other minorities.[531]

Israeli-Arabs are politically represented, as well as preferentially accepted into universities that exist on Israeli and Jewish money from around the world.[532] I have never encountered, or heard of, an Israeli-Arab (or any other Arab for that matter) who has contributed money to any Israeli university --- yet, they are more than willing to enrol and enjoy the Israeli State subsidies.

The situation is so absurd, that many of these Israeli-Arab politicians are able to openly support terrorism --- and hail terrorist organizations such as Hamas and Hezbollah --- without

---

[531] "Freedom House: Israel only free state in the Middle East - Israel News ...."
http://www.jpost.com/Israel-News/Politics-And-Diplomacy/Freedom-House-Israel-only-free-state-in-the-Middle-East-480295. Accessed 28 Jan. 2018.
[532] "$400 million gift to Ben-Gurion University is largest bequest ever ...." 25 Jun. 2016,
https://www.haaretz.com/israel-news/ben-gurion-univerity-gifted-400-million-1.5401016. Accessed 28 Jan. 2018.

any measure taken against them by the Israeli Government.[533] For such actions against The State in an Arab country, they would have normally been executed (and in a best case scenario, they would have definitely been jailed for treason).

The Islamic fundamentalists --- and famous Imams from the Arab and Islamic world --- also preach that Jews come from monkeys and pigs; while at the same time they themselves live as primates with 3 or 4 wives, and --- like pigs --- devour the little resources that their communities have to offer to the general population (without any consideration for the weak and fragile).[534] They also firmly believe in an awaited paradise for suicide bombers and terrorists, with 72 virgins to entertain them.[535]

Third World countries and their leaders are also drawn to the anti-Semitic frenzy; believing in their entitlement to riches that have been 'taken' by the world conspiracy of Jewish and White-man oligarchy.[536]

While it may be true that world resources are not priced fairly, said Third World countries are not entitled to receive more resources in their current corrupt and nepotistic regimes. The enormous wealth and aid flowing into these countries over the years has found its way to their leaders' personal bank accounts and lifestyles; with very little improvement to their people's lives.[537]

Then there are the armies of 'politically correct' individuals, who have only done harm to Third World developing countries --- and have only empowered terrorist organizations --- by trying to appease their generally ignorant and pretentious leaders (who are themselves racists and, at times, anti-Semitic). These 'Social Justice Warriors' eternalise the dire situation of the general population in those Third World countries --- leaving them in ignorance, poverty, and helplessness under: corrupt; lazy; nepotistic, and terrorist regimes.[538]

The main point of all this is that everyone in this world --- in one way or another --- is responsible for: anti-Semitism; racism; terrorism, and cultural warfare.

---

[533] "Bill aims to ban MKs who support terror against Israel | The Times of ...." https://www.timesofisrael.com/bill-aims-to-ban-mks-who-support-terror-against-israel/. Accessed 28 Jan. 2018.
[534] "Egyptian President Calls Jews 'Sons of Apes and Pigs'; World Yawns ...." 14 Jan. 2013, https://www.theatlantic.com/international/archive/2013/01/egyptian-president-calls-jews-sons-of-apes-and-pigs-world-yawns/267131/. Accessed 28 Jan. 2018.
[535] "Virgins? What virgins? | Books | The Guardian." 11 Jan. 2002, https://www.theguardian.com/books/2002/jan/12/books.guardianreview5. Accessed 28 Jan. 2018.
[536] "Blaming Jews won't solve SA's ills | The Star - IOL." 7 May. 2015, https://www.iol.co.za/the-star/blaming-jews-wont-solve-sas-ills-1855347. Accessed 28 Jan. 2018.
[537] "How Much Aid is Really Lost to Corruption? | Center For Global ...." 23 Jan. 2017, https://www.cgdev.org/blog/how-much-aid-really-lost-corruption. Accessed 28 Jan. 2018.
[538] "Jeremy Corbyn says he regrets calling Hamas and Hezbollah 'friends ...." 4 Jul. 2016, https://www.theguardian.com/politics/2016/jul/04/jeremy-corbyn-says-he-regrets-calling-hamas-and-hezbollah-friends. Accessed 28 Jan. 2018.

The cultural warfare is ongoing around the world, and will never stop (since one's cultural beliefs is another's perceived bad culture that should be fought off). One's heroic culture, is another's villainous culture.

Therefore, my claim is that anti-Semitism is forever --- just as: racism; Islamophobia; Islamofascism; anti-Americanism; ethnic hate, and many more ills in this world are here to stay. The golden path of tolerance yet firmness --- and above all, education --- are the tools to combat these ills. The right education --- not a biased one.

Who can change this situation, and how it will ever happen, is one of those monumental questions of humanity.

Finally, I would like to point out that anti-Semitism can be found in any human being from any culture --- this includes Jews who exhibit anti-Semitic views, or assimilated Jews who even try to give credibility to their anti-Semitic views by mentioning their distant origins as Jews. One specific example was Obama's secretary of foreign affairs, Mr. John Kerry --- faulting everything on Israel, including the war in Syria and the formation of Isis; using the most illogical arguments, while flaunting his partial distant Jewish ancestry as justification for his 'understanding' of Jews and the State of Israel. What privileged Mr. Kerry does not reveal, is all the other ancestors he had; and *their* inherent anti-Semitic views about Jews. He is by no means the only assimilated Jew who is vehemently anti-Semitic.

In my life, I have encountered various levels, degrees, and shades of anti-Semitism. When it comes to Jews or Israel, the hardcore anti-Semite will exhibit no logic whatsoever. He may be a very logical and well-educated individual in his profession, and in his attitude towards life in general; yet when it comes to Jews, or Israel --- any trace of his logic seems to be thrown out the window.

This phenomenon of anti-Semitic illogicality was well observed and captured by the former liberal British prime minister Lloyd George[539], who was quoted as follows:

"Of all extreme fanaticism that plays havoc in man's nature, there is none as irrational as anti-Semitism. The Jews cannot vindicate themselves in the eyes of these fanatics. If the Jews are rich, they are victims of theft and extortion. If they are poor, they are victims of ridicule. If they take sides in a war, it is because they wish to gain advantage from the spilling of non-Jewish blood. If they espouse peace, it is because they are scared and anxious by nature or traitors to their country. If the Jew dwells in a foreign land he is persecuted and expelled. If he wishes to return to his own land, he is prevented from doing so." - Lloyd George, 1923

The obvious illogicality of hardcore anti-Semites can only point to the thought that perhaps anti-Semitism is a very logical phenomenon; within a multitude of human beings who seem to have an issue with Jews in general, and Israel's right to exist in particular. Perhaps it is a

---

[539] "Quotes on Anti-Semitism – The Wickens." http://www.thewickens.info/2012/06/quotes-on-anti-semitism/. Accessed 30 May. 2018.

genetic phenomenon; built over many years of history, by interactions and conflicts of survival between Jews and their non-Jewish/assimilated Jewish neighbors.

If Jewish intellectual and business prowess can be attributed by some researchers to genetics; why should anti-Semitism be any different? If anti-Semitism is a genetic condition, it would --- first of all --- explain the futility of arguing with an anti-Semite; and secondly, indicate how difficult it is to modify anti-Semitic minds. It may take many years to uproot anti-Semitism, if at all possible.

This may also explain the difficulties of reaching peace agreements with Palestinian leaders who blatantly exhibit their anti-Semitism; or peace agreements with Iranian Shia clergy, who openly declare their desire to exterminate the Jewish State of Israel.

Chapter 15

Concluding Remarks

It has been the aim of this book to investigate the reasons for some ethnic Jews being so dominant in this world in business and intellectual pursuits.

In this final chapter, there will be an attempt to sum up and organise what has been learned and discovered by reviewing the journey of the Jewish people throughout history; and the ample examples given of their conduct over the years.

From the onset of recorded Judaic history, it was shown that Jewish people had sought after, and are still seeking, wisdom. The invention and use of the ancient Hebrew alphabet --- which is a precursor to the Western world's alphabet --- is a testimony to Jewish People's drive to gain and record knowledge; as well as their drive to pass this knowledge on to future generations. The pursuit of knowledge is also referred to by the Jewish Bible as King Solomon's greatest asset, and an example of good governance --- a model for all human beings.

Literacy, and the pursuit of knowledge, has accompanied the Jewish people every step of the way during their historical journey. From the times of Babylon, when the Bible had probably been written, right up until modern times. In all fields of technology and the humanities, Jews feature as dominant figures.

The Jewish people wrote the Bible; which had been a unique work of literature for ancient times. This was followed by the Talmud, which had enhanced their knowledge regarding human behaviour, moral justice, and a myriad of philosophical thought. The Talmud's strength still resonates, to this day, within modern legal and moral issues. The Judaic scriptures had also accumulated and disseminated family laws, guidance, and advice for good-living. These Talmudic studies had enhanced Judaic people's family-and-learning-oriented culture --- a culture that has proved to be beneficial to intellectual and business pursuits.

Then came the innovation of compulsory education for every child from the age of six. This innovation --- which became a religious duty --- had accompanied Jewish people's lives for nearly two thousand years until its adoption by the Western world. Thousands of years of: literacy; reading; writing; and intellectual pursuits, have contributed to intellectual capacity. This includes: memory; speed reading; deep thinking, and analysis. Moreover, a culture of encouraging small children to think and express their thoughts and feelings without fear had been a pillar of this drive for education. This has contributed to the development of many learning and creating capabilities --- of which imagination is central.

The drive for literacy had included numerical literacy components. These aspects of literacy served Judaic people well, in trade and business (and later on in free occupations such as accounting, finance, and banking). It had also enhanced their calculating skills, which were further sharpened following the occupation of money-lending in Europe --- an occupation that also requires management and risk assessment skills.

The combination of all these accumulated cerebral skills --- which had been passed down over generations --- combined with tightly-knit communities had also allowed Jewish people to innovate banking and financial instruments. This further enhanced their intellectual wealth, as well as their material wealth and its preservation.

The continuous reading, writing and driving the brain for performance must have increased/improved memory, the thinking process, and problem solving. This would have resulted in neurological processing abilities that had been instrumental to success in law and medicine --- fields that require enormous brain capacity. It further made Jewish people good doctors and lawyers with an imaginative flair.

This unique and enhanced imagination that had been developed as a result of the continuous yearning for knowledge is what had eventually created the most famous intellectuals such as Professor Einstein, Professor Freud, and Karl Marx --- as well as many others who are not mentioned in this book.

Can other things be learned from this amazing historical journey of the Jews? Anything about human genetics or psychological lessons? Can the Jewish experience be enhanced for the benefit of individuals, communities, and even countries? Perhaps for the benefit of businesses at least? Some of the following analyses may be considered:

Genetic variation

Contrary to modern popular belief and presumptuous academic articles, we can clearly realise that during thousands of years of history spanning most of: Europe; North Africa; and the Middle-East, Jewish people may have been infused with genetic material from a wide array of human groups. The Ashkenazi-Jews suffer from genetic diseases that are mostly encountered in Eastern-Europe (such as a high prevalence of breast cancer)

One needn't be a geneticist to observe the phenotype of Jews in Israel to notice that. Even among Ashkenazi-Jews you will find: white and dark-skinned people; blonde and dark-haired individuals; people with brown or blue eyes; heavy and skinny built people --- with a wide spectrum of colours and shapes.

It may be true that some genetic diseases --- such as Tay-Sachs --- have developed in some community of Jews, and are distinct; but these diseases are also present in other minority French-origin populations in Canada (Quebec) and the USA (New-Orleans). It may be possible that those French communities had some European-Jewish ancestors.

Genes from non-Jewish populations had been transferred to Jewish populations --- either by force during: Egyptian; Babylonian; Greek; and Roman occupations, or during countless anti-Semitic pogroms which included rape (which could perhaps be the real reason why Rabbinical Judaism regarded the mother's identity as a prerequisite to Judaism). Also by will, since Jewish merchants had taken foreign wives (or assimilation, and the return of assimilated populations to their Judaic core).

Genetic theorists consider genetic variance to be a benefit to populations --- increasing the chances of survival. Beyond the various and multiple genetic diseases that are found in Jewish populations, many Jews who live in secure environments manage to live a very long life. The long history of the survival of Jews in all aspects of life is by all means second-to-none.

Cultural variation, and cultural warfare

From the days of the Egyptian occupation of Canaan, and the invention of modern writing through: Babylonian input; Persian religious influences; Hellenistic and Roman exposure, Jews have been absorbing various cultural influences from their occupiers; all the while fighting a cultural war, in order to survive said occupiers rules.

This cultural exchange can only be understood with the use of proper analytical mechanisms. Cultural exchange has benefits which improve certain aspects of societies; however, in the long run, it also diminishes the value of other aspects of the new society.

It has been demonstrated that Jewish culture is extremely rich in: family values; education; diversity, and the development of life skills. Economically, it spans from pure capitalism (in relation to the outside business environment) to practices of socialism (for the benefit of the community members). Religiously speaking, Judaism's diversity is evident in the sense that one will find ethnic-Jews in the most atheistic circles; as well as within ultra religious ones. Jewish people today demonstrate this highly versatile culture by their achievements in all walks of life. Perhaps the secret to vast Jewish wealth lies within its diverse, as well as extremely wealthy and rich, culture. Money is simply a by-product of this tremendous cultural wealth (which is based on knowledge and intellect).

Competitive traits

Innovation

The first Jewish innovation that had been discussed was the alphabet --- an innovation that, since its inception, had changed humanity forever .

The Bible was also is the best-selling novel of all time. In the early chapters, the Bible's uniqueness had been demonstrated. It had certainly been an advanced piece of writing for its time in history. When compared to: Egyptian; Babylonian; or Greek mythology, the Bible had been a cut above the rest --- with unprecedented progressive ideas about slavery, family laws, and how to conduct a fruitful life. The Talmud had also been a well thought-out innovation for its time; and a precursor to modern Legal reasoning. Jews' innovations in the banking, investments, and financial worlds have been extensively discussed in this book.

From Mark Twain's open letter about the Jews --- as well as from historical records --- we know that European-Jews had been restricted from pursuing virtually all occupations. However, they had still found new niches in the areas that they *had* been permitted to work. Money lending is the most notorious occupation that Jews had been permitted to engage in for their livelihood. From this humiliating starting point, Judaic people had still managed to come out on top; by developing banking, investments, international finance and financial risk management tools --- tools that, today, govern Western business. Earlier in history --- and to this day --- ethnic-Jews are renowned for being the most astute traders and fierce competitors in all of those financial fields.

The nobel prize awards to many ethnic-Jews for their contributions to science and technology --- contributions that had improved the lives of billions of people around the world --- is also a living proof of their profound ability for innovation. Hollywood, Silicon Valley, Wall Street, and the High-Tech industries in Israel, are all testimonies to the Jews' ability to possess highly imaginative and innovative capabilities --- the building blocks of the ethnic-Jewish entrepreneurial spirit.

Today's involvement of many ethnic-Jews in technological innovation in the Silicon Valley, and in Israel's 'Silicon Wadi', is another living proof of the ethnic-Jewish cultural drive for innovation and excellence. It is a precursor to what is to be expected from ethnic-Jewish people in the future of computer and cyber technologies.

Tenacity

The tenacity of Jews over centuries can hardly be doubted. They stuck to their beliefs through 'fire and water' so to speak. Many had succumb to life pressures and had converted and assimilated; but the ones who had remained on the path, true to their beliefs, are characters of tenacity of the highest order.

This tenacious stand over generations encompasses a strong mental will-power and stamina, as well as a high level of ambition --- all geared to achieve intellectual ability first and foremost. Compounded over many generations, it could only have yielded some highly effective people in business and intellect. All those attributes, and many other hidden ones, have elevated ethnic-Jews to become the wealthiest and richest people on the planet --- the ultimate survivors of humanity. I hope that this book has revealed the true secret to Judaism, its survival, and its success.

The ordinary person can learn much from this survival story; as well as for governments and countries around the world who would like to change the future of their nation. Building a legacy of diversity in thinking, and freedom, can be a good start. Cultural lessons of history can also be compiled and taught to young people in schools and other institutions.

Recently, the Spanish government had announced that they would be considering granting citizenship to people who had Sephardic-Jewish ancestry. Portugal has already been acting in this regard since 2013. My personal opinion is that Judaic people are entitled to that and more. As a true cosmopolitan people who had lived and contributed to many countries and civilizations, Jews should be entitled to live wherever they want in this world. They should be welcomed. They are more than entitled to have their own country in the ancient land of Israel. The Arab-Israeli conflict should be addressed by the International community with more innovation; as it is more of an education/change of heart and mind problem. The fact that vast amounts of land had been vacated in what was Syria, and millions of refugees had flooded Europe in recent years, is testimony to that land not being the main issue in that area --- the changing of people's hearts and minds is the main issue. This, unfortunately, can only be achieved by educating the young members of the society.

The Israeli-Palestinian conflict can also be addressed, and solved, by changing people's hearts and minds. Any assistance to Palestinians should involve a conditional change in their mindset. Israel is not going to vanish . . . and it is definitely not the sole source of all the Palestinians' problems.

Business Advancement, Teamwork, and Networking

What must a businessman contend with, and how do Judaism's history lessons provide an answer for this? The multi-faceted needs for any business venture is embedded within the Jewish culture. It can be described as follows:

The first factor is the need to make money in a new fashion, or within an improved model for the existing way of conducting business. The need for imaginative powers is absolutely key to success. The best example that comes to mind is the personal computer breakthrough; and Microsoft pioneering the software for the personal computer. Amazon is an example of an improved retail system using the internet and technology. Business is about making money in a new and innovative way. The second factor is the deployment of the entrepreneurial spirit --- the will to take initiative and plan the steps needed to achieve the success of that business.

The third factor is finance --- many small businesses will implode if they cannot finance their operations. Jewish people would always approach other wealthy Jews to receive finance. Usually the older experienced financier would have a good feeling if the business is viable or not, as they would already be a seasoned business person themself. Apart from the finance, they may act as a mentor to the new venture.

Once these three steps have been completed, the mental and physical discipline to build the business comes next --- dedication to the business, long hours of work, and achieving the goals of the business (whether those goals be the successful manufacturing and distribution of a product, or the trade/supply of services). This will include disciplines such as: marketing and execution plans; persuasion skills; judgement of customers' characters and the financial risk of dealing with them; calculating skills and buying at the right prices; wise spending of funds, e.t.c . . . all these processes must be achieved within an environment of good teamwork and management, and the development of networks. Once there is success and money begins flowing into the business, the need for financial management and wealth preservation becomes another factor for the continuation --- and future success of --- the business.

Throughout this book, it has been demonstrated how Jewish culture has developed Jewish individuals to become intellectual, knowledgeable, and imaginative. It has been demonstrated how Jews had always thought of new ways to make money; as doing so had been the lifeline to their survival. It has been shown how Jews had become entrepreneurial, due to a lack of work and restriction from their environment. How they had become organised and worked as a team within small communities, in the face of large hostile environments. They had developed networks with other Jews over continental Europe, and later America. The Talmud had taught them the basics of business contracts. They had become good storytellers, which is a prerequisite for the marketing, selling, and buying of goods. They had dealt with money, and had developed their calculation skills to spend wisely and always preserve their wealth. Their lives --- which had always revolved around their family and community --- had helped them stay focused, sober, and modest; always ready for the next day's challenges. Jews had kept a healthy lifestyle; with low alcohol consumption, and no drugs. They had engaged with, and drove, their children to pursue intellectual achievements.

All the above aspects of Judaism have promoted a deep culture of learning; and have developed a heightened, limitless imagination within individuals --- the secret for Jewish success in intellect and business. Unfortunately, for all the other people of the world who feel unlucky --- and for all assimilated ethnic-Jews who, over the years, have lost many of those values --- there are no shortcuts. The Jews had earned their skills through blood, sweat, and tears --- through terrible restrictions and unspeakable persecution. The sacrifices of their forefathers is what had shaped their capabilities today.

Like Profesor Einstein has said before: Jews need to stop apologizing for being who they are. They should be proud of their achievements. Achievements which have contributed to humanity's health and well-being.

When nearly a quarter of Nobel prize awards are achieved by ethnic-Jews --- and scores of major cutting-edge medical and technological developments come from the U.S.A. and Israel --- I would think that perhaps an apology should come from all the anti-Semites of the world who had recently, via the United Nations, attempted to sever the link between Jews and their ancestral land of Judea (and especially their eternal capital of Jerusalem).

The most problematic issue, and a great challenge, is the fact that as Jews continue to prosper and flourish; large numbers of growing populations around the world are getting poorer and more frustrated --- mostly due to their own culture. This is a breeding ground for: ignorance; jealousy; hate, and a future of heightened anti-Semitism.

This challenge of anti-Semitism is a world challenge, which will need a global plan --- perhaps better systems of uplifting poor populations around the world. A multi-faceted approach is required; one that includes population growth control, and upgrading the environment. But, as was mentioned earlier, education is key for changing psyches --- building a world culture of learning, which also focuses on promoting good and healthy family values.

This is what big organisations like the United Nations should be busy with --- not the useless and hopeless activities that have encouraged corruption and nepotism; nor the shameful political ramming of the only Jewish state in the world --- the State of Israel.

Lessons for the individual citizen of the world

No shortcuts. If it's not you who will experience the breakthrough, it will be your children or your grandchildren. That had clearly been shown in history by even other nations who had a vision for change in their countries. The most logical first step should be a moral and healthy family-oriented lifestyle; coupled with the development of a learning culture. Learn, learn, learn --- whether it be a new: language; skill; Legal skill; human behaviour skill; life management skill; musical instrument; brain-enhancement game like chess, or word and mathematical games . . . anything that can enhance you and your children; anything that will help in your profession, or improve your lifestyle. Always keep interested. Try and write a book, or at least some short essays. Live a healthy life. Keep away from harmful substances and bad company. Join people and communities who share your interests.
All these things seem to be trivial, but it is so easy to stray of the path and fall into bad habits in this modern consumer driven capitalist world. Some of these bad habits such as drugs can only offer a one way ticket to ruin and destruction.

The Great genetic debate

Finally, I have chosen to address the Jewish genetic issue; as many people in the modern world are firm believers that it is just a matter of genetics that certain people have better capabilities than others in certain areas. While this may be true to a certain extent, one should always be keep in mind that genetics and the environment constantly interact with one-another. The classic approach was that genetic variations of animals or plants are produced. The ones that are most suited to the environment survive and continue breeding and spreading the wanted genes, while the others die out --- but recently, there are more in-depth theories regarding the human genetics of the brain.[540] Most studies will admit that the mechanisms of brain genetics are largely unknown;[541] so again we are in the dark, and can only rely on empirical knowledge.

Empirically, it is suspected that even identical twins who are seperated and reared apart, have a 50% chance to become dissimilar when it comes to religious tendencies or other

---

[540] "Genetic basis of human brain evolution - NCBI - NIH." 8 Oct. 2008, https://www.ncbi.nlm.nih.gov/pmc/articles/PMC2715140/. Accessed 29 Jan. 2018.
[541] "The genetic basis of human brain structure and function: 1,262 ...." 21 Aug. 2017, https://www.biorxiv.org/content/early/2017/08/21/178806. Accessed 29 Jan. 2018.

factors of personality.[542] This may indicate to the strong impact and influence that the environment has on brain development. Therefore, there is a good reason to believe that environmental changes in culture are high contributors to the development of the individual and the community --- not much different to what this book has shown . . . that is, the historical progression of the Jewish learning culture, which had eventually produced high calibre intellectual and business individuals.

Other compelling empirical evidence, which I had stressed in the beginning of the book, is the fact that most of the individuals discussed had been secular ethnic-Jews (such as Einstein and Marx for example) --- not ultra-religious ones. It was also mentioned that IQ is by all means not the only factor that can explain the phenomenon of ethnic-Jewish success. When balancing all this information regarding IQ and cultural environment, it may be suspected that there is an ongoing interplay between genetics and social culture that eventually molds the type of high-achieving individuals this book describes.

So, if a person has been raised in a very religious Jewish family and: their mind had been sharpened due to the study of the Torah and Talmud; their family values were of high standards; and even if they had lived a healthy family life within their community but never engaged in academic studies, they will always remain a very sharp person in the Torah and the Talmud, and would never become an Einstein or a Freud. On the other hand, if such an individual became engaged in academic pursuits early enough in life; he may become a very good academic. If his children continue this trend, they too may become even more successful academically; and perhaps even in business.

But then comes the trade off. As the descendants venture into the secular world --- which is comprised of many cultures --- do they begin losing their cultural heritage? I suspect that some do. As they carry on drifting and assimilating, do they further lose some original values? Yes, they probably do. Within a few generations, not only has the culture changed, but the genetics have probably changed as well.

This process, which I have just described, is reversible; and social cultures can be modified. One such excellent example is the nation of Singapore.[543] Most of the articles about Singapore will hail the economic miracle of Singapore. Very few will understand that this miracle first involved a fundamental change of culture --- a change that had not even taken so long (when considering the length of human lifetimes). That is a clear message to other people. If you start the change, you may see it in your lifetime; whether the success will manifest with you, with your children, or with your grandchildren. Start the change today, and you will bear the fruits in the future.

My next book

I hope that my readers have enjoyed this book. I hope that every sentence made your mind tick; and that after reading this book, you feel as though many puzzling questions about Jewish people and Judaism are now satisfactorily answered. I hope that the book has enhanced your understanding about life-processes and human development in general --- but above all, I

---

[542] "Twins Separated at Birth Reveal Staggering Influence of Genetics." 11 Aug. 2014, https://www.livescience.com/47288-twin-study-importance-of-genetics.html. Accessed 29 Jan. 2018.
[543] "How Lee Kuan Yew engineered Singapore's economic miracle - BBC ...." 24 Mar. 2015, http://www.bbc.co.uk/news/business-32028693. Accessed 29 Jan. 2018.

hope that the lessons of this book have enhanced your understanding about how to approach life and create wealth for yourself and generations to come.

During the writing of this book, I have realized that my attempt to solve the puzzle of Judaic people's wisdom and success may have advanced my imaginative and intellectual skills further.

I have realized that the Jewish story is a remarkable survival story, and --- like any human quest for survival in history --- the human brain has featured as the main tool of survival. This has prompted me to write a second book . . . a book which will again use the best tool available to humans --- their process of imagination (which is generated by their mind).

In my second book, I aim to try and solve many questions about humanity and its patterns of behaviour. It will be a journey into the mind itself, and perhaps it will be able to unlock the secret to many things that we cannot explain --- such as feelings, beliefs, and thought processes (one of them being the process of imagination itself). I invite my readers to read my second book --- a book which I truly believe may contribute to every human being's personal advancement.

If the Jewish secret for intellectual and financial success could be summed up, it would be the long historical construction of a specific culture --- a family and community oriented culture of learning and knowledge. One that enhances its members' imagination to achieve, discover, and innovate. One that drives initiative and bold decisions. A culture . . . of wealth.

www.ingramcontent.com/pod-product-compliance
Lightning Source LLC
Chambersburg PA
CBHW030627220526
45463CB00004B/1445